D1757001

TURNING IMAGES IN PHILOSOPHY, SCIENCE, AND RELIGION: A NEW BOOK OF NATURE

TURNING IMAGES IN PHILOSOPHY, SCIENCE, AND RELIGION: A NEW BOOK OF NATURE

EDITED BY
CHARLES TALIAFERRO
AND JIL EVANS

OXFORD
UNIVERSITY PRESS

OXFORD
UNIVERSITY PRESS

Great Clarendon Street, Oxford OX2 6DP

Oxford University Press is a department of the University of Oxford.
It furthers the University's objective of excellence in research, scholarship,
and education by publishing worldwide in

Oxford New York

Auckland Cape Town Dar es Salaam Hong Kong Karachi
Kuala Lumpur Madrid Melbourne Mexico City Nairobi
New Delhi Shanghai Taipei Toronto

With offices in

Argentina Austria Brazil Chile Czech Republic France Greece
Guatemala Hungary Italy Japan Poland Portugal Singapore
South Korea Switzerland Thailand Turkey Ukraine Vietnam

Oxford is a registered trade mark of Oxford University Press
in the UK and in certain other countries

Published in the United States
by Oxford University Press Inc., New York

British Library Cataloguing in Publication Data
Data available

Library of Congress Cataloguing in Publication Data
Data available

Typeset by SPI Publisher Services, Pondicherry, India
Printed in Great Britain
on acid-free paper by
MPG Books Group, Bodmin and King's Lynn

ISBN 978-0-19-956334-0

10 9 8 7 6 5 4 3 2 1

Contents

Acknowledgements

We are deeply grateful to Tom Perridge and Elizabeth Robottom of Oxford University Press for their encouragement and support for this project. We are very grateful to Gwen Daniels, Tricia Little, Eric Erfanian, Conner Westby, Therese Cotter, Rachael Wolanski, and Elisabeth Granquist for assistance in preparing this manuscript. We also thank Christine Baeumler, Stephen Carpenter, Anthony O'Hear, Karen Evans, Mara Naselli, and Todd R. Evans, for invaluable advice and edits. We thank Susan Frampton and Nicola Sangster for their expert copyediting and proofing, and Tessa Eaton for her help with the production.

In this book and a sister, co-authored book *The Image in Mind* (2011), we have sought to think critically and creatively about aesthetics, imagination, and the natural world. We dedicate our share of the work to a senior art critic and philosopher, Dore Ashton, who embodies the Platonic ideal of critical and creative thought. She has been a wonderful inspiration to us both since Jil met and worked with her in 1994.

Charles Taliaferro and Jil Evans

June 2011

Notes on Authors

Conor Cunningham is assistant director of the Centre of Theology and Philosophy, University of Nottingham. He is the author of *Genealogy of Nihilism* (Routledge, 2002), and *Darwin's Pious Idea* (Eerdmans, 2010), which is being translated into French and Spanish. He also wrote and presented the multi award-winning BBC2 documentary *Did Darwin Kill God?* Along with Peter M. Candler Jr., he is editor of two book series: *Interventions* (Eerdmans), and *Veritas* (SCM).

Jil Evans is an American artist based in Minneapolis. She has exhibited her paintings and prints nationally and internationally. Her work is in many private and public collections including the Minneapolis Institute of Arts, Halle Ford Museum of Art, Harry and Margaret Anderson Collection of Art, and Walker Art Center. She has received grants including: Jerome Foundation Grant, Arts Midwest/National Endowment for the Arts, two Minnesota State Arts Board grants, the Pew Grant to study and paint in Italy and residencies at the American Academy in Rome and Atlantic Center for the Arts. She is a founding member of Form + Content Gallery. She is the co-author of *The Image in Mind: Theism, Naturalism, and the Imagination* (Continuum, 2011).

Geoffrey Gorham is associate professor of philosophy at Macalester College and resident fellow at the Minnesota Center for Philosophy of Science, University of Minnesota. He is the author of numerous articles on the history and philosophy of science in journals such as *Philosophy of Science, Journal of the History of Philosophy, Studies in the History and Philosophy of Science, Perspectives on Science*, and *Early Science and Medicine*. He recently published a book, *Philosophy of Science, A Beginners Guide* (Oneworld, 2010) and is at work on another on the concept of time in early modern natural philosophy.

Gordon Graham is Henry Luce III Professor of Philosophy and the Arts at Princeton Theological Seminary, where he is also director of the Center for the Study of Scottish Philosophy. His philosophical interests range widely and he has published extensively in the philosophies of art, education, ethics, politics and religion. His most recent books include *The Re-enchantment of the World: Art versus Religion* (Oxford University Press, 2007) and *Theories of Ethics* (Routledge, 2010).

Dr Douglas Hedley was educated at the universities of Oxford and Munich and has been lecturing at the University of Cambridge since 1996. He is Reader in Hermeneutics and Metaphysics in the Faculty of Divinity and a fellow of Clare College, University of Cambridge. He was visiting professor at the Sorbonne and delivered the Teape Lectures in India in 2007. He is author of *Coleridge, Philosophy and Religion* (2000), *Living Forms of the Imagination* (2008) and *Sacrifice Imagined* (2011).

Dale Jacquette is *Lehrstuhl ordentlicher Professur für Philosophie, Schwerpunkt theoretische Philosophie* (senior professorial chair in theoretical philosophy), at the University of Bern, Switzerland. He is the author of numerous articles on logic, metaphysics, and philosophy of mind, and has recently published *Symbolic Logic, Philosophy of Mind: The Metaphysics of Consciousness, Ontology, Wittgenstein's Thought in Transition, David Hume's Critique of Infinity*, and *Logic and How it Gets That Way*. He has edited the *Cambridge Companion to Brentano*, the *Blackwell Companion to Philosophical Logic*, and for North-Holland the volume on Philosophy of Logic in *the Handbook of the Philosophy of Science* series.

Martin Kemp FBA is the professor emeritus of history of art at Trinity College, University of Oxford. He was trained in natural sciences and art history at the University of Cambridge and the Courtauld Institute, London. He was British Academy Wolfson Research Professor (1993-98). For more than 25 years he was based in Scotland (universities of Glasgow and St. Andrews). He has held visiting posts in Princeton, New York, North Carolina, Los Angeles, Montreal and Harvard (I Tatti). He has written, broadcast and curated exhibitions on imagery in art and science from the Renaissance to the present day. Books include, *The Science of Art: Optical Themes in Western Art from Brunelleschi to Seurat* (Yale University Press, 1990), and *The Human Animal in Western Art and Science* (Chicago, 2007). He has published extensively on Leonardo da Vinci, including the prize-winning *Leonardo da Vinci: The marvellous works of nature and man* (1989 and 2006). His book on the newly discovered Leonardo portrait, *La Bella Principessa*, written with Pascal Cotte, is published by Hodder and Stoughton (2010). Increasingly, he has focused on issues of visualizations, modeling and representation. He writes a regular column for *Nature* (published as *Visualizations* (Oxford University Press, 2000) and developed as *Seen and Unseen* (Oxford University Press, 2006) in which his concept of "structural intuitions" is explored). He is currently writing a book on iconic images, *Christ to Coke: How Image Becomes Icon*.

E. J. Lowe is professor of philosophy at Durham University, UK, specializing in metaphysics, the philosophy of mind and action, the philosophy of logic and language, and the philosophy of John Locke. His books include *Subjects of Experience* (Cambridge University Press, 1996), *The Possibility of Metaphysics* (Oxford University Press, 1998), *The Four-Category Ontology* (Oxford University Press, 2006), *Personal Agency* (Oxford University Press, 2008), and *More Kinds of Being* (Wiley-Blackwell, 2009).

Anthony O'Hear is professor of philosophy at the University of Buckingham, director of the Royal Institute of Philosophy and editor of *Philosophy*. His books include *Beyond Evolution: Human Nature and the Limits of Evolutionary Explanation* (Clarendon Press, 1997), *The Great Books* (Icon Books, 2007; and ISI Books, 2009), and *The Landscape of Humanity: Art, Culture and Society* (Imprint Academic, 2008).

Daniel N. Robinson is a member of the Philosophy Faculty, University of Oxford and Distinguished Professor, Emeritus, Georgetown University. He is the author of eighteen books and editor of more than thirty published volumes in a wide variety of subjects, including moral philosophy, the philosophy of psychology, legal philosophy, the philosophy of mind, intellectual history, and history of psychology. He is past-president of two divisions of the American Psychological Association, the Division of the History of Psychology and the Division of Theoretical and Philosophical Psychology, receiving lifetime achievement awards from both. His most recent book is *Consciousness and Mental Life* (Columbia University Press, 2008).

Charles Taliaferro, professor of philosophy, St. Olaf College, is the author or editor of fifteen books. He is on the editorial board of *Faith and Philosophy*, *Religious Studies*, *Sophia*, *Religious Studies Review*, *Philosophy Compass*, and *Ars Disputandi*. His most recent books are *Aesthetics: A Beginner's Guide* (Oneworld, 2011), the co-authored *A Brief History of the Soul* (Wiley-Blackwell, 2011), and the co-authored *The Image in Mind: Theism, Naturalism, and the Imagination* (Continuum, 2011).

Mark Wynn is senior lecturer in philosophy of religion in the Department of Theology and Religion at the University of Exeter. He is the author of *God and Goodness* (Routledge, 1999), *Emotional Experience and Religious Understanding* (Cambridge University Press, 2005), and *Faith and Place* (Oxford University Press, 2009).

Illustrations

Introduction

Charles Taliaferro and Jil Evans

Our ideas about the cosmos can be seen as the history of different images of nature: nature as organism, soul (the *anima mundi* or world soul), creation or artifact, animal or machine. With the advent of Christianity in the West, the natural world was seen as a great artifact: a book of nature. Nature was and is God's first book, the second being the Bible. This traditional portrait of the natural world reached its zenith in late medieval philosophy and it had currency in modern science. Charles Darwin himself began *On the Origin of Species* with a passage from Francis Bacon that fully supports the study of the Bible as God's book and the study of nature as the other book of God: "To conclude, therefore, let no man out of a weak conceit of sobriety, or an ill-spirited moderation, think or maintain, that a man can search too far or be too well studied in the book of God's word, or in the book of God's works; divinity or philosophy, but rather let men endeavour an endless proficience in both."[1]

While the image of nature as an artifact of God has proponents, especially in light of the revival of philosophical theism since the last quarter of the last century, a different image of nature has gained momentum after Darwin. The natural world may *appear* to be an artifact (nature functions as if designed) but there is no designing mind or intentional, purposive, good Creator. For some contemporary naturalists, the cosmos is, as it were, a book without an author. Richard Dawkins' book title *The Blind Watchmaker* is apt given his view that the world may appear to be an intentional object like a watch or a book, but the forces that made it are non-intentional and non-purposive.

1. Charles Darwin, *On the Origin of Species* (New York: D. Appleton, 1860), 1.

The role of images and the imagination in philosophy and religion is being given greater attention in recent years. Suzanne Langer was particularly insightful when she observed: "Religious thought operates primarily with images....Images only, originally made us aware of the wholeness and overall form of entities, acts and facts in the world; and little though we may know it, only an image can hold us to a conception of a total phenomenon, against which we can measure the adequacy of the scientific terms wherewith we describe it."[2] As part of this new attention to images and imagination, some philosophers have been led to consider what may be called the aesthetics of inquiry. In the debate between theism and naturalism, for example, we may investigate which worldview is more beautiful or ugly, which enhances or enriches our understanding of consciousness and values or which obscures and overshadows our experience of each other and the world. We began an investigation of the aesthetic dimension of images as employed by science and religion in our co-authored book *The Image in Mind: Theism, Naturalism, and the Imagination.*

This book, *Turning Images in Philosophy, Science, and Religion: A New Book of Nature*, grew out of our desire to bring together some of the best philosophers who are working on images, imagination, and aesthetics, to address the comparative strengths and weaknesses of the theistic and secular naturalist images of the natural world. We are delighted that four of the philosophers who have helped lead the renewed look at aesthetics and imagination in philosophy of religion agreed to contribute: Gordon Graham, Douglas Hedley, Anthony O'Hear, and Mark Wynn. Five other diverse, outstanding philosophers, Conor Cunningham, Geoffrey Gorham, Dale Jacquette, E.J. Lowe, and Daniel N. Robinson, were invited to cover vital terrain in the philosophy of religion and science to assist in the exploration of theism and naturalism. The other two writers are Martin Kemp and Jil Evans. Kemp has written extensively on the relationship of art and science and Evans is a practicing studio artist who has explored these ideas in her work and writing.

Martin Kemp begins the book by looking at D'Arcy Thompson's vision of the natural world, combining poetry and visual images to set the stage for thinking about nature along either teleological or non-purposive

---

2. Langer, *Mind: An Essay of Human Feelings*, Vol 1 (Baltimore: Johns Hopkins University Press, 1967), xviii–xix.

lines. Geoffrey Gorham then offers an overview and analysis of the images of nature found in early modern science and philosophy. Gorham explores the ways in which early modern thinkers were passionately committed to re-conceiving the relationship of God and nature in light of modern science. In chapter three, Anthony O'Hear takes up the problem of accounting for the origin of mind or consciousness, highlighting some of the limitations of Darwinian evolutionary biology in terms of values. Dale Jacquette offers a thoroughgoing, naturalistic account of the emergence of intentionality and a unique argument about the emergence of art and the aesthetic appreciation of nature. For Jacquette, the evolution of intelligence and imagination does not constitute an obstacle for naturalism. E.J. Lowe, on the other hand, advances some difficulties facing a naturalist approach to mental life. Lowe contends that human perception, meaning, and structured thought are difficult to account for in scientific naturalism. Douglas Hedley offers a cognitive account of the imagination and also advances reasons why naturalism faces deep challenges. Hedley's Platonic conception of imagination is in the tradition of Coleridge. Daniel N. Robinson offers a sweeping account of nature and naturalism, historically engaging Aristotle, Kant, Hegel and others. Robinson is intent on questioning the concept of nature as found in contemporary naturalism, and he hints at the end of his chapter at the promising alternative of theism. Conor Cunningham's chapter is a take-no-prisoners critique of contemporary naturalism. Gordon Graham investigates the resources of naturalism in accounting for our sense of the sacred. Mark Wynn provides a subtle account of the imagination and perception, outlining how these may play into the theism–naturalism debate. The book concludes with Jil Evans' reflections on the Galapagos Islands, that key, almost mythic place that became instrumental in shaping Darwin's development of his theory of evolution. Evans compares two images of the Galapogos Islands, one is naturalistic, the other theistic.

A brief note on terminology: "theism" and "naturalism" may be defined in different ways, and we have not imposed strict common usage. Roughly, "theism" is the view that there is an all good, omnipotent, omniscient, omnipresent, necessarily existing God who created and sustains the cosmos. "Naturalism" has been advanced in strict terms in which only the natural sciences are recognized as reliable sources of knowledge. But naturalism has also been defended in broad terms in which the social sciences

are worthy sources of knowledge, and there are forms of naturalism that
are broader still, recognizing irreducible normative facts, consciousness,
free will, and so on. For the purposes of this book, the essential idea to
keep in mind is that whatever the form of naturalism, all forms assume or
assert the falsehood of theism.[3]

3. All forms of naturalism also deny the soul as an immaterial reality, miracles, and afterlife, and so
on. For an overview of different forms of naturalism, see *Naturalism* by Stewart Goetz and
Charles Taliaferro (Grand Rapids: Eerdmanns, 2008).

ONE

"Loving Insight": D'Arcy Thompson's Aristotle and the Soul in Nature

Martin Kemp

For so work the honey-bees,
Creatures that by a rule in nature teach
The act of order to a peopled kingdom.
They have a king and officers of sorts;
Where some, like magistrates, correct at home,
Others, like merchants, venture trade abroad,
Others, like soldiers, armèd in their stings,
Make boot upon the summer's velvet buds;
Which pillage they with merry march bring home
To the tent-royal of their emperor:
Who, busied in his majesty, surveys
The singing masons building roofs of gold,
The civil citizens kneading up the honey,
The poor mechanic porters crowding in
Their heavy burdens at his narrow gate,
The sad-eyed justice, with his surly hum,
Delivering o'er to executors pale
The lazy yawning drone.[1]

Thus spoke the Archbishop of Canterbury—educationally—to Shakespeare's King Henry V. It is to this speech that D'Arcy Wentworth Thompson refers in his magisterial Spencer Lecture "On Aristotle as a Biologist" at Oxford on St Valentine's day in 1913:

1. Shakespeare, *Henry V*, I. 2.

> Plato saw philosophy, astronomy, even mathematics, as in a vision; but Aristotle does not know this consummation of a dream. The bees have a king, with Aristotle. Had Plato told us of the kingdom of the bees, I think we should have had Shakespearian imagery. The king would have had his "officers of sorts, his magistrates, and soldiers, his singing masons building roofs of gold."[2]

Characteristically Thompson does not spoon-feed his audience with a reference to his source. Nor does he provide references for many of the philosophical and cultural quotations and allusions in his *magnum opus* of biophysics, *On Growth and Form* (1917).[3] He deigns to translate his numerous quotations and pithy tags from Greek, Latin, German, and French. Thompson expects his readers to *know*. He also expects us to handle techniques in mathematics, most especially geometry, which are beyond most educated persons. Unrealistic as his demands might seem, he was not asking us to do anything he could not do himself. Professor of Biology at Dundee from 1884 until taking up the chair of Natural History at St. Andrews, which he held for sixty-four years, he was a recognized scholar of Greek and Latin classics and was widely respected by professional mathematicians and philosophers.[4] For us, later and lesser mortals, it would be good to have an annotated edition.[5]

Thompson inserted biology into culture as a whole, and saw it as capable of shedding light on the very nature of nature, both in itself and in its cultural translations over the centuries. His model for the centrality of biology to human understanding was Aristotle. Botany and zoology, Thompson believed, conduct us to the edge of the mysteries of consciousness, the soul and the infinite deity. They speak not just of the technicalities of how diverse plants and animals are formed and how they function but are also the bearers of *value*. In nature we can witness the beauties of form fitting function according the principles of mathematical physics and see that they are "good":

---

2. *On Aristotle as Biologist with a Proemium on Herbert Spencer*, the Herbert Spencer Lecture, Oxford, 1913, 16–17 (hereafter as *Aristotle as Biologist*).
3. I have used throughout *On Growth and Form* (Cambridge, 1917), hereafter *On Growth*. Cambridge proceeded to publish three other editions: an expanded and revised edition in 1942, and an abridged version by John Tyler Bonner in 1961, and finally the abridged edition with an introduction by the great Thompsonian, Stephen Jay Gould in 1992.
4. The best compact introduction to Thompson's biography is http://www-groups.dcs.st-and. ac.uk/~history/Biographies/Thompson_D'Arcy.html
5. I have here attempted to trace those of the unsourced quotations that seemed most important. A full-scale tracing of all the allusions in Thompson's publications would be a massive but instructive job.

the physicist proclaims aloud that the physical phenomena which meet us by the way have their manifestations of form, not less beautiful and scarce less varied than those which move us to admiration among living things. The waves of the sea, the little ripples on the shore, the sweeping curve of the sandy bay between its headlands, the outline of the hills, the shape of the clouds, all these are so many riddles of form, so many problems of morphology, and all of them the physicist can more or less easily read and adequately solve: solving them by reference to their antecedent phenomena, in the material system of mechanical forces to which they belong, and to which we interpret them as being due. They have also, doubtless, their immanent teleological significance; but it is on another plane of thought from the physicist's that we contemplate their intrinsic harmony and perfection, and "see that they are good."[6]

The allusion here is not a precise quotation (unless I have missed the actual source), but seems to be to Genesis 1:31: "And God saw every thing that he had made, and, behold, it was very good. And the evening and the morning were the sixth day." In any event, Thompson would have expected us to be alert to the allusion to the first book of the Bible.

This sense of the intrinsic "goodness" of the mathematics of nature as comprehended "on another plane of thought" is not something most modern biologists would own up to. However, if we interpret "goodness" in terms of an instinctive delight in the look and performance of the subjects they study, and add to that their feeling of the worth of communicating their discoveries, we can understand that value is still implicit in biology. We could call it "aesthetic" value, but I would prefer not to, particularly because I regard the term too period-specific to be useful in our present context. Instinctive delight is certainly important in driving what I have called "structural intuitions"; that is to say the deeply involving interplay between orders in nature and the perceptual-cognitive systems that we use to discern the orders, however obscurely veiled they are behind natural appearance. I am also for the most part avoiding the term "design," although it is very germane, because the "argument from design" has been hijacked by extreme creationists in a way that Thompson would have regarded as absurd. Indeed, he does not himself use such an argument, even by implication, to explain the manifold *variety* of natural form. "Goodness" in his sense resides in the relationship between the great mysteries of God's *decrees* in nature and our human ability to relate to these mysteries. In biology, the mysteries that are

6. Thompson, *On Growth*, 7.

accessible to us are the recurrent "riddles of form" that run in a shared way across the organic and inorganic worlds.

Over the centuries generations of philosophers and biologists have been drawn to a special set of natural phenomena that exhibit evident, if often complex, geometries. I am thinking of things like phyllotaxis in plants, the spirals of shells, the nests of certain birds, the packing of cells in honeycombs, the branching of trees and rivers, the symmetries of flowers and snowflakes, the patterned patches of giraffes and the stripes of zebras, the tensile structures of thin films and foams, the turbulent flows of liquids and particulate materials, the geometry of crystals, the self-generated designs of chemical interactions, the beguiling arrays of diffusion and aggregation, and, more recently, the wide range of overtly chaotic phenomena that have become the focus of the sciences of complexity as played out on computers.[7] Even if the investigators are not thinking in any conscious way at the level of Thompson's other "plane of thought," the inherent satisfaction the biologist feels in seeing and analyzing such geometries remains an implicit source of potent motivation, even without any explicit religious dimension.

In this essay I will explore the nature of Thompson's "vision" (to use the term he applies to Plato) both in itself and as having a broader bearing on biology and visual knowledge before and after his era. His enduring relationship with Aristotle will help shape our quest. The headings will be "the physical mathematics of nature"; "unity"; "teleology and the evolution of form"; and "beyond explanation." On all these topics Thompson himself expresses himself with such eloquence and, for the most part, with such elegant clarity that I make no apology for using an unusually high quotient of quotations.

The physical mathematics of nature

Thompson indeed expounds pattern in nature, if we understand pattern as an expression of force and process. *On Growth and Form* is about the visible manifestation of force in nature, not about nature's obvious "appearance."

---

7. For reviews of these and related phenomena in contemporary and historical contexts, see P. Ball's trilogy, *Shapes, Flow* and *Branches*, 3 vols. (Oxford: Oxford University Press, 2009); see also M. Kemp, *Seen/Unseen. Art, Science, and Intuition from Leonardo to the Hubble Telescope* (Oxford: Oxford University Press, 2006).

He is the first to advocate biophysics (rather than biomathematics, as it is often called) as a central discipline in biology:

> As soon as we adventure on the paths of the physicist, we learn to weigh and to measure, to deal with time and space and mass and their related concepts, and to find more and more our knowledge expressed and our needs satisfied through the concept of number, as in the dreams and visions of Plato and Pythagoras; for modern chemistry would have gladdened the hearts of those great philosophic dreamers.[8]

Though Thompson certainly would not align himself with these "philosophic dreamers" in their more metaphysical modes, he recognized the glory of the ancient tradition to which his quest for the mathematics of nature belonged.

He shared Aristotle's vision of the essential embeddedness of mathematics in the fabric of things rather than its separate and divine meta-existence in the Platonic manner. His mathematics follows Aristotle's in its essentially dynamic nature:

> Evermore his [Aristotle's] world is in movement. The seed is growing, the heart beating, the frame breathing. The ways and habits of living things must be known: how they work and play, love and hate, feed and procreate, rear and tend their young; whether they dwell solitary, or in more and more organized companies and societies. All such things appeal to his imagination and his diligence.[9]

In his "Proemium to Herbert Spencer" that opens his Spencer lecture, Thompson characteristically emphasizes the sweep of tradition to which this vision belongs: "As in former days Descartes, and as Democritus and Epicurus in days of old, so did Spencer find in matter and in motion, or rather in matter and in force, the fabric of a world." It is more than tradition, however. Thompson also knew about the kind of modern physics that was to give rise to Einstein:

> All the while Spencer recognizes that Space, Time, Motion, and Matter itself are remote from Absolute Reality, and have their source in our own Empiricism. The "Persistence of Force" is the only truth which transcends experience; and what we ultimately mean by the persistence of force is a cause which transcends our conception and our knowledge.[10]

---

8. Thompson, *On Growth*, 2.   9. *Aristotle as Biologist*, 15.   10. *Aristotle as Biologist*, 7.

There is a direct echo here of James Clerk Maxwell, Thompson's fellow Scot, to whom he looks for non-classical theories of atoms and energy. Maxwell is indexed eight times in *On Growth and Form* compared to Plato's surprisingly lowly three.

In two respects, however, Thompson is closer to Plato than Aristotle. The first, as he noted himself, was in the poetry of expression, of which his own writings are a supreme example. The second is in an instinctual reverence for the beauty and rule of mathematics, above all, geometry. In 1904 he published an erudite study on "Plato's Theory of the Planets" for the astronomy journal, the *Observatory* (later revised for the *Classical Review*), in which he delighted in both the poetic figuration and implicit precision of Plato's astronomical understanding. He looks at the allegory of the Vision of Er in the tenth book of *The Republic*, where the Greek philosopher envisages the heavenly Spirits bearing privileged witness to the glories of the astronomical universe: "now the first and outermost whorl had the broadest circular rim, that of the sixth was second, and third was that of the fourth, and fourth was that of the eighth, fifth that of the seventh, sixth that of the fifth, seventh that of the third, eighth that of the second." After a learned overview of Greek writings on the subject, Thompson concludes that "Plato utilized all the astronomic science of his time, simplifying it for the purposes of his allegory."[11] Here is a tantalizing glimpse of Plato as the Shakespeare of the mathematical sciences.

But poetry does not sanction wooly metaphysics. Thompson holds no truck with Pythagorean mysticism, old or new. He is often cited as a source of inspiration for those who wish to find the "golden section" as ubiquitous in nature (and in art). This cannot be sustained if we take the trouble to read what he actually wrote:

> the fact that the successional numbers, expressed as fractions, 1/2, 2/3, 3/5, represent a convergent series, whose final term is equal to 0-61803 . . . , the *sectio aurea* or "golden mean" of unity, is seen to be a mathematical coincidence, devoid of biological significance; it is but a particular case of Lagrange's theorem that the roots of every numerical equation of the second degree can be expressed by a periodic continued fraction. The same number has a multitude of curious arithmetical properties. It is the final term of all similar series to that with which we have been dealing, such for instance as 1/3, 3/4, 4/7, etc., or 1/4, 4/5, 5/9, etc. It is a number beloved of the circle-squarers, and of

11. Plato, *The Republic,* book 10, 616 E, quoted in "On Plato's Theory of the Planets," *Observatory* 27(1904), 363–66.

all those who seek to find, and then to penetrate, the secrets of the Great Pyramid. It is deep-set in Pythagorean as well as in Euclidean geometry. It enters (as the chord of an angle of 36°), into the thrice-isosceles triangle of which we have spoken on p. 511 [gnomon of triangle is isosceles]; it is a number which becomes (by the addition of unity) its own reciprocal; its properties never end. To Kepler (as Naber tells us) it was a symbol of Creation, or Generation. Its recent application to biology and art-criticism by Sir Theodore Cook and others is not new. Naber's book, already quoted, is full of it. Zeising, in 1854, found in it the key to all morphology, and the same writer, later on, declared it to dominate both architecture and music. But indeed, to use Sir Thomas Browne's words (though it was of another number that he spoke): "To enlarge this contemplation into all the mysteries and secrets accommodable unto this number, were inexcusable Pythagorisme." If this number has any serious claim at all to enter into the biological question of phyllotaxis, this must depend on the fact, first emphasized by Chauncey Wright, that, if the successive leaves of the fundamental spiral be placed at the particular zimuth which divides the circle in this "sectio aurea," then no two leaves will ever be superposed.[12]

Amongst the dense cluster of allusions, we may particularly note those to Henri Adrien Naber's obscure 1908 exposition of Pythagoreanism, *Das Theorem des Pythagoras, in seiner ursprünglichen Form und wiederhergestellt betrachtet as Grundlage der geese Pythagorean Philosophie* (The Theory of Pythagoras, Restored to Its Original Form and Considered as the Foundation of the Entire Pythagorean Philosophy), and to Theodore Andrea Cook's more popular *Spirals in Nature and Art* (1903) and *The Curves of Life* (1914). While respecting the diligence, mathematical skill, historical erudition and ingenuity of Naber's and Cook's labors, he rejected their metaphysical bases. Cook's advocacy of the golden ratio as the key to beauty in nature and art, be it in the spiral formations of shells or the proportional glories of such masterpieces as Botticelli's *Venus*, Hals's *Laughing Cavalier,* or Turner's *Fighting Temeraire*, did not stand up to the kind of empirical scrutiny that Thompson demanded.[13] Thompson was all too aware that a functional explanation of the mathematics of process that have shaped a biological form, such as a spiral phyllotaxis, could be subject to pretty mathematical embroidery that becomes airily detached from the realities of cause and effect. We will encounter this principle of economy of explanation again in the section on teleology and form.

12. *On Growth*, 649.
13. For a comparative study of Thompson and Cook, see M. Kemp, "Spirals of Life: D'Arcy Thompson and Theodore Cook, with Leonardo and Dürer in Retrospect," in *Physis* 32 (1995), 37–54.

Unity

The nature of Thompson's quest played towards morphologies shared across apparently very different species, organs and parts rather than classificatory differentiation. Indeed, his emphasis upon physical process exploited many instances of similarity between organic and inorganic forms, such as the configurations adopted by viscous fluids when they fall into less viscous substances, which he saw as analogous to sea creatures without skeletons or shells, such as medusoid bells. Or we could cite structural parallels between clusters of bubbles and aggregates of cells. Evolutionary theory and genetics, by contrast, naturally play towards the heritable differences that differentiate parts, individuals, families, species, and so forth. In looking towards commonalities Thompson was swimming against the biological tide of his era, and indeed of much of the twentieth century.

Again Aristotle is fundamental in how we understand Thompson's way of observing patterns in the movement and forces of natural processes:

> the quest of physical causes merges with another great Aristotelian theme,— the search for relations between things apparently disconnected, and for "similitude in things to common view unlike." Newton did not shew the cause of the apple falling, but he shewed a similitude between the apple and the stars.[14]

Thompson's gift for the telling sentence or phrase is unsurpassed in the sciences and would stand up well in any context. A likely though not precise source for the quotation is Quintilian's discussion of varied kinds of "similitude" using biological examples in *Institutio oratoria*.[15]

His reverence for unity depends not least on Aristotle's *Metaphysics*, particularly book 3, through which it runs as a leitmotif. Thompson typically casts his Aristotelian net far and wide:

> The biologist, as well as the philosopher, learns to recognise that the whole is not merely the sum of its parts. It is this, and much more than this. For it is not

---

14. *On Growth*, 6.
15. Quntilian, *Institutio oratoria*, V, 11, 30: "I am aware that some writers have shown pedantic zeal in making a minute classification of similes, and have pointed out that there is lesser similitude (such as that of a monkey to a man or a statue when first blocked out to its original), a greater similitude (for which compare the proverb "As like as egg to egg"), a similitude in things dissimilar (an elephant, for instance, and an ant both belong to the genus *animal*), and dissimilitude in things similar (puppies and kids, for example, are unlike the parents, for they differ from them in point of age)."

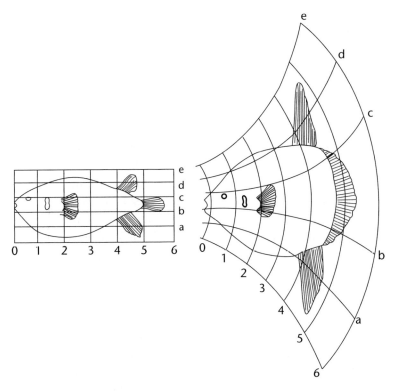

Figure 1.1 D'Arcy Thompson, *The Geometrical Transformation of a Porcupine Fish into a Sunfish*, from *On Growth and Form*, 1917, figs. 381 and 382

a bundle of parts but an organisation of parts, of parts in their mutual arrangement, fitting one with another, in what Aristotle calls "a single and indivisible principle of unity"; and this is no merely metaphysical conception, but is in biology the fundamental truth which lies at the basis of Geoffroy's (or Goethe's) law of "compensation," or "balancement of growth."[16]

The French pioneer of evolutionary thinking, Etienne Geoffrey de Saint-Hilaire, argued for an essential unity of plan in animals with differential development of parts, in which one highly developed part was compensated by lesser development in another. This has an obvious relevance to Thompson's idea of "transformation," which described the formation of various species through the skewing and warping of the same bodily template (Fig. 1.1).

16. *On Growth*, 714.

Goethe, the famous universalizer, was undoubtedly admired for his engagement with commonalities of form and phenomena, and as an example of the shared cultural reach of science, literature, and art. At the start of chapter 17 in *On Growth and Form*, "On the Theory of Transformations," Thompson explains, "We have learned in so doing that our own study of organic form, which we call by Goethe's name of Morphology, is but a portion of that wider Science of Form which deals with the forms assumed by matter under all aspects and conditions, and, in a still wider sense, with forms which are theoretically imaginable." However, there is no reference in *On Growth and Form* to Goethe's *Metamorphosis of Plants*, in which a notional *ur*-leaf (not a Platonic form) was seen as the template for all the diverse parts of the plant, ranging from sepals to stamens. This omission is somewhat surprising, but Thompson may well have felt that Goethe's theory erred too much on the side of mysticism rather than mathematics.[17]

Goethe was perhaps more admired as an author than a scientist. Earlier in *Growth and Form*, when Thompson analyzes the rules that placed a limit on the height of trees, citing Galileo and Ruskin amongst others, he characteristically quoted (in German) an essentially literary passage from Goethe's imaginative autobiography, *Aus Meinem Leben: Dichtung und Wahrheit* (From My Life: Poetry [or Fiction] and Truth). The lines read to the effect that "care is taken that even the tallest trees shall not in invade the heavens."[18] This is immediately followed by a classic Thompsonian aside: "But Eiffel's great tree of steel (1,000 feet high) is built to a very different plan [to trees]; for here the profile of the tower follows the logarithmic curve, giving equal strength throughout, according to a principle which we shall have occasion to discuss when we come to treat of 'form and mechanical efficiency' in connection with the skeletons of animals."

Thompson's great text of seventeen chapters, approaching 800 pages even in the first edition, is less an exploration of a variety of topics, or even of a series of linked themes, than a sustained exposition of the mathematical warp and woof that underlies the diverse creatures and plants depicted in the prodigious tapestry of nature.

17. For Goethe, see M. Kemp, *Seen/Unseen*, 190–3.   18. *On Growth*, 20–1.

Teleology and the evolution of form

Thompson accepted Darwin's theory of natural selection only unenthusiastically, regarding it as insufficient as an explanation of morphology. For Thompson, natural selection undermined classic teleology, in which *telos* as the "end" or "purpose" is seen as the governing principle behind the study of natural form. Thompson was skeptical of attempts to reconcile Darwinism and teleology:

> In a very curious way, we are told that teleology was "refounded, reformed or rehabilitated"[19] by Darwin's theory of natural selection, whereby "every variety form and colour was urgently and absolutely called upon to produce its title to existence either as an active useful agent, or as a survival" of such active usefulness in the past. But in this last, and very important case, we have reached a "teleology" without a τέλος [*telos*].[20]

In Thompson's view, a Darwinian "final cause," in the Aristotelian sense, becomes little more, if anything, than the mere expression or resultant of a process of sifting out the good from the bad, or the better from the worse, in short a process of mechanism. The apparent manifestations of "purpose" or adaptation become part of a mechanical philosophy, according to which "chaque chose finit toujours par s'accommodera à son milieu."[21] In short, by a road which resembles but is not the same as Maupertuis's road, we find our way to the very world in which we are living, and find that if it be not, it is ever tending to become, "the best of all possible worlds."[22]

The allusion here is to Pierre Louis Moreau de Maupertuis's "principle of least action," which decreed a fundamental economy of action between causes and effects in the dynamics of the universe. It was a principle adduced first in relation to astronomy but was also applied by Maupertuis to motion in the natural world, such as the movement of animals and the growth of plants. The causes were governed by a limited set of mathematical laws that testified to the wisdom of God.

Thompson was deeply sympathetic to Maupertuis's view, since teleology could be retained with respect to the *telos* of underlying laws decreed by God

---

19. Thompson's footnote in *On Growth* is to Ray Lankester's article, "Zoology," *Encyl. Brit.,* 9th ed. (1888), 806.
20. *On Growth*, 4.
21. Thompson's footnote in *On Growth* is to Paul Janet, *Les Causes Finales* (1876), 350.
22. Thompson's footnote in *On Growth* refers to Leibniz's *Théodicée.*

and to which all things in motion were necessarily obedient, rather than advocating the more crude teleology of organisms or components of organisms designed in a detailed way to perform predetermined functions. Thus, the neck of a giraffe did not grow longer and longer according to a prescribed purpose, but the evolution of its advantageously long neck must be structured and constrained by a set of physical laws. Thus Thompson provides a hypothetical analysis of the "whole girder-system" of the giraffe's vertebral column.[23]

Thompson is not altogether explicit about how teleology can be saved in the face of natural selection, but it seems that a more abstract and general teleology allows him to save the "great vision" of the "final cause" in nature:

> Time out of mind, it has been by way of the "final cause," by the teleological concept of "end," of "purpose," or of "design," in one or another of its many forms (for its moods are many), that men have been chiefly wont to explain the phenomena of the living world; and it will be so while men have eyes to see and ears to hear withal. With Galen, as with Aristotle, it was the physician's way; with John Ray, as with Aristotle, it was the naturalist's way; with Kant, as with Aristotle, it was the philosopher's way. It was the old Hebrew way, and has its splendid setting in the story that God made "every plant of the field before it was in the earth, and every herb of the field before it grew." It is a common way, and a great way; for it brings with it a glimpse of a great vision, and it lies deep as the love of nature in the hearts of men.

He seems to shift the basis of teleology from the "story" in *Genesis*, which retains its allegorical truth, and from the detailed adaptation of forms to specific functions, to a final cause that generates the manifold of nature through the laws of physico-chemical action. The laws do not just belong to the realm of physics; they are integral to our passionate human insight into the majestic order of creation. The values of biophysics are thus mathematical *and* spiritual. They serve the theological *telos* of allowing us to participate in the wonder of God's creation.

The *locus classicus* of the geometrical cells of the bees' honeycomb will serve to exemplify Thompson's approach showing how it related to tradition and, in a more problematic way, to the new principles of Darwinian biology. In Thompson's account, or rather in the accompanying footnote, the tensions with Darwin are apparent:

> The question is, to what particular force are we to ascribe the plane surfaces and definite angles which define the sides of the cell ..., and the ends of the cell

23. *On Growth*, 705.

in cases where one row meets and opposes another. We have seen that Bartolin suggested, and it is still commonly believed, that this result is due to simple physical pressure, each bee enlarging as much as it can the cell which it is a-building, and nudging its wall outwards till it fills every intervening gap and presses hard against the similar efforts of its neighbour in the cell next door.[24] ...But it is very doubtful whether such physical or mechanical pressure, more or less intermittently exercised, could produce the all but perfectly smooth, plane surfaces and the all but perfectly definite and constant angles which characterise the cell, whether it be constructed of wax or papery pulp. It seems more likely that we have to do with a true surface-tension effect; in other words, that the walls assume their configuration when in a semi-fluid state, while the papery pulp is still liquid, or while the wax is warm under the high temperature of the crowded hive.[25] Under these circumstances, the direct efforts of the wasp or bee may be supposed to be limited to the making of a tubular cell, as thin as the nature of the material permits, and packing these little cells as close as possible together. It is then easily conceivable that the symmetrical tensions of the adjacent films (though somewhat retarded by viscosity) should suffice to bring the whole system into equilibrium, that is to say into the precise configuration which the comb actually presents. In short, the Maraldi pyramids which terminate the bee's cell are precisely identical with the facets of a rhombic dodecahedron, such as we have assumed to constitute (and which doubtless under certain conditions do constitute) the surfaces of contact in the interior of a mass of soap-bubbles or of uniform parenchymatous cells; and there is every reason to believe that the physical explanation is identical, and not merely mathematically analogous.[26]

In the footnote, Thompson explains the distinctions:

Darwin had a somewhat similar idea, though he allowed more play to the bee's instinct or conscious intention. Thus, when he noticed certain half-completed cell-walls to be concave on one side and convex on the other, but to become perfectly flat when restored for a short time to the hive, he says: "It was absolutely impossible, from the extreme thinness of the little plate, that they could have effected this by gnawing away the convex side; and I suspect that the bees in such cases stand on opposite sides and push and bend the ductile and warm wax (which as I have tried is easily done) into its proper intermediate plane, and thus flatten it."

The heart of the tension lies between Darwin's desire to exploit natural selection as the core explanation for all form and function in nature, governing

24. Thompson's footnote in *On Growth* is to Darwin's *Origin of Species*, chap. 8, quoted below.
25. Thompson's note in *On Growth* reads, "Since writing the above, I see that Mülenhoff gives the same explanation, and declares that the waxen wall is actually a *Flüssigkeitshäuchten*, or liquid film."
26. *On Growth*, 332.

intentional and non-intentional acts, and Thompson's conviction that phys-ico-chemical laws held sway over the parameters of natural form. The geom-etry of a honeycomb, for Thompson, was the necessary result of the mechanism decreed by the laws—what would now be called a "self-organizing" process.

The balance between the factors intrinsic and extrinsic to the bee—and it is clearly a matter of balance rather than a crude "either-or"—is still very much a matter for debate. It seems to me unlikely that there is a specific set of genes for geometrical design that govern in every detail the collective building operations. Equally the wax does not spontaneously arrange itself. If we watch the bees at work, they collaboratively build the bases and walls flake-by-flake. The bees seem to be equipped genetically with a set of direc-tional and gravitational skills that work with the physical parameters. These parameters act both to shape and to set constraints whilst "the singing masons" build their "roofs of gold." At present we are better at explaining how the form is optimal than precisely how the "inner bee" works with the outer wax to reach the geometrical end. The inner and outer types of explanation are both necessary, but each is insufficient on its own if we wish to have a rounded understanding of this particular riddle of form.

Figure 1.2 D'Arcy Thompson, *Liesgang's Rings*, from *On Growth and Form*, 1917, fig. 205

An even more direct clash between Thompsonian process and Darwinian natural selection occurs when he discusses the "ocelli" or eyespots of the emperor moth. Looking at the concentric rings of pigments of different hue and tone within the ocelli, Thompson sees a marked affinity with Liesgang rings (Fig. 1.2). Named after the German chemist, Raphael Liesgang, the rings are formed by chemical processes of diffusion and precipitation, as described in *On Growth and Form*:

> If we dissolve, for instance, a little bichromate of potash in gelatine, pour it on to a glass plate, and after it is set place upon it a drop of silver nitrate solution, there appears in the course of a few hours the phenomenon of Liesegang's rings. At first the silver forms a central patch of abundant reddish brown chromate precipitate; but around this, as the silver nitrate diffuses slowly through the gelatine, the precipitate no longer comes down in a continuous, uniform layer, but forms a series of zones, beautifully regular, which alternate with clear interspaces of jelly, and which stand farther and farther apart, in logarithmic ratio, as they recede from the centre.[27]

Thompson naturally attributes the ocelli in the wings of the emperor moth to this kind of process, whereas Darwin looks towards sexual selection: "Darwin's well-known disquisition on the ocellar pattern of the feathers of the Argus Pheasant, as a result of sexual selection, will occur to the reader's mind, in striking contrast to this or to any other direct physical explanation."[28] He later records ironically that the ocelli in "the jewelled splendour of the peacock and the humming-bird, and the less effulgent glory of the lyre-bird and the Argus pheasant, are ascribed to the unquestioned prevalence of vanity in the one sex and wantonness in the other." It is with some relief that Thompson records in a footnote that William Bateson, the dedicated Darwinian and Mendelian who coined the term "genetics," "appears inclined to suggest a purely physical explanation of an organic phenomenon: 'The suggestion is strong that the whole series of rings (in Morpho) may have been formed by some one central disturbance, somewhat as a series of concentric waves may be formed by the splash of a stone thrown into a pool, etc.'"[29]

Thompson would have gained much comfort from the creation of novel eyespots and eyespot distributions in butterfly wings by the Portuguese art-

27. *On Growth*, 427.

28. *On Growth*, 431, Thompson's note is to the *Descent of Man*, Vol. 2 (1871), 132–53.

29. Thompson's note is to Bateson's *Variation* [*Materials for the study of variation: treated with special regard to discontinuity in the origin of species*], chap. 12.

Figure 1.3 Marta de Menezes. "*Nature?*" Live *Bicyclus anynana* butterfly with modified wing pattern, 2000

ist Marta de Menezes (Fig. 1.3). She has used a thin needle coupled to a heat generator to intervene in a very minor way with the development of the patterns while the butterflies were still in their cocoons. The eyespots self-organized in new ways that were not due to genetic dictate and that were not heritable.

The second of Thompson's discussions of the eyespots triggers a notably rhapsodic footnote:

> Delight in beauty is one of the pleasures of the imagination; there is no limit to its indulgence, and no end to the results which we may ascribe to its exercise. But as for the particular "standard of beauty" which the bird (for instance) admires and selects (as Darwin says in the Origin, p. 70, edit. 1884), we are very much in the dark, and we run the risk of arguing in a circle: for well-nigh all we can safely say is what Addison says (in the 412th Spectator)[30] later—that each different species "is most affected with the beauties of its own kind....*Hinc merula in nigro se oblectat nigra marito;...hinc noctua tetram Canitiem alarum et glaucos miratur ocellos.*"[31]

30. See J. Addison, "Pleasures of Imagination," *Spectator*, 412 (Monday, 21 June 1712).
31. *On Growth*, 671.

Addison's own translation of the relevant section in his Latin poem, published later in the 1744 edition of the *Spectator*, runs:

> The black-bird hence selects her sooty spouse;
> The nightingale her musical compeer,
> Lured by the well-known voice: the bird of night,
> Smit with her dusky wings and greenish eyes,
> Woos his dun paramour.

As we have noted, Thompsonian biology is a cultural pursuit. And teleology is at the human heart of the culture of biology.

Beyond explanation

Thompson acknowledges that there are strict practical limits to what he could accomplish in determining the physical processes behind each form in nature, just as there were limits to the physicists' explanation of complex phenomena. He comes very close at one point to the modern sciences of complexity in realizing that hugely varied and variable phenomena ("unpredictable" as we would say) can result from a simple set of initial causes. Here he is speaking of the "structure of the cell":

> The fact that the germ-cell develops into a very complex structure, is no absolute proof that the cell itself is structurally a very complicated mechanism: nor yet, though this is somewhat less obvious, is it sufficient to prove that the forces at work, or latent within it are especially numerous and complex. If we blow into a bowl of soap suds and raise a great mass of many-hued and variously shaped bubbles, if we explode a rocket and watch the regular and beautiful configuration of its falling streamers, if we consider the wonders of a limestone cavern which a filtering stream has filled with stalactites, we soon perceive that in all these cases we have begun with an initial system of very slight complexity, whose structure in no way foreshadowed the result, and whose comparatively simple intrinsic forces only play their part by complex interaction with the equally simple forces of the surrounding medium.[32]

He is optimistic that physics can ultimately solve these problems of complex appearance arising from simple causes, but there remains something beyond the reach of even the most complete physical explanation:

32. *On Growth*, 159.

How far, even then, mathematics will suffice to describe, and physics to explain, the fabric of the body no man can foresee. It may be that all the laws of energy, and all the properties of matter, and all the chemistry of all the colloids are as powerless to explain the body as they are impotent to comprehend the soul. For my part, I think it is not so. Of how it is that the soul informs the body, physical science teaches me nothing: consciousness is not explained to my comprehension by all the nerve-paths and "neurones" of the physiologist; nor do I ask of physics how goodness shines in one man's face, and evil betrays itself in another. But of the construction and growth and working of the body, as of all that is of the earth earthy, physical science is, in my humble opinion, our only teacher and guide.[33]

Aristotle again plays a central role in defining the role and limits of explanation in the physical sciences (including biophysics). Thompson quotes a substantial passage from Aristotle's *De partibus animalium*:

Doubtless, he [Aristotle] says, "the glory of the heavenly bodies fills us with more delight than we get from the contemplation of these lowly things; for the sun and stars are born not, neither do they decay, but are eternal and divine. But the heavens are high and afar off, and of celestial things the knowledge that our senses give us is scanty and dim. On the other hand, the living creatures are nigh at hand, and of each and all of them we may gain ample and certain knowledge if we so desire. If a statue please us, shall not the living fill us with delight; all the more if in the spirit of philosophy we search for causes and recognize the evidences of design. Then will Nature's purpose and her deep-seated laws be everywhere revealed, all tending in her multitudinous work to one form or another of the Beautiful."[34] In somewhat similar words does Bacon, retranslate a familiar saying: "He hath made all things beautiful according to their seasons; also he hath submitted the world to man's inquiry."[35] On the other hand, a most distinguished philosopher [James Ward] of to-day is struck, and apparently perplexed, by "the awkward and grotesque, even the ludicrous and hideous forms of some plants and animals."[36] I commend him, with all respect, to Aristotle or to that Aristotelian verity given us in a nutshell by Rodin, "Il n'y a pas de laideur!"[37]

The precise source of the Rodin tag is elusive, but it is in keeping with the great sculptor's declared view that "for the artist, nothing in nature is ugly." The same is evidently true for the Thompsonian biologist. The Rodin

---

33. *On Growth*, 8–9.
34. Thompson's footnote in *On Growth* is to [Aristotle's] *De Part. Anim.* i. 5.
35. Thompson's footnote in *On Growth* is to Bacon's *De Sapienta Veterum* (Eccles. 3: 11).
36. Thompson's footnote in *Aristotle as a Biologist* is to James Ward's *The Realm of Ends or Pluralism and Theism* (Cambridge: Cambridge University Press, 1912) 85.
37. *Aristotle as a Biologist*, 15–16.

reference confirms that Thompson was more alert to and engaged with the visual arts than has generally been recognized.[38] His particular interest in Rodin may have been triggered by the award of an honorary degree to the sculptor in Scotland by the University of Glasgow in 1905.

Thompson follows the Rodin tag with the passage that leads up to the Plato-Shakespeare conjunction that we have already quoted:

> To be sure, Aristotle's notion of beauty was not Rodin's. He had a philosopher's comprehension of the Beautiful, as he had a great critic's knowledge and understanding of Poetry; but wise and learned as he was, he was neither artist nor poet. His style seldom rises, and only in a few such passages as that which I have quoted, above its level didactic plane. Plato saw philosophy, astronomy, even mathematics, as in a vision…[39]

Even if Aristotle did not speak with the poet's voice, he was, Thompson insists, fully aware that our poetic engagement with the realm of the beautiful leads us infallibly to the nature of the rational soul of human beings and its transcendent superiority to the sensitive soul of animals and the nutritive soul of plants:

> At length the reasoning soul, the νους or *nous* emerges in man, as the source of his knowledge and his wisdom. In a brief but very important passage, with a touch of that Platonic idealism never utterly forgotten by him (and so apt to bring Wordsworth to our own minds), Aristotle tells us that this soul "cometh from afar" μόνον θύραθεν επεισιέναι, θείον είναι μόνον [that comes afterward, from without, and hence it is considered as the only one of divine substance]."[39] Yes, in very plain Greek prose, this is no less than to assert that "trailing clouds of glory," "it cometh from afar."[40]

Thompson overtly contrasts "Spencer's colder catalogue of facts and Aristotle's more loving insight into the doings and into the hearts, into the motives and the ambitions, of men…. Aristotle … is the great Vitalist, the student of the Body with the Life thereof, the historian of the Soul."[41] Towards the end of his Spencer lecture, Thompson expresses wonder at how Aristotle's profound and early immersion in biology led him to develop his most profound ideas:

---

38. See Matthew Jarron's and Cathy Caudwell's valuable *D'Arcy Thompson and His Zoology Museum in Dundee* (Dundee: 2010), 45–7; also Jarron's lecture in Oxford. I am grateful to Jarron for the text of his lecture.
39. Thompson's reference in *On Growth* is to *De Gen. An.* Ii, 3, 736 b 27.
40. *Aristotle as a Biologist*, 26.   41. *Aristotle as a Biologist*, 25.

I can only see dimly, and cannot venture to explain, how his lifelong study of living things led to his rejection of Plato's idealistic ontology, and affected his whole method of classification, his notion of essentials and accidents, his idea of "Nature" that "makes nothing in vain," his whole analysis of causation, his belief in, and his definition of, Necessity, his faith in design, his particular form of teleology, his conception and apprehension of God.[42]

We began with Shakespeare as quoted by Thompson. Let us end by picking up his allusion to Wordsworth, who spoke of the soul coming "from afar." Into such far realms, the poet and the biologist both reach out through faith rather than reason. The reference is to Wordsworth's ode, *Intimations of Immortality from Recollections of Early Childhood*:

> Our birth is but a sleep and a forgetting:
> The Soul that rises with us, our life's Star,
> Hath had elsewhere its setting,
> And cometh from afar:
> Not in entire forgetfulness,
> And not in utter nakedness,
> But trailing clouds of glory do we come
> From God, who is our home:
> Heaven lies about us in our infancy!

42. *Aristotle as a Biologist*, 30.

TWO

Early Scientific Images of God: Descartes, Hobbes, and Newton†

Geoffrey Gorham

I n medieval philosophical theology, God was balanced delicately between transcendence and immanence. On the one hand, God could not be entirely removed from the world since he was the continuous source of its being and powers.[1] And yet God's literal presence within space and time seemed manifestly incompatible with divine attributes such as simplicity and immutability. If God was in space and time the way bodies are, God

† *Abbreviations:* AT= Descartes, René, *Oeuvres de Descartes* 11 vols., ed. C. Adam and P. Tannery (Paris: J. Vrin, 1976), citation by volume and page number. The standard English translations of Descartes' philosophical works and correspondence are: Descartes, R., *The Philosophical Writings of Descartes* 2 vols., ed. and trans. J. Cottingham, R. Stoothoff, and D. Murdoch (Cambridge: Cambridge University Press, 1984–85), and *The Correspondence*, ed. and trans. J. Cottingham, R. Stoothoff, D. Murdoch, and A. Kenny (Cambridge: Cambridge University Press, 1991). EW = Thomas Hobbes, *English Works* 11 vols., ed. W. Malmesworth (London: J. Bohn, 1839–1845), citation by volume and page number. AW = Thomas Hobbes, *Thomas White's De Mundo Examined*, ed. H. Jones (London: Bradford University Press, 1976), citation by chapter and page number. L = Thomas Hobbes, *Leviathan with Selected Variants from the Latin Edition of 1668*, ed. E. Curley (Indianapolis: Hackett Publishing, 1994), citation by part and chapter. C = Thomas Hobbes, *Appendices* i-iii, in *Leviathan with Selected Variants from the Latin Edition of 1668*, ed. E. Curley (Indianapolis: Hackett Publishing, 1994), citation by appendix and page number. EL = Thomas Hobbes, *Elements of Law*, ed. J. C. A. Gaskin (Oxford: Oxford University Press, 1994), citation by part, chapter, paragraph and page number. DG= Newton, Isaac, "De Gravitatione et aequipondio fluidorum," in *Newton: Philosophical Writings*, ed. and trans. A. Janiak and C. Johnson (Cambridge: Cambridge University Press, 2004).

1. As St. Anselm observed, the divine Being must be "in every place and time, inasmuch as all other existing things are sustained by its presence in order that they not fall away into nothing." Anselm, St. *Monologion*. Vol. 1, 22. J. Hopkins and H. Richardson, ed. (Toronto: The Edwin Mellen Press, 1974), 38.

would have distinct parts—left and right sides, before and after—and therefore be at risk of corruption and change. So theologians like Augustine and Boethius developed a compromise whereby God is always and everywhere, but in a manner appropriate to a perfect and incorporeal being: all at once and entirely. This metaphysical template for divine eternity and immensity remained intact through centuries of scholastic refinement.[2] With the revival of ancient systems, Renaissance philosophers tilted to divine immanence, comparing God's worldly presence to illumination or ensoulment. But the seventeenth century moved beyond such metaphors as God was enlisted directly into various ambitious scientific programs.[3] Descartes, for example, derived his law of rectilinear motion from the fact that God "always conserves the motion in the precise form in which it is occurring at the very moment when he conserves it" (AT 8A 63–4). God's sustenance was no longer all at once but moment-by-moment. Similarly, emerging theories of absolute space called upon God to fill an actually infinite void. Newton's teacher Isaac Barrow observed that since "God is infinite in essence, he must subsist beyond the bounds of matter. . . . Therefore something is beyond, i.e. some sort of space."[4]

If God's essence is actually present in time and space, the question arises whether this essence is disclosed to empirical science as a direct object of sense, measurement, and imagination. In this chapter, I argue that the most powerful and influential thinkers of the seventeenth century encouraged a conception of God as strongly continuous with nature, but they also strongly resisted the implication that God was therefore known by the senses and imagination. The attitude of Descartes, Hobbes and Newton will be found similar to Spinoza, who thoroughly collapsed the distinction between God

---

2. Thus, Augustine already conceived of God's immensity as a real presence that permeates the universe though "not having one part here and another there, but being whole everywhere and present everywhere." Augustine, St., *The Manichean Debate* ed. S. J. Roland Teske (New York: New City Press 2006), 245. Similarly, along the temporal dimension, Boethius offered the famous definition of God's eternity as "a possession of life simultaneously entire and perfect, which has no end." Boethius, *Consolations of Philosophy*, trans. J. C. Relihan (Indianapolis: Hackett Publishing, 2001), 144. Two recent, more detailed studies of corporeal God's relation to Hobbes's metaphysics and natural philosophy, which however differ in numerous ways from my approach and from one another, are: A. Lupoli, "*Fluidismo e Corporeal Deity nella filosofia naturale di Thomas Hobbes*," *Revista di Storia della filosofia* 54 (1999), 573–609; C. Leijenhorst, "Hobbes's Corporeal Deity," *Revista di Storia della filosofia* 59 (2004), 73–95.

3. See Gorham, "God and the Natural World in the Seventeenth Century: Space, Time and Causality," *Philosophy Compass* 4 (2009), 1–14 for an overview of this development.

4. Isaac Barrow, *Mathematical Lectures*, X in *Mathematical Works*, ed. W. Whewell (Cambridge: Cambridge University Press, 1860), 170.

and nature but nevertheless warned that men are often frustrated in their attempt to understand God "because they cannot imagine God, as they can bodies, and have joined the name *God* to the images of things."[5]

Descartes' unimaginable God

Descartes and Hobbes, in spite of mutual philosophical and personal antagonism, were able to find some common ground in the "objections and replies" to Descartes' *Meditations*. They after all shared a fundamental commitment to the mechanical philosophy, as Descartes recognized: "Like me, he wants to restrict his attention to shapes and movements" (AT 3 283). Moreover, although each made God the ultimate source of these shapes and movements they both denied that God could be known in the same way as bodies. The empiricist Hobbes maintained that although we posit God as first cause, we simply have "no idea or image corresponding to the sacred name of God" (AT 7 180). Descartes insisted that we have a clear idea of God but it is not "depicted in the corporeal imagination" since God is absolutely incorporeal (AT 7 183; AT 5 272). Moreover, since he is not united to a body in the way humans are, "God does not possess any corporeal imagination" (AT 7 181). However, beginning with Descartes, I would like to argue that neither philosopher is able to keep God entirely out of the imagination.

The imagination plays a crucial role in the *mathesis universalis* expounded by Descartes in the early, unpublished *Regulae*. In Rule 12, we are told that the intellect must "be assisted by the imagination" in the attainment of truth (AT 10 411). For example, "we do not form two distinct ideas in our imagination, one of extension the other of body; but just the single idea of extended body" (AT 10 444). We run into the error of a vacuum because we employ, instead of a "corporeal idea," merely "an incorrect judgment of the intellect alone" (AT 10 443).[6] In Descartes' later philosophy the imagination is downgraded somewhat as a means of grasping extended nature but remains important for the investigation of the properties of particular

5. Spinoza, *Ethics* II P 47 Schol, in *A Spinoza Reader*, ed. and trans. E. Curley (Princeton: Princeton University Press, 1994), 145.
6. For detailed discussion of Descartes' early theory of the imagination, see Sepper, *Descartes' Imagination: Proportion, Images and the Activity of Thinking* (Berkeley: University of California Press, 1996).

material things. In the Fifth Meditation (concerning the "Essence of Material Things") Descartes explains, "I distinctly imagine the extension of the quantity (or rather of the thing which is quantified) in length, breadth and depth" (AT 7 63). So while I can understand a chiliagon and a pentagon without the imagination, "I can also imagine a pentagon by applying my mind's eye to its five sides and the area contained within them" (AT 7 73). The intellect furnishes the abstract ideas of "extension," "chiliagon," and so on; the imagination supplies particular shapes and motions. In this sense "body (extension, shapes and motion) can likewise be known by the intellect alone, but much better by the intellect aided by the imagination" (AT 3 691).[7] But Descartes always holds, even in the *Regulae*, that when it comes to things "in which there is nothing corporeal... the senses must be kept back and the imagination must, as far as is possible, be divested of every distinct impression" (AT 417). Thus, Descartes' comments about the ideas of God and the soul: "[T]rying to use one's imagination to understand these ideas is like trying to use one's eyes to hear sounds or smell colors" (AT 6 37). Similarly, he chastises Gassendi that since imagination is restricted to corporeal images, "If anyone thus represents God, or the mind, to himself he is trying to imagine something that is unimaginable" (AT 7 385).

Since God is unimaginable, it follows for Descartes that religious pictures and stories that depict corporeal things and events are inherently misleading. This point is broached in the replies to Hobbes: "Nothing we attribute to God can have been derived from external objects as a copy is derived from its original since nothing in God resembles what is to be found in external, that is corporeal, things" (AT 7 188). It is explained more thoroughly in Descartes' attack on his fallen disciple, Regius, who had dared to assert that the idea of God derives from "the observation of things or in verbal instruction" (AT 8B 345). Descartes offers a cutting rejoinder: "No one can assert that we know nothing of God other than his name or the corporeal image which artists give him, unless he is prepared to admit openly that he is an atheist and totally lacking in intellect" (AT 8B 360). Strictly speaking, corporeal images do not depict God at all and that is why merely imagining God is no better than atheism.

Nevertheless, I suggest that Descartes cannot altogether avoid imaginary representations of God, even at the very foundations of his natural philosophy.

---

7. See further Nolan, "Imagination in Rationalist Mathematics," in *A Companion to Rationalism*, ed. A. Nelson (London: Blackwell, 2005).

In the *Principles of Philosophy* (1644), he derives his three laws of motion from the assumption that "God imparted various motions to the parts of matter when he first created them, and he now conserves all this matter in the same way" (AT 8A 61). But the various "parts of matter" in the Cartesian plenum are mutually distinguished only by relative motion: "by "one body" or one "part of matter" I mean whatever is transferred at a given time" (AT 8A 33–4). So imparting various motions to the parts of matter involves a division of extension into various shapes and sizes through relative motions. But how could God, lacking a corporeal imagination, represent to himself this carving up of generic matter? For, as we saw above, the imagination seems to be the faculty by which particular figures are cognized. Furthermore, it is unclear whether we can represent this creation to ourselves using only the purely intellectual idea of God as infinite and immutable mind. It does not seem to be contained in this idea that God should affect some particular division within extension. There is some indication Descartes was aware of such problems with his creation model since he notes that we may need to rely on "divine revelation" and "faith" to grasp how "certain changes take place without any change in the creator" (AT 8A 61).

In a more elaborate version of the creation story in the earlier *World* (1633), Descartes supposes that God first creates in "imaginary space" undifferentiated matter and then "really divides it into many such parts, some larger and some smaller, some of one shape and some of another, however we care to imagine them" (AT 11 34). Descartes repeatedly insists that we are to conceive this creation story in the imagination, "fashioning this matter as we fancy." Moreover he characterizes the account as a mere "fable" about a "new world" rather than the actual world. Elsewhere, Descartes remarks on the charming power of fables to "awaken the mind" (AT 6 5) but subsequently warns that fables can also "make us imagine many events as possible when they are not" (AT 6 7). The reason the creation of matter must be presented as a fable, I suggest, is because it requires us to apply our imagination beyond its limits. God would need to conceive a particular division of bare extension into parts; but nothing in our idea of God makes this intelligible to us. This fable about the initial creation of bodies may be contrasted with the subsequent derivation of the laws of nature in the *World*, which Descartes says "follow inevitably from the eternal truths" in such a way that "if God had created many worlds they would be as true in each of them as in this one" (AT 11 47). These eternal truths include facts about the essence of God, especially his immutability, which are known by the mind alone: "The knowledge of these truths is so natural to our souls that we cannot but hold them infallible" (ibid.). Whether we rely on revelation, or settle for a fable, we are unable to conceive intellectually how an absolutely incorporeal and immutable being produces the diverse shapes and motions of this world.[8]

It is worth noting that Descartes' creation fable reveals that the Cartesian imagination outstretches the senses in a certain respect. It assumes we are capable of imagining very clearly the boundless matter whose only attribute is three-dimensionality: "The idea of this matter is included to such an extent in all the ideas that our imagination can form that you must necessarily conceive it or else you can never imagine anything at all" (AT 11 35). Undifferentiated extension is unique among the objects of Cartesian imagination: it is presupposed in all imaginings of bodies but lacks any sensible qualities of its own. The potentially infinite, insensible, and ubiquitous nature of Cartesian extension might seem almost divine, as Henry More in fact suggested to Descartes in a 1649 letter (AT 5 241). Descartes predictably replied that this is impossible since "God is not imaginable or divisible into parts" (AT 5 272). Nevertheless the notion that God is imaginable (if not strictly sensible) because he constitutes space and time becomes an attractive doctrine in the wake of Descartes, as we shall see below.

Hobbes's corporeal God

In his 1641 objections to the *Meditations*, Hobbes contends that although we are inevitably led to posit God as the uncaused, eternal cause of the causes of our ideas, strictly speaking "there is no idea of God in us" (AT 7 180; see also L 1, 11; EW 3 92–3). He implies, by analogy with angels ("immaterial and invisible creatures who serve God") that this is because God is incorporeal. But by the time of *Leviathan* (1651) Hobbes has embraced wholesale materialism: "Every part of the universe, is body, and that which is not body, is no part of the universe: and because the universe is all, that which is no part of it, is *nothing*" (L 4, 46; EW 3 672). The Cartesian notion of "incorporeal substance," he now maintains, is not only false but "contradictory and inconsistent" (L 1, 4; EW 3 27).

---

8. For a different, but I think compatible, account of the role of imagination in the earlier creation fable, see Sepper, *Descartes's Imagination*, chap. 6.

Hobbes holds back from drawing the seemingly unavoidable conclusion that God himself is corporeal (or nothing at all). He finally makes this unorthodox theology explicit in the appendix to the Latin translation of *Leviathan*, published almost two decades after the original, when Hobbes was 80 years old. Using dialogue form, Hobbes has the interlocutor ("A") ask what it is to deny incorporeal substance except "to deny that God exists or to affirm that God is a body." "B" answers on behalf of Hobbes, as if it were a mere afterthought: "He affirms, of course, that God is a body" (L Appendix iii; C 540). The discussion turns quickly to the authority for such a doctrine in Scripture and the Church Fathers. A more detailed philosophical defense of Hobbes's corporeal God is found in his reply to Bishop Bramhall's *Catching the Leviathan* (1658), which included the charge:

> They who deny all incorporeal substances can understand nothing by God but either nature (that is, not *naturam naturantem* a real author of nature, but *naturam naturatam* that is the orderly concourse of natural causes) as T.H. seems to intimate or a fiction of the brain without real being (Bramhall *Works*, 526).

Hobbes's posthumous *Answer to Bramhall*, probably written the same year the Latin *Leviathan* was published, firmly grasps one horn of Bramhall's dilemma: "To his lordship's question here *what I leave God to be*, I answer: I leave him to be a most pure, simple invisible spirit corporeal" (EW 4 313). This corporeal God, Hobbes explains is also "infinite" and "eternal" (EW 4 306).

Scholars on both sides of the long debate about the sincerity of Hobbes's theism have generally dismissed his corporeal God as either inconsistent with his more orthodox theological pronouncements or incoherent in itself.[9] Consider God's infinite body. In *Leviathan*, Hobbes defines a body as "that

---

9. Those who view Hobbes as a sincere theist tend to emphasize the orthodox aspects of his professed theology. See Glover, "God and Thomas Hobbes" in *Hobbes Studies* ed. K. Brown (Oxford: Blackwell, 1965); Martinich, *The Two Gods of Leviathan: Thomas Hobbes on Religion and Politics* (Cambridge: Cambridge University Press, 1992); Geach, "Hobbes' Religion" in *Thomas Hobbes: Critical Assessments Vol. IV: Religion* ed. P. King (London: Routledge, 1993); Paachi, "Hobbes and the Problem of God" in *Perspectives on Thomas Hobbes* ed. G. A. J Rogers and A. Ryan (Oxford: Oxford University Press, 1998). Those who consider Hobbes a closet atheist tend to hold that his corporeal God is incoherent. See E. Curley, " 'I Durst Not Write So Boldly': or How to Read Hobbes' Theological-Political Treatise," ed. Emilia Giancotti, *Proceedings of the Conference on Hobbes and Spinoza, Urbino* (Naples: Bibliopolis, 1992); Jesseph, "Hobbes's Atheism" in *Midwest Studies in Philosophy* 26 ed. P. A. French and H. K. Weinstein (2002): 140–66; Berman, *A History of Atheism in Britain: From Hobbes to Russell* (Kent: Croom Helm, 1988), and Tuck "The 'Christian Atheism' of Thomas Hobbes" in *Atheism from the Reformation to the Enlightenment* ed. M. Hunter and D. Wooton (Oxford: Oxford University Press, 1992), both consider Hobbes an atheist, at least from *Leviathan* onwards, but neither discusses his corporeal God. Nor does

which filleth, or occupieth some certain room, or imagined place" (L 3, 34, 2; EW 3 381). Here Douglas Jesseph, a proponent of the atheist Hobbes, objects: "Hobbes's ontology admits only bodies, each of which is coincident with some bounded, determinate part of space; God however is infinite and incomprehensible and this rules out the possibility that God could be a body in the sense defined by Hobbes" (144). But this ignores an explicit distinction drawn in the *Answer to Bramhall*: "*Body* is that substance which hath magnitude indeterminate and is the same with corporeal substance; *A body* is that which hath magnitude determinate and so is understood to be a *totum* or *integrum aliquid*" (EW 4 309). It is clear that he intends God to be *body* rather than *a body*, since he goes on to explain what it means for indeterminate body to be "pure and simple," terms included in his earlier definition of God. Since body as such need not have determinate magnitude, Hobbes is not after all inconsistent in holding God to be infinite body.

Another problematic implication of corporeal theism cannot be so easily accommodated: the attribution of parts and division to God. In the *Leviathan* Hobbes himself says we ought not "attribute to him parts or totality, which are the attributes of things finite" (L 2, 31; EW 3 51). In his answer to Bramhall, Hobbes is at pains to show he is not on this point "inconsistent and irreconcilable" with himself, that is, "a forgetful blockhead" (EW 4 286–7). He expressly disavows Bramhall's traditional "partless" or "holenmerist" conceptions of God's ubiquity and eternity as total presence in every place and instant—as if God were "no greater than to be wholly contained within the least atom of earth . . . and that his whole duration is but an instant of time" (EW 4 300. See also L 4, 46; EW 3 675–7). Referring to certain condemned Trintarian heresies, he agrees that God is not divisible

Hepburn, though he notes a tension between the immanent and transcendent tendencies in Hobbes's theology, "Hobbes on the Knowledge of God" in *Rousseau and Hobbes: A Collection of Critical Essays* ed. M. Cranston and R. S. Peters (New York: Anchor Books, 1972), nor Springborg, who nevertheless concludes that Hobbes's religious beliefs "ultimately remain a mystery," "Hobbes on Religion" in *Cambridge Companion to Hobbes* ed. T. Sorell (Cambridge: Cambridge University Press, 1996), 369. Mintz adopts a similar stance in *The Hunting of Leviathan* (Cambridge: Cambridge University Press, 1962), 44. Zarka, specifically mentioning the corporeal God doctrine, insists on the theological foundations of Hobbes's thought but concedes that this foundation remains "open and uncertain," "First Philosophy and the Foundations of Knowledge" in *Cambridge Companion to Hobbes*, 80. Duncan takes the corporeal God doctrine to support the sincerity of Hobbes's theism, though he does not analyze it in detail, "Knowledge of God in Leviathan." *History of Philosophy Quarterly* 22 (2005): 31–48. Strauss comes closest to the analysis I will present, although he does not broach the question of coherence in *What is Political Philosophy?* (New York: The Free Press, 1959).

into numerically distinct individuals "as the name of man in divisible into "Peter" and "John" (EW 4 302; see also EW 4 398).[10] The corporeal extension of God does not imply, however, that God is really divisible in this way. For he insists that any spatial part of God is itself infinite. By this he seems to mean when we consider any part of God's presence we do not really, but only conceptually, distinguish it from the rest of its infinite expanse:

> But that in a substance that is infinitely great it should be impossible to consider anything that is not infinite I do not find there condemned. For certainly he that thinks God is in the every part of the church does not exclude him out of the churchyard. And is this not considering him by parts. For dividing a thing which we cannot reach nor separate one part thereof from another is nothing but considering of the same by parts. So much concerning indivisibility from natural reason ... (EW 4 302)

God has spatial parts, just as he has successive duration, but not in a way that allows him to be really separable into finite parts or "discerptible" as Henry More would say. This conforms not only to natural reason, but to Scripture, since, "God is nowhere said in Scriptures to be indivisible, unless his Lordship [i.e. Bramhall] meant division to consist only in separation of parts" (ibid.). The "block-headed" inconsistency with *Leviathan* is therefore avoided.

Hobbes's corporeal theism is not pantheism, a doctrine he specifically derides as tantamount to atheism: "Those philosophers who said the world (or the soul of the world) was God spake unworthily of him, and denied his existence" (L 2, 31; EW 3 351).[11] In Hobbes's view, God is one, very special body among others. He is remarkably explicit about this to Bramhall: "I mean by the universe the aggregate of all things that have being in themselves and so do all men else. And since God has a being it follows that he is either the whole universe or part of it" (EW 4 349). God happens to be that part of the universe which is the uncaused cause of the rest: "God is properly the hypostasis, base and substance that upholdeth all the world, having subsistence not only of himself but from himself, whereas other substances have their subsistence only in themselves not from themselves" (EW 4 308). God's being part of the world is also consistent with his being infinite since one can easily distinguish infinity from totality, just as

---

10. This of course raises the issue of the Trinity, about which Hobbes had a good deal to say. See Springborg "Hobbes on Religion" for a concise summary.
11. Glover, "God and Thomas Hobbes"; Jesseph, "Hobbes's Atheism."

philosophers were accustomed to distinguishing the spatial infinity of the created world from its eternity.[12]

To understand how Hobbes's corporeal God "upholdeth" the world, we need to recall that God is defined as a pure and simple spirit. Hobbes explains that a body is pure and simple when it is perfectly homogeneous, that is, "One and the same kind in every part throughout" (EW 4 309). Such a body, he says, can be mixed with other bodies while retaining its simplicity, like wine in water. He next explains that spirit is "thin, fluid, transparent, invisible body" (ibid.). He then illustrates how such a "spiritual" body might mix with ordinary matter to produce change and diversity in the world:

> I have seen, and so have many others, two waters, one of the river and the other mineral water, so that no man could discern one from the other from his sight; yet when they are both put together the whole substance could not be distinguished from milk. Yet we know the one was not mixed with the other, so as every part of the one to be in every part of the other, for that is impossible, unless two bodies can be in the same place. How then could the change be made in every part, but only by the activity of the mineral water, changing it everywhere to the sense and yet not being everywhere and in every part of the water? (EW 4 310)

If there is any doubt that Hobbes is here venturing, however clumsily, a model of God's operation in nature, he quickly puts it to rest. Like the mineral water in the river, it is precisely by virtue of being thoroughly interspersed with matter that God is able to affect all the natural changes we observe:

> If such gross bodies have such great activity what then can we think of spirits, whose kinds be as many as there are kinds of liquor, and activity greater? Can it then be doubted that God, who is infinitely fine spirit, and withal intelligence, can make and change all species and kinds of bodies as he pleases? (EW 4 310)

Hobbes says little about the source of God's activity. But it seems to be consistent with his physical principles that corporeal God acts on finite bodies

---

12. Hobbes discusses both spatial and temporal infinity in *De Corpore* 2, 7, 12; EW 1 99–100. On this last point I am in disagreement with Curley, "'I Durst Not Write So Boldly'". Curley's impressive paper includes a comprehensive discussion of Hobbes's reaction to Spinoza's *Theological-Political-Treatise,* reported by his early biographer John Aubrey: "He told me he had out-thrown him a bar's length, for he durst not write so boldly." But there is no reason to think Spinoza's pantheism had any influence on Hobbes: the *Ethics* was published just before Hobbes's death, long after his theological views were fully settled. Cf. Glover "God and Thomas Hobbes," 166.

by an endeavor or conatus that stretches to the past eternally and outward infinitely.[13]

As the featureless substrate of natural change, Hobbes's corporeal God is reminiscent of Aristotelian prime matter. Indeed, in *De Corpore* Hobbes comments that the notion of prime matter as "body without the consideration of any form or accident but only magnitude or extension" is "not of vain use" in accounting for radical change in bodies, for example, from water to ice. But he then considered it a purely conceptual being, a "mere name" that designates the notion of "body in general" abstracted from any property other than bare quantity (*De Corpore* 2, 8, 24; EW 1 118).[14] But later, body in general is reified and made to serve a purpose similar to the undifferentiated extension of Descartes' creation stories. Both are conceived as unbounded and undivided material plenums, lacking any qualities besides Euclidean dimension, through which God operates to produce the observable properties and interactions of ordinary, gross bodies. But whereas Descartes separates God from the plenum, as agent from patient or mind from body, Hobbes's God is an immanent cause of change.

Even though God is a body according to Hobbes's late theology, he consistently asserts that God is unimaginable. As mentioned above, his original reason for asserting this seemed to be the immateriality of God. Later, when his wholesale materialism is in place, he prefers to invoke a different reason: "Whatever we imagine is finite. Therefore there is no idea or conception of anything we call infinite..." (L 1, 3; EW 3 17). But this seems a rather weak reason. It is plausible that we cannot imagine or picture an actual or complete infinity, and in that sense God's body is incomprehensible by finite minds. But why aren't we able to imagine or conceive God in part, just as we could sense or imagine part of an infinite ocean? There is another weak sense in which corporeal God is unimaginable. In the Latin *Leviathan*, he explains that angels, like all spirits, "because of the transparency of spiritual substances, are invisible" (L Appendix iii; C 543). And the analysis is extended to God in the *Answer to Bramhall*: God is an "invisible spirit corporeal"

13. Hobbes says that the propagation of any endeavor, whether in empty space or a plenum, is temporally instantaneous and spatially infinite (*De Corpore* 3, 15, 7; EW 1 216). Hobbes says, "for as it is true that nothing is moved by itself; so it is also true that nothing is moved but by that which is already moved" (*De Corpore* 4, 26, 1; EW 1 412).
14. For more on Hobbes's use of prime matter, and other Aristotelian concepts, in his natural philosophy, see Leijenhorst, *The Mechanisation of Aristotelianism: The Late Aristotelians Setting of Thomas Hobbes' Natural Philosophy* (Leiden: Brill, 2002).

(EW 4 313). God is unimaginable simply because he is the subtlest of spirits and so invisible and intangible. Thus, God is unknowable in the same sense as the smallest bodies that compose things, not because his being is of a different order than gross bodies but because his dimensions are invisible to human senses. Still, as for Descartes, it follows that any attempt to represent him with an image is futile in itself and also "against the second commandment and of no use to worship" (L 4, 45; EW 3 658; see also AT 7 180).

In *Leviathan*, Hobbes maintains that religion arises from fear of "power invisible." This religion is *true*, he says, "when the power we allege is truly such as we imagine" (L 1, 6; EW 3 45).[15] The *Answer to Bramhall* provides a more detailed, and more naturalistic, gloss of true religion: ignorance of second causes made men fly to some first cause, the fear of which bred devotion and worship" (EW 4 292). In other words, the lack of an adequate science of natural or finite ("second") causes inspires religion; if science eventually produces a true conception of the first cause underlying all secondary causes (Hobbes's corporeal God) then religion is true. Under the corporeal God, science is not the exclusion of religion but the culmination of its original instinct. In the end, Hobbes finds a place for God in his materialist, mechanistic world as the indeterminate but dimensional, all-pervasive plenum underlying and governing physical changes and interactions. So conceived, we can take quite literally Hobbes's assertion that "it is impossible to make any profound enquiry into natural causes, without being inclined thereby to believe there is one God eternal; though they cannot have any idea of him in their mind, answerable to his nature" (L 1, 11; EW 3 92).

Newton's spatio-temporal God

Owing to his materialism, staunch royalism, and love of polemic, Hobbes was alienated from the mainstream intellectual world of seventeenth-century England.[16] But the close association he makes between God and the world

15. Curley notes that Hobbes revises the definition of true religion in the Latin edition so that the invisible powers really are as we "allow" rather than as we "imagine" in order to avoid the implication that something invisible is imaginable C 31 n3; See also C 542; Appendix iii, 9–10.
16. See Shapin and Schaffer, *Leviathan and the Air-Pump: Hobbes, Boyle and the Experimental Life* (Chicago: University of Chicago Press, 1989), for a stimulating account of Hobbes's relation to Boyle and the Royal Society. See also Westfall, *Science and Religion in Seventeenth Century England* (New Haven: Yale University Press, 1958). See Taliaferro, *Evidence and Faith: Philosophy*

is made by more respected figures such as Henry More and Isaac Newton. Remarking on Newton's famous characterization of infinite space as God's "sensorium," Leibniz wondered whether this placed Newton among those "modern Englishmen" who hold space to be "God himself or one of his attributes."[17] Leibniz was right to be suspicious. With increasing force and openness through the last decades of his life, Newton identified God's attributes of immensity and eternity with space and time themselves, and so his God became, in effect, the absolute inertial frame of his mechanics. Moreover, like Hobbes, Newton considered this partial assimilation of God and nature a step towards a more authentic brand of theism than was available from scholastic theology or the dominant churches.

Newton's spatio-temporalization of God seems to have begun in his philosophically rich, but unpublished, tract known as *De gravitatione et aequipondio fluidorum* (c.1865). *De grav* opens with a powerful critique of Descartes' relationist conceptions of place and motion, from which Newton concludes: "It is necessary that the definition of places, and local motion, be referred to some motionless thing—extension alone or space alone insofar as it can be seen truly distinct from bodies" (DG 20–21). This "space alone" is immobile, homogeneous, infinite, eternal, and independent of bodies; time alone is constant, the same everywhere, lacking beginning or end, and independent of motions. Furthermore, they are neither substances nor accidents but rather "emanative effects" of God. Here is Newton's gloss of this relationship:

> Space is an emanative effect of the first existing being, for if any being whatsoever is posited, space is posited. And the same may be asserted of duration: for certainly both are affections or attributes (*affectiones sive attributa*) of a being according to which the quantity of any thing's existence is individuated to the degree that the size of its presence and persistence is specified. So the quantity of existence of God is eternal in relation to the time in which he persists; and infinite in relation to the space in which he is present. (DG 25)

While they are necessary consequences of his infinite and eternal existence, and therefore uncreated, Newton seems to retain a distinction between God and the world: space and time are the "effects" of God. But we will see that eventually this gap is erased.

and Religion since the Seventeenth Century (Cambridge: Cambridge University Press, 2005), chap. 1 on Hobbes's relation to the Cambridge Platonists.

17. G. W. Leibniz and S. Clarke, *Correspondence,* ed. R. Ariew (Indianapolis: Hackett Publishing, 2000), 14.

In the wake of the first edition of *The Principia* (1687), which says almost nothing about God, the connection between God and space and time becomes even more intimate. In the unpublished work from the early 1690s, "Tempus et Locus," Newton lists numerous religious advantages of a spatial and temporal God versus the scholastic's transcendent God. The fourth of these emphasizes that it is preferable that "creatures share so much as possible the attributes of God (*attributa Dei*)."[18] The implication is that we share in God's attributes of space and time, no less than his attributes of will and intellect. And in the General Scholium to the second edition of *The Principia* (1713), Newton declares that God is "omnipresent not only *virtually* but *substantially*." Furthermore: "He endures always and is present everywhere and by existing always and everywhere he *constitutes* duration and space."[19] "Constitutes" could be taken in either a metaphysical or the legislative sense.[20] Yet he describes the relation of finite things to God in just the way one would characterize the relation of bodies to absolute space: "In him all things are contained and move but he does not act on them nor they on him."[21]

The queries to the *Opticks* (which so puzzled Leibniz) provide additional evidence that Newtonian space and time are divine attributes. Newton proposes that just as animals directly perceive the "sensible species" or ideas of things in their "sensorium," in the same way "there is a being incorporeal, living, intelligent, omnipresent, who in infinite space, as it were his sensory (*tanquam sensorium*), sees the things themselves intimately, and thoroughly perceives them."[22] God perceives things directly in absolute space just as we perceive ideas directly in our sensory field. The same analogy also accounts for God's omnipotence: "Being in all places, [God] is able to move the bodies within this boundless uniform sensorium, and thereby to form and

18. McGuire, J. E., "Newton on Place, Time, and God: An Unpublished Source," *British Journal for the History of Science* 11 (1978), 114–29, 121. Cited henceforth as "Tempus et Locus."

19. Newton, Isaac, *The Principia: Mathematical Principles of Natural Philosophy* ed. and trans. I. B. Cohen and A. Whitman (Berkeley: University of California Press, 1999), 941.

20. For a recent legislative reading, see Carriero, "Newton on Space and Time: Comments on J. E. McGuire" in *Philosophical Perspectives on Newtonian Science* ed. P. Bricker and R. I. G. Hughes (Cambridge, MA: MIT Press, 1990), 109–34, 131 n. 23. On the rich theological backdrop to the General Scholium, particularly its voluntarism and anti-trinitarianism, see Snobelen, " 'God of Gods, and Lord of lords': The Theology of Isaac Newton's General Scholium to *The Principia*," *Osiris* 16 (2001), 169–208.

21. *The Principia*, 941–2.

22. Newton, *Philosophical Writings*, ed. and trans. A. Janiak and C. Johnson (Cambridge: Cambridge University Press, 2004), 130.

reform the parts of the universe."[23] On this model absolute space is not distinct from God, no more at least than the sensorium is distinct from sentient beings. The analogy makes rather vivid the line from Acts (17: 28) that Newton liked to quote: "In him we live and move and have our being." We live and move in the space of God's imagination.

If Newtonian space and time are divine attributes, it follows that physical considerations can settle, or clarify, certain theological questions.[24] For example, it makes no sense for absolute space, as the frame for all other motions, to move. This explains Newton's rather surprising remark in a theological manuscript that God "being immoveable . . . is necessarily in all places alike so that no place can subsist without him or be emptier or fuller of him."[25] Nor do the parts of space and time move relative to one another since they are individuated by their mutual location: "If any two could change their locations they would change their individuality at the same time and each would be converted numerically into the other" (DG 25). For this reason, Newton argues, there is no need to fear that God, as infinite extension and duration, becomes divisible: "lest anyone should imagine that for this reason God to be like a body, extended and made of divisible parts, it should be known that spaces themselves are not actually divisible" (DG 26). From the physical structure of space and time it will likewise follow that God is infinitely extended, eternal and uncreated.

Newton also embraces a consequence of his "physico-theology" that not even Spinoza would countenance, namely that God will have inherent measure and dimension.[26] In a remarkable passage from *De grav.* Newton observes

23. Newton, *Philosophical Writings*, 138. See also "Tempus et Locus": "understanding everything to the utmost, freely willing good things, by his will affecting all possible things, and containing all other substances in Him as their underlying principle and Place; a substance which by his own presence discerns and rules all things, just as the cognitive part of man perceives the forms of things brought into the brain and thereby governs his own body," 123.

24. The overall conception of Newtonian space and time that I defend here was earlier more common among Newton scholars but has fallen out of favor. See e.g. Burtt, *The Metaphysical Foundations of Modern Science* (Atlantic Highlands: Humanities Press, 1952), 259; Koyré, *From the Closed World to the Infinite Universe* (Baltimore: Johns Hopkins University Press, 1957), 227; Grant, *Much Ado About Nothing: Theories of Space and Vacuum from the Middle Ages to the Scientific Revolution* (Cambridge: Cambridge University Press, 1981), 243–4.

25. *Irenicum*: Keynes MS. 3, fol. 3. "The father is immoveable no place being capable of becoming emptier or fuller of him than it is by the eternal necessity of nature: all other beings are moveable from place to place." Keynes MS. 8, Art. 5. See also Mclachlan, *Sir Isaac Newton: The Theological Manuscripts* (Liverpool: The University Press, 1950), 56.

26. This is not Newton's term but Kant's: *Critique of Pure Reason*, A 632/B 660. But the seventeenth and early eighteenth century saw a barrage of "physico-theologies" putting the new science in the service of traditional religion, e.g., Charleton: *The Darkness of Atheism Dispelled*

that in absolute space "there are everywhere all kinds of figures, everywhere spheres, cubes, triangles, straight lines...even though they are not disclosed to sight" (DG 22). Like the body of Hobbes's corporeal God, the divine attributes of space and time have dimension and quantity in their own right: "So the quantity of the existence of God is eternal in relation to duration, and infinite in relation to the space in which he is present" (DG 25). God's duration and presence fall within the scope of mathematical physics.[27]

Nevertheless, Newton's God is not directly observable or imaginable. Absolute space and time, since they are independent of any body or motion, are not "capable of inducing any change of motion in body or change of thought in the mind" (DG 33). So we perceive all the figures embedded within space only through bodies that occupy it, like ink in water. Or, as he puts it in *The Principia*, absolute space and time are known only by their "sensible measures."[28] In terms of the *Opticks* analogy, our perceptions of bodies provide a sort of indirect perception of God's imagination since it is within his sensorium that God is able to "form and reform the parts of the universe."[29] So corresponding to the scientific distinction between absolute space and time, which cannot be seen, or distinguished from one another by our senses, and the bodies and motions which serve as their sensible measures is the theological distinction between God and creation: "The father is the invisible God whom no eye hath seen or can see, all other beings are sometimes visible."[30] As Hobbes insisted, we do not perceive the invisible God, even though he is substantially present and continually active.

In the General Scholium, Newton draws an important religious lesson from the absolute immateriality and imperceptibility of God's space and time: "He totally lacks any body and corporeal shape and so he cannot be

by the Light of Nature: A Physico-Theologicall Treatise (1652), and Boyle, Physico-Theological Considerations about the Possibility of the Resurrection (1675). See Manuel, The Religion of Isaac Newton (Oxford: Clarendon Press, 1974), 24, and Harrison, "Physico-Theology and the Mixed Sciences" in The Science of Nature in the Seventeenth Century, ed. P. R. Anstey and J. Schuster (Dordrecht: Springer, 2005).

27. Spinoza strongly resisted the implication that because God was extended he was also quantifiable or measurable. Those of his "adversaries" who make this inference wrongly "suppose an infinite quantity to be measurable and composed of parts." Ethics I P15 Schol, in A Spinoza Reader, 95.

28. Principia, 408.

29. Sepper makes a similar observation concerning the sensorium analogy. "Goethe, Newton and the Imagination of Modern Science," Revue Internationale de Philosophie 63 (2009), 261–77, 276.

30. Keynes MS 8, Article 2.

seen nor heard nor touched nor ought to be worshipped in the form of something corporeal."[31] Although God's way of knowing and our own bear "a similitude of some kind," the similitude is very weak. [32] In terms nearly identical to Hobbes, Newton warns: "As a blind man has no idea of colors, we have no ideas of the way in which the most wise God understands and senses all things."[33] In one of his theological manuscripts, "A Short Scheme of the True Religion," Newton declares the sin of idolatry—"making and worshipping the images of dead men or of other things in heaven above or in the earth beneath"—a much greater threat to true religion than atheism. For whereas atheism is patently "senseless and odious" idolatry is easily exploited by kings, "it seeming very plausible to honour the souls of heroes & saints."[34]

The sources of idol worship, as well as the origin of true religion, are explained in more detail in another theological manuscript on which Newton labored privately for years. In the "Origins of Religion," Newton speculates that idolatry arose when the souls of dead heroes were imaginatively projected into various planets and stars. Deification was eventually extended to animals and sculptures, and "Thus was the world soon filled with Gods."[35] According to Newton's genealogy, this worship of particular men, planets, and icons was an historical corruption of "the most universal and the most ancient of all religions." This original religion conceived the temple of God as "the whole system of the heavens" partially illuminated by a central light source (Prytaneum):

> The whole heavens they reckoned to be the true & real Temple of God & therefore that a Prytaneum might deserve the name of his Temple they framed it so as in the fittest manner to represent the whole system of the heavens. A point of religion than which nothing can be more rational.[36]

Since the system of heavens and its source of illumination are the subjects of natural philosophy—specifically astronomy, mechanics and optics (three

31. *Philosophical Writings*, 91. See also the *Opticks*, where God is said to be "incorporeal" (*Philosophical Writings*, 130) and "void of any members or parts" *Philosophical Writings*, 138. See also Article 2 of the "Twelve Articles," Keynes MS 8; *Newton's Theological Manuscripts*, 56.
32. *Principia*, 943.
33. *Principia*, 942.
34. Keynes MS 7.
35. Yahuda MS 41, f 9–10; Westfall, "Isaac Newton's *Theologiae Gentiles Origines Philosophicae*," in *The Secular Mind*, ed. W. W. Wager (New York: Holmes & Meier, 1982), 25.
36. Yahuda MS 41, f 6; *Theologiae Gentiles*, 24.

of Newton's favorites)—it follows that the original, pure religion (of which he conjectures even Stonehenge may be a remnant) was science in pristine form: "Thence it was that the Priests anciently were above other men well skilled in the knowledge of the true frame of Nature & accounted it a great part of their Theology."[37] Like Hobbes, Newton considers the "true religion," at least until "the nations corrupted it," to consist simply in the pious pursuit of natural knowledge: "For there is no way (without revelation) to come to knowledge of the Deity but by the frame of nature."[38]

As an historical thesis, the original coincidence of science and theism is obviously speculative and Newton was not inclined to espouse it publicly. But as a philosophical idealization, he repeats it openly, if more soberly, in later published works. Thus, in Query 31 of the *Opticks* (one of the two queries that likens space to the "sensorium" of God), Newton expresses confidence that science will promote religious morality, "so far as we can know by natural Philosophy what is the first cause, what Power he has over us, and what benefits we receive from him, so far our duty towards him will appear to us by the light of nature." Physics can also help us correct and prevent perennial religious corruptions like "worship of false gods," "transmigration of souls," deification of the "sun and moon and dead heroes," and so on.[39] With the "frame of the nature" properly recognized as the divine attributes of absolute space and time, and with the bodies it contains illuminated by the sun in accordance with the universal laws of optics, natural philosophy is restored to its proper place as the ground and arbiter of the true, primordial religion: "to treat of God from phenomena is certainly a part of natural philosophy."[40]

Newtonian physico-theology is fallible. As mentioned, because the parts of absolute space and time cannot be distinguished by our senses, "we use sensible measures in their stead." For example, Newton observes that astronomers correct the slightly unequal terrestrial days by referring to the eclipses of the Jovian moons or a pendulum clock: "in order to measure celestial motions on the basis of a truer time." But he concedes, "it is possible that there is no uniform motion by which time may have an exact measure."[41] So although empirical science can provide real quantitative knowledge of the divine attributes, these measurements are approximate and tentative.

37. Yahuda MS 41, f7.
38. Yahuda MS 41, f7; *Theologiae Gentiles*, 25. See further Manuel, *The Religion of Isaac Newton* 42–5.
39. *Philosophical Writings*, 140.   40. *Principia*, 943.   41. *Principia*, 410.

Thus, he concludes Query 28 of the *Opticks* with a telling profession of hope in the potential of "true religion": "Though every step in this philosophy brings us not immediately to the knowledge of the first cause, it brings us nearer to it, and on this account is to be highly valued."[42] Still there remains room for revelation and faith.[43]

Conclusion

According to the historiographical critique developed by Talal Asad, Charles Taylor and others, "secularism" is a form of ideology that isolates the sacred and religious elements of traditional culture from ascendant statist and capitalist forms of life, thereby empowering the latter and marginalizing the former. On this analysis, the scientific revolution is a crucial step in the process of "disenchantment." The rise of mechanistic science removes God, and his agents, from direct involvement in natural processes, thereby encouraging deism, materialism and finally the "death of God." The highly transcendent, rationalistic theology of scholastic Christianity is seen as a necessary precursor to this sidelining of God. As Asad has put it, "The representation of the Christian God as being quite apart in "the supernatural world" signals the construction of a secular space that begins to emerge in early modernity."[44]

---

42. *Philosophical Writings*, 130.

43. The epistemological parallels between the progressive, falliblist attitude of seventeenth-century English science, as typified by "virtuosi" of the Royal Society like Newton and Boyle, and the moderate, rationalistic theological orientation of liberal Anglican movements like Latitudinarianism, have been documented in detail by numerous scholars. See Shapiro, "Latitudinarianism and Science in Seventeenth-Century England." *Past and Present* 40 (1968): 16–41, 35. See also Westfall, *Science and Religion in Seventeenth Century England*; Mulligan, "Anglicanism, Latitudianrianism and Science in Seventeenth Century England," *Annals of Science* 30 (1973): 213–19; Manuel, *The Religion of Isaac Newton*; Force and Popkin, *Essays on the Context, Nature and Influence of Isaac Newton's Theology* (Dordrecht: Kluwer Academic Publishers, 1990), esp. chap. 7; M. Jacob, *The Cultural Meaning of the Scientific Revolution* (New York: McGraw-Hill, 1987); Shapin and Schaffer, *Leviathan and the Air-Pump* (Princeton, NJ: Princeton University Press, 1986), chap. 7; Harrison, *The Bible, Protestantism and the Rise of Early Modern Science* (Cambridge: Cambridge University Press, 1988). What I have emphasized here is the metaphysical side of this same important parallel (at least for Newton). Similar recent gestures along these lines include Funkenstein, *Theology and the Scientific Imagination from the Middle Ages to the Seventeenth Century* (Princeton: Princeton University Press, 1986); Cunningham, "Getting the Game right: some Plain words on the Identity and Invention of Science," *Studies in the History and Philosophy of Science* 19 (1988): 365–89; Ducheyne, "Newton's Secularized Onto-theology versus Descartes' and Leibniz', or on the Importance of Unifying Tendencies in the Secularization-process," *Theology and Science* 4 (2006): 71–86.

44. T. Asad, *Formations of the Secular: Christianity, Islam, Modernity* (Stanford: Stanford University Press, 2003), 27.

The next step is taken by the new science, which reveals that such a God is irrelevant to strictly mechanistic operations of natural systems. Thus, Charles Taylor writes: "Mechanism undermines enchantment, the expression-embodiment of higher reality in the things which surround us and thus made the presence of God in the cosmos something which was no longer experience-near, or at least not at all in the same way."[45] He invokes Newton's system as the culmination of this mechanistic disenchantment.

I hope it is now clear that Newton's aim was precisely the opposite: to draw God back into the world from which he had been alienated by obscure theology and make us constantly conscious of his presence and power. In the General Scholium Newton rails against abstract theology, which emphasizes God's attributes rather than his providence: "a being, however perfect, without Dominion is not the Lord God."[46] The greatest figure of the scientific revolution is not at all inclined to relegate God to the realm of mystery or the supernatural. The view of Hobbes, another hero of the Enlightenment, is remarkably similar. He also derides scholastic abstractions concerning God's transcendence: "When the nature of a thing is incomprehensible I can acquiesce in the scripture; but when the signification of words is incomprehensible I cannot acquiesce in the authority of the schoolmen" (EW 4 314). Invoking the familiar line from Acts about being in God, Hobbes wonders, "Can a being which has quantity be in a being which does not have quantity?" (*Leviathan* Appendix iii; C 541). His God could hardly be more present in the cosmos, constantly directing and producing empirical things by a kind of mixing. Descartes' God better fits Taylor's image of the mechanical philosophy's distant, impersonal divinity. Indeed, his co-religionist Blaise Pascal scolded Descartes for this: "He had to make Him give a 'fillip' to set the world in motion; beyond this, he has no further need of God."[47] But even Descartes' abstract God is constantly called upon to give the world its motions and diversity. And in order to convey this engagement with the world, the rationalist Descartes was obliged to rely on imaginative fables.

But even if Taylor is wrong about the religious aims of the early modern natural philosophers, the critique of secularism is essentially correct about the ultimate impact of early modern science on religious culture. While God re-enters the world in the seventeenth century, following his

---

45. C. Taylor, *A Secular Age* (Cambridge, MA: Harvard University Press, 2007), 329.
46. *Principia*, 940–1.
47. B. Pascal, *The Provincial Letters, Pensées, Scientific Treatises*, trans. W. F. Trotter (Chicago: Denton Publishers, 1952), 186.

supernatural sojourn through the high Middle Ages, he returns in the service of very different needs and in a form that would have been unfamiliar to the Homeric Greeks or the Biblical Jews. Absolutely lacking any body, and with inscrutable ends, the Cartesian God is clear to the intellect but unrelated to sense or imagination. Except for those concerned to provide a metaphysical grounding for physics, or an escape from demon skepticism, such a God is simply irrelevant. And even Descartes concedes that he spends only "three or four hours a year" in purely intellectual meditation. Hobbes's God is simply the undifferentiated material plenum required by his mechanist natural philosophy, a geometrical version of Aristotelian "prime matter" needed to "uphold the world" but otherwise beyond sense and reason. Newton's God is an invisible yet substantial and infinite presence that frames and grounds universal law by constituting space and time while freely producing matter and motion. His will and attributes can be apprehended and quantified through experimental inquiry—certainly better than by revelation, mystical communion or priestly mediation—but only to an approximate degree. While such a God answered to the ideals of an empiricist, Arian, and physicist such as Newton (much as Spinoza's impersonal *deus sive natura* later inspired Einstein), it could hardly substitute for the familiar saints, rituals, narratives, and social structures of traditional religion. In this way, Newton's hope to reinstall the "most universal and ancient of all religions" in place of the idolatrous corruptions of the churches no doubt encouraged the deists, atheists, and secularists of the early eighteenth century. His fanciful and self-serving genealogy of religion was simply no match for his elegant and revolutionary physico-theology. Prior to God's decline and demise in the eighteenth century, God did not first enjoy a quiet retirement from worldly concerns. During the seventeenth century he was re-employed by well-intentioned theists in a thankless and invisible job: grounding mathematical science.

THREE

Darwinian Tensions

Anthony O'Hear

All evolutionists now

In a broad sense, I suppose, we all accept evolution, if by "we" we mean anyone likely to be reading this. Of course, if "we" includes the whole world, we all do not; and many who do accept the theory of evolution probably have only the vaguest notion of why they should. How much this matters is another question, but quite clearly to anyone who looks at the evidence without any preconceptions it is hard not to think that life on Earth has come about through evolutionary processes. In particular, all that we know of geology and its related disciplines tells us that the Earth is very old, and has itself been subject to a process of continuous development. From the fossil record, we can also conclude that life itself is very old, and that its earliest forms were very simple compared to much of what we see around us today. We also see evidence of species long since extinct. Then, from biology and from the remains of older, now extinct forms of life, we see remarkable similarities among natural forms and their embryos, which strongly suggest common ancestries. We know from experiments and observations that a process very similar to what is described in evolutionary theory (to put it no stronger) actually does occur in the world today. From genetics and microbiology, we know a great deal about the mechanisms of hereditary transmission and about the relationships between genes and behavior, and between genes and morphology. And no doubt there is much more and in very great detail which contributes most impressively to filling out the evolutionary picture and to its broad credibility.

To be sure there are problems. The fossil record is incomplete, but in what we see, we do not see a process of continuous evolutionary development, by constant little changes, as Darwin suggested. Quite large changes seem to happen rather quickly and suddenly, followed by long periods of comparative stability. One wonders, if that is so, how big changes to species, requiring more or less synchronized development in a lot of genetic sites could have occurred by purely random trial and error; the classic random variation and selective retention beloved by Darwinian theorists seems far more appropriate for the gradual accretion of small changes, step by step (which is what we do see in the breeding of fruit flies and the like). And maybe, connected to this point, there is the more general point that many basic evolutionary changes seem to depend on whole complexes of genes being in situ, so to speak, ready for the change, but without contributing anything to the organism's well-being in advance of the future change.

Intelligent Design

This last point is the one hammered away at by theorists of what has become known as Intelligent Design Creationism, much to the irritation of the Darwinists, who insist that the examples adduced by their opponents either can be brought within standard evolutionary explanations or will be. As a non-biologist I am not competent to judge the plausibility of these claims—on either side. However, as a philosopher I can make three critical points about Intelligent Design, two of which are quite independent of the detailed examples, and the third is an entirely general point about the nature of the examples. I should underline that in making these critical remarks, I am not at all saying that it might not be quite rational for someone to look at the world as if it were designed, and to see aspects of it that contribute to the coherence of that view. What I am questioning is the use of the considerations adduced by proponents of Intelligent Design to produce a rationally compelling argument to the effect that naturalism is intrinsically inadequate to explain the order and life we find around us. My own position is that there are no such arguments, one way or the other. Whether one sees the universe as designed or not will depend to a great extent on one's prior commitments, commitments which are not irrational on either side, but which cannot themselves be conclusively established through argument. My quarrel, such as it is, with the so-called Intelligent Design theorists is that they tend to present their picture as if it is a quasi-empirical argument, on the same epistemological and scientific footing as Darwinism itself, as if it could be established not just by argument in a general sense, but by appealing to various supposed empirical defects in the neo-Darwinian picture, against which they propose their own view as another empirical hypothesis. It is this latter point in particular which I find less than convincing.

Having said that, the first critical point I would make about Intelligent Design is that in some of its expositions (e.g. Dembski's), heavy reliance is made on probability, namely, whether the type of complexity found in biological organisms is more or less likely to have occurred through natural selection or through the guiding hand of a designer. The problem here is actually an old one, and is not in any way peculiar to the specific examples adduced by Behe, Dembski and the like.[1] It is that, in the absence of examples of sets of universes with and without designers, we simply have no basis for making the relevant judgments of probability. Universes are not, as C. S. Peirce was fond of saying, as plentiful as blackberries, so we cannot tell whether features of this universe—the only universe—are more or less likely to have emerged randomly or with an intelligent designer.

In reply to this, it would then be said by defenders of the Intelligent Design argument that from what we know of natural processes an "irreducibly complex" system is not likely to have occurred by a blind evolutionary process, and is far more likely to have been produced by a designer as least as intelligent as a human being, which brings me on to the second point. The fact, if it is a fact, that one explanation (blind evolution) is unlikely does not by itself make another explanation (intelligent designer) more likely. And the postulation of an immaterial intelligent designer outside the universe in connection with things in the universe is something of which we have no experience whatever and is, in addition, beset with all kinds of problems of its own, which was Hume's point from long ago. So, if their proposal is to have any *empirical* force (as opposed to being religiously suggestive on a different level altogether), the proponents of Intelligent Design will have to tell us rather more about the nature of the designer and his operation than they are actually in a position to do. My point is that God is not the sort of being who can be arrived at the end of a chain of quasi-scientific reasoning, for, apart from the problem raised by Hume, that would make God as a being among beings, as opposed to being on a different

---

1. Michael Behe, *Darwin's Black Box: The Biochemical Challenge to Evolution* (New York: Free Press, 2nd ed., 2006). William Dembski, *The Design Inference: Eliminating Chance Through Small Probabilities*, (Cambridge: Cambridge University Press, 1998). The whole controversy is usefully analysed and discussed in *Intelligent Design Creationism and its Critics*, edited by Robert T. Pennock (Cambridge, Mass: MIT Press, 2011).

ontological level altogether. (This, incidentally, is my reaction to Antony Flew's late espousal of a form of design thinking.)[2]

And then, thirdly, we are assuming that "blind evolution" cannot do the job required. Not only is this a risky "god of the gaps" maneuver, involving a deal of question-begging on the part of the Intelligent Design theorists— for the Darwinists will (and do) vigorously attempt to close the gaps by producing explanations within their framework, showing, for example, that the supposedly independent bits within an "irreducibly complex" biological set-up are not biologically independent at all. Remember that Behe's favourite image is of the bits of a mousetrap lying around on the ground, with the implicit question as to how such independent entities could ever have been lying around like that without the activity of the mousetrap designer, who then, of course, puts them together. But biological systems are not made up of independent bits in that way; their elements are already living and working together, allowing the systems to take on new functions with quite small changes. Behe would probably say that this *is* his point: how are we to explain the living, holistic aspects of biological development? But the argument may still go against him here. The organs and tissue of an already existing living organism are not like the components of an inanimate mousetrap, and could take on new functions with comparatively small changes in structure.

Genocentrism

The complaint about the mousetrap analogy is that it suggests too mechanistic a picture of the biological world. But it may be that standard neo-Darwinism is guilty of a similar defect (which may, incidentally, conspire to make Intelligent Design creationism look more plausible than it should). What I am referring to is the tendency of neo-Darwinism to explain everything—evolution itself, morphology of individual organisms, and behavior, individual and social—in terms of genes and their supposed striving to replicate themselves. This tendency has been dubbed by Brian Goodwin *genocentrism*, and according to Goodwin, for all its power and success, it fails to account for or to credit the extent to which living things

---

2. Antony Flew and Roy Abraham Varghese, *There Is a God: How the World's Most Notorious Atheist Changed His Mind* (New York: HarperCollins, 2008).

are complex systems, wholes exercising a top-down effect on the bits which make them up.[3]

So genes are not, as it were, individual atoms or billiard balls pursuing their own independent ends, and entering into complex organizations only to further their own ends, and turning those organizations to their own ends. Such, of course, is the picture given by talk of selfish genes, but, even assuming it makes sense to think of genes as striving to do anything or that we understand just where they got their impetus to reproduce themselves, this picture is no more true at the genetic level than an analogous form of individualism is true at the social level (Hobbes). An alternative view is being developed currently according to which there is an emergent biological order, in which organisms are seen as wholes, governing their own development from embryonic origins to adulthood. In this new model, the lives of complex organisms take on an intrinsic value and quality quite apart from their efficacy at survival and reproduction. It thus stands in opposition to the reductionism of neo-Darwinism, taking organic form and complexity to be irreducible to the parts of the organism, and seeing these forms as guiding the development, the existence and even the creativity of the organism as it makes its way through life.

In a way the emergent complexity view will provide an answer to the Intelligent Design theorists, for the "irreducible complexity" which so baffles them will now be seen as a fundamental property of biological life, just as natural as the physics of gravitational attraction. What we actually have here is a *tertium quid*, between the question-begging reductionism of the selfish gene and the miraculous and inexplicable activity of the intelligent designer within the created realm. We will also have a view of life and of biology that goes beyond the characteristic Darwinian tropes of the survival of the fittest and of the "rigid destruction" of variations with characteristics "in the least degree injurious"—in Darwin's own words. (Did anyone, even in the heyday of Darwinism, really believe this last thesis, even though Darwin himself took it to be virtually synonymous with Natural Selection? The fact that they didn't shows that for all the claims about Darwin's theory being scientific, in its innermost core it was never taken as refutable.)

It is claimed by its advocates that the recasting of biology in terms of holistic morphogenetic analyses helps us to account for the large-scale

---

3. Brian Goodwin, *How the Leopard Changed Its Spots* (Princeton: Princeton University Press, 2nd ed., 2001).

evolutionary developments which caused Darwin problems. They will also point to the fact that the molecular composition of chromosomes does not in itself determine the forms of the things the chromosome goes on to instruct; principles governing the organization of the organism in question have to be in play, including both the presence of other features elsewhere in the organism and even environmental influences. One of these environmental influences is good mothering, which can in some cases turn genes in their young on, so to speak. The key point is that some of the things genes do are not in themselves determined by the composition of the molecules of the chromosome, but depend for their functioning on feedback mechanisms from within the whole organism in which the genes exist and on influences from outside the organism. Moreover, segments of DNA only replicate themselves fully, without reverting to simpler and simpler forms, in the context of whole systems of cells. Then there is the striking fact that chemically very similar bits of DNA behave differently within organisms, depending on the cellular context and the function of the phenotypical bit they are producing or upholding.

The neo-Darwinist picture is one of genes determining form and behavior from the bottom up, so to speak, and in a kind of Hobbesian universe in which already existing contractors help each other but only to further their own ends. As already mentioned, this picture may inadvertently have given ammunition to the proponents of Intelligent Design, by making the complexity of whole organisms and even their parts seem more mysterious at the biological level than it really is. In contrast, some biologists are coming to see the organism as a whole, as a "functional *and* a structural unity in which the parts exist for *and by means of* one another in the expression of a particular form. This means that the parts of an organism—leaves, roots, flowers, limbs, eyes, heart, brain—are not made independently and then assembled, as in a machine, but arise as a result of interactions within the developing organism."[4] So we should not see what we take to be the parts of organisms, including their genes, to have an independent existence apart from the wholes of which they are parts; and some would extend the notion of the whole here to include the ecology of the environments in which organisms exist, which would suggest a far less confrontational model of the organism-environment relationship than is suggested by classical Darwinism.

4. Goodwin, *How the Leopard Changed Its Spots*, 197.

We can and indeed should accept a generally evolutionary account of the living world, even if we are ready to contemplate some significant shifts from Darwinian and neo-Darwinian orthodoxy, including the use of the ever burgeoning study of complexity and complex organizations in many areas, from mathematics and chemistry to the social sciences and the study of artificial life. So far, though, much of what I have been pointing to touches on aspects of biology that are beyond my competence to do more than report on in a rather journalistic manner. In my conclusion, though, I will have something to say about the implications of a potential shift from a genocentric biology to a biology of emergent complexity, which focuses on the forms and organization of organisms as a, or even the primary explanatory tool. I want now, though, to look at what strikes me as an unresolved tension which runs through much of Darwin's own thought, and which bears particularly, though not exclusively, on the application of his theory to the human species. The tension derives from Darwin's own understanding of evolution.

Evolution and progress

According to one strand of Darwinian thinking, evolution is fundamentally a relative notion, and that there is in Darwin's theory no necessity that the development of evolutionary processes should be progressive in any sense other than being "better at surviving and reproducing." Proponents of this interpretation will point out that in *The Origin of Species* Darwin hardly uses the term "evolution" (which definitely has connotations of progress in a more general sense), but tends to speak of the laws of variation, natural selection and descent with modification. "Descent with modification" carries with it no implication that the modifications brought about through natural selection will necessarily be bigger or more complex or more beautiful or more intelligent. Indeed they definitely would not be any of these things if the costs of greater complexity, intelligence, and so on, in terms of energy consumption and so on outweigh the survival advantages they bring.

On this austere understanding of what is going on, success in the struggle for survival is all that really counts, and all that natural selection guarantees, and that may come in all sorts of ways. The theory says that variations benefiting their possessors in the struggle for survival will do better and eventually displace their competitors and their less successful con-specifics.

But success is always relative to a given environment, and may not require greater complexity or perfection viewed in absolute terms. Thus, a longer neck might benefit its possessor if there are tall food-bearing trees, but not if the trees all die out. If that happened, the very same characteristic that was once an advantage will later prove a disadvantage. This effect can be quite radical in leading to the shedding of costly characteristics within a species when they are no longer required. Thus, we see cave-dwelling descendents of sighted creatures with no sight, or flightless birds in New Zealand (before humans arrived with their rodent followers). In each case, the effort and energy needed to produce sight and flight was not necessary for survival, so the faculties in question simply dropped off. They consti- tuted a cost with no consequent advantage, and so long as there is no better equipped competitor there will be no evolutionary impetus towards what we might regard as an improvement, or what might indeed be an improve- ment, absolutely speaking.

Darwin was well aware of all of this: "As natural selection acts by compe- tition, it adapts the inhabitants of each country only in relation to the degree of perfection of their associates. . . . Nor ought we to marvel if all the con- trivances of nature be not, as far as we can judge, absolutely perfect; and if some of them be abhorrent to our idea of fitness." And having mentioned bees being killed by their own stings, drones being produced in vast num- bers for just one act, then to be slaughtered, ichneumonidae feeding in the bodies of live caterpillars, and other examples of waste, profligacy and worse in nature, he concludes "the wonder indeed is, on the theory of natural selection, that more cases of the want of absolute perfection have not been observed."[5]

Logically what Darwin says here is impeccable. Relative fitness and non- progressive development, fit enough just for the relevant environment, is all that is strictly implied by the theory of natural selection. Indeed, we could argue that if species longevity and geographical spread are the criteria of evolutionary success the most successful species may well be certain types of insect. Certainly mammals in general and human beings in particular will be nowhere near the most successful. And, more generally, Darwin is keen on occasion to point out that our own ideas of what constitute perfection in a species might just be a little, shall we say, anthropocentric: he wrote in a letter that while to us intelligence may seem the chief mark of progress, to

5. Charles Darwin, *The Origin of Species* (Harmondsworth: Penguin Books, 1982), 445.

a bee it would no doubt be something else. This last sentiment might well seem to some to put Darwin in a favorable light, as immune to the race and species progressivism characteristic of his age. Unfortunately, (perhaps) Darwin turns out to have had no such immunity, nor did he see evolution in general in strictly relative terms.

This is actually perfectly evident from the closing pages of *The Origin of Species*. "As natural selection works solely by and for the good of each being, all corporeal and mental endowments will tend to progress towards perfection," he writes at the end of the penultimate paragraph. What he says there is something of a *non sequitur*, especially given our earlier observations on the logic of natural selection, which would license no such perfectionist optimism. One wonders, moreover, what was Darwins's own standard of progress and perfection. Is a horse more perfect than a dinosaur, a fish than an amoeba? Is mankind more perfect than the bee? If we think we know what Darwin's answers might be to at least some of these questions, there is more than a hint that in his judgments he would be implicitly judging the animal kingdom by the human characteristics of intelligence, rationality, morality, brain complexity and the rest.

Darwinism and the Creator

At the start of the paragraph just quoted, Darwin had spoken (as he always did in all editions of *The Origin of Species*) of his system as being in accordance with "the laws impressed on matter by the Creator." We can argue about just what Darwin meant at the various stages of his life by "the Creator;" but it would be hard to have a mind-set which could make any reference, however metaphorical, to a creatorial mind which did not take some tendency towards the better as being inherent in creation. Darwin may have become an agnostic theologically speaking, as he tells us quite explicitly in his *Autobiography*, even while admitting "the extreme difficulty or even impossibility" he has "of conceiving this immense and wonderful universe, including man and his capacity of looking far backwards and far into futurity, as the result of blind chance or necessity."[6] And even granted Darwin's steady drift towards personal agnosticism—"The mystery of the beginning of all things is insoluble by us; and I for one must be content to

6. Darwin, *The Autobiography of Charles Darwin*, Nora Barlow, ed. (London: Collins, 1958), 92.

remain an Agnostic."[7]—in his core theorizing there are significant traces of (dare we say?) design thinking.

It is not just that nature *mimics* human livestock breeders, which is what Darwin argues in his less exuberant moments. In a striking, but not atypical passage from the Natural Selection chapter in *The Origin of Species*, Darwin says: "Natural selection is daily and hourly scrutinising [sic], throughout the world, every variation, even the slightest; rejecting that which is bad, preserving and adding up all that is good; silently and insensibly working, whenever and wherever opportunity offers, at the improvement of each organic being…"[8] Natural selection *scrutinizing, rejecting, preserving, adding, silently working at the improvement of each (!) organic being, and doing it all daily and hourly.* Falls of sparrows notwithstanding, the Gospels never imply so much; nor is Thomas Aquinas's all-sustaining First Cause quite so busy and officious here on earth. Metaphor, all metaphor, we will be told, no doubt correctly. But metaphors reveal and metaphors are powerful; and this one is all of a part of Darwin's attempt to hold on to natural selection as a progressive, beneficent force, an attempt which all but forces him to envisage it anthropomorphically, as a displaced intelligent designer, doing the Creator's work for him, through the laws he has impressed on it. (Although it would take us too far afield here, it is worth noting briefly that the God envisaged in the best traditional theology is not an interfering being at all, so not the one Darwin is replacing with natural selection, but rather one whose rain falls on the just and the unjust alike; not a being among beings, but the source of all that is who has withdrawn from creation precisely in order to allow things to develop and emerge according to the order of creation.)

In the closing passage of *The Origin of Species* Darwin says this:

> Thus, from the war of nature, from famine and death, the most exalted object which we are capable of conceiving, namely, the production of the higher animals, directly follows. There is a grandeur in this view of life, with its several powers, having been originally breathed into a few forms or into one; and that, whilst this planet has gone on cycling according to the fixed law of gravity, from so simple a beginning endless forms most beautiful and most wonderful have been, and are being, evolved.

Yes, we may think, but this is some distance from the earlier dispassionate nod in the direction of more cases of the want of absolute perfection. And life breathed in? How? By whom? And stylistically the endless forms most

---

7. Darwin, *Autobiography*, 94.   8. Darwin, *The Origin of Species*, 133.

beautiful and most wonderful will certainly outweigh in the reader's mind the war, the famine, the death which led to this inspiring result, and displace them from the forefront of his consciousness, as much as in any traditional theodicy.

But what of the writer's mind? We know that in fact even as early as 1856 Darwin lamented the "clumsy, wasteful, blundering, low, and horribly cruel works of nature." In 1865 he reflected on the certainty of the extinction of all life: "To think of millions of years, with every continent swarming with good and enlightened men, all ending in this, and with probably no fresh start until this our planetary system has been again converted into a red-hot gas. *Sic transit gloria mundi* with a vengeance." And in 1881 he told Wallace that even with everything to make him happy and contented, "life has become very wearisome to me", partly surely because of his growing agnosticism.[9] For all Darwin's pointing up of aspects of sympathy among us and other creatures, and his talk of grandeur in his vision notwithstanding, one can easily become depressed, as Darwin seemed to be himself, with the fundamentally cruel and bleak aspects of his re-imagining of nature.

Our knowledge of reality

Actually rather more hangs on agnosticism at this point than Darwin's personal mood, as Darwin himself recognized. If natural selection is all that there is, and if the human mind can be explained in purely evolutionary terms, as deriving from that of the lower animals, why should we accept that what we think about ultimate reality has any objective validity? "A dog might as well speculate on the mind of Newton," Darwin wrote in 1881. He went on to express a "horrid doubt" as to whether "the convictions of man's mind, which has been developed from the mind of the lower animals, are of any value or at all trustworthy. Would anyone trust the convictions of a monkey's mind, if there are any convictions in such a mind?"[10]

Part of the point here is that just like a bee, a monkey might have a very different perspective on the world from us; and, in the case of scientific and philosophical speculation, compared to us, a very limited one. But equally, ours might seem even more limited to our distant descendents or to creatures

9. All quotations are from John C. Greene, *Debating Darwin: Adventures of a Scholar* (Claremont: Regina Books, 1999), 53–4.
10. Darwin, *Letter to William Graham, July 3, 1851, in The Life and Letters of Charles Darwin*, vol.1, Francis Darwin, ed. (London: John Murray, 1888), 285.

with higher intellectual powers. Darwin hopes that natural selection will eventually produce people who would look on him and Lyell and Newton as "mere barbarians;" but while that does seem to follow from the point about natural selection's program of relentless scrutinizing and improving, what confidence would that leave us in the theories of Darwin, Lyell and Newton? Will their theories, in the future, seem no more reliable than those of the primitive and barbaric Tierra del Fuegans Darwin encountered on his epic voyage did to him, and who caused him to remark in his journal for 17 December 1832 on how wide was the difference between savage and civilized man, greater than that between wild and domesticated animals, "inasmuch as in man there is a greater power of improvement"? So what would an improved Darwin or Lyell of 500 years hence think of what will no doubt seem to be the primitive ramblings and superstitions of their predecessors from the nineteenth century?

If these were not sufficient grounds for skepticism on our existential and metaphysical convictions, we also have to consider the nature of Darwinian explanations. As we have already pointed out, the theory of natural selection tells us that a creature's physical and mental development is conditioned by what will aid survival and reproduction—and that is all. Why are we to suppose that speculating on our own nature has anything to do with that, or, even more, that the faculties we have developed to help us get round the savannah and find mates in earlier times are going to help us in coming to the truth in advanced scientific and philosophical investigations? Or indeed in the looking long into the past and into the future, which Darwin himself saw as part of our capacities? How did these come about through natural selection alone? And apart from the scope of our enquiries, surviving and getting mates are different aims from a disinterested pursuit of truth, and techniques and perceptual media which work well at the level of basic survival and reproduction may be pretty sketchy, if not actually misleading, when it comes to investigating areas remote from everyday experience.

Darwin's point is put with telling directness by Thomas Nagel: "If, *per impossibile*, we came to believe that our capacity for objective theory were the product of natural selection, that would warrant serious scepticism [sic] about its results beyond a very limited and familiar range."[11] Nagel concludes that the development of the human intellect—which can go beyond the limited and the familiar—probably provides a counter-example to the

11. Thomas Nagel, *The View From Nowhere* (New York: Oxford University Press, 1986), 79.

view that natural selection explains everything. I would concur, adding two further points. The first is that even if we add the role of the intellect in sexual selection, saying that our minds have developed partly in order to attract mates through story telling and other mental performances neither validates those performances or explains why it is that potential mates value those who pursue objective theory (if they do). The theory of natural selection needs supplementing at both these points to give a satisfactory account of our pursuance of objective theory.

Then secondly, as Darwin himself acknowledged, the theory of natural selection is in danger of self-destructing. If that theory explains what we think and do in terms of the value things have for us in promoting survival and reproduction, saying in effect that we accept them because they promote survival and reproduction, the same must be true of the theory of natural selection itself. We accept it, if we do, because it helps us in the struggle for existence, not because it is true, which would of course provide no rational argument against the creationist or the Islamist who might, not unconvincingly, find great support for survival in the following of his creed. So Darwinism undermines its own claims to be true (just as in analogous ways do the theories of Marx, Nietzsche and Freud if we take them at face value).

Faced with these problems, one could, of course, take a completely different tack at this point. Maybe, as Nagel suggests, the mind and our searching for truth shows that natural selection is not the whole story. Along with other human capacities (for cooperation, for the appreciation of beauty, to name but two), our acquiring of knowledge for its own sake might be something rooted in nature, something to which evolution in the broad sense has been tending, and even something anticipated in earlier forms of life. After all, it might seem to the dispassionate observer, not already convinced of the truth of strict Darwinism, that much in the behavior of the "lower" animals is done for its own sake, for amusement, play and curiosity, and hard to bring within the procrustean bed of the promotion of survival and reproduction. To the dispassionate observer, not already committed to selfish genery and the like, the human mind might come to seem not an anomaly whose self-centered classificatory schemes unjustifiably overestimate mind in general and the human mind in particular, but as something indeed cued into reality itself in a way which transcends the demands of survival and reproduction. If we do follow this tack—which we are surely not barred from doing by anything in biology in the strict sense, as opposed to the dogmas of neo-Darwinism—then we would not have to worry about our theories of nature self-destructing. But we would, of course, have to pay the price of admitting that at least one of them, that is the Darwinism that would see everything as either anomalous or conducive only to survival and reproduction, is false.

Savages and civilized races

Let us, though, for the moment assume that Darwinian explanations are in general true and do not apply to the Darwinian theory itself, and let us see what that theory implies about human development. It turns out that Darwin's early reaction to the Tierra del Fuegans was not an anomaly, but is all of a piece with the core doctrine of continuous improvement through natural selection. He refers to them again at the end of *The Descent of Man* in 1871: "They possessed hardly any arts, and like wild animals lived on what they could catch; they had no government, and were merciless to everyone not of their tribe." And opening out his discussion, he goes on to say that he would prefer to be descended from a monkey or a baboon who manifested traits of loyalty and self-sacrifice as from "a savage who delights to torture his enemies, offers up bloody sacrifices, practices infanticide without remorse, treats his wives like slaves, knows no decency, and is haunted by the grossest superstitions."[12]

Earlier in the main body of *The Descent of Man*, Darwin had written a whole chapter on the way inferior races had been replaced by superior ones; even "at the present day civilized nations are everywhere supplanting barbarous nations, excepting where the climate opposes a deadly barrier."[13] This is due, he suggests, to the working out via natural selection of the effects of better intellectual and moral faculties and sensibilities, which give their possessors advantages in the struggle for survival, which, together with their "daring and persistent energy" (also a product of natural selection) go some way to explaining the "remarkable success of the English as colonists" and "the wonderful progress of the United States."[14] Indeed part of chapter 5 of *The Descent of Man* is devoted to rebutting the contrary suggestion that all races started at the same level, with some declining over time. For Darwin,

12. Darwin, *The Descent of Man* (London: John Murray, 2nd ed., 1898), Vol II, 440.
13. Ibid, Vol I, 197.   14. Ibid, Vol I, 218.

as an evolutionarily progressive thinker, the descent of man implies *ascent* both from lower species and from lower stages of human development. As early as 11 October 1859, in a letter to Charles Lyell, Darwin had written "I look at this process as now going on with the races of man; the less intellectual races being exterminated."[15]

As late as 1881 Darwin wrote: "The more civilized so-called Caucasian races have beaten the Turkish hollow in the struggle for existence. Looking to the world at no very distant date, what an endless number of the lower races will have been eliminated by the higher civilized races throughout the world." Admittedly, this is in a letter (the one to William Graham already referred to), but that remark (redolent as it may be of the contemporaneous talk of "Bulgarian atrocities" and of "sick men of Europe") is precisely in reply to a correspondent who was doubtful that the struggle for survival and natural selection had done much to contribute to human progress. In 2011, it is hard not to be disturbed by Darwin's casual reference to the elimination of endless numbers of lower races, and even more by the way this sort of thinking was taken up by his followers such as Haeckel and von Treitschke, who in turn influenced Hitler. (The fact that Hitler himself wrote critically of Darwin does nothing to show that Darwinian thinking, particularly on eugenics, had not become a significant part of the intellectual sea in which Hitler and his ideologues and supporters swam.) Moreover, the remark in question is all of a piece with the teaching of *The Descent of Man,* even if more forcefully expressed.

The question we have to face here is not whether Darwin held the views ascribed to him. He clearly did. The question is whether those views follow from the theory of natural selection. The inescapable conclusion is that, if that theory is to be applied to human history, it is hard to see how, in some form, it can fail to do so.

The very first chapter of that book is entitled "The Descent of Man from Some Lower Form," so clearly no species egalitarianism there. It is indeed just what we had been led to expect from the conclusion of *The Origin of Species* where we were promised that the theory of natural selection would throw light on the origin of man *and his history.* For if natural selection is a doctrine of progress and if it applies to human history as well as to human origins we must expect that humans will be better than animals in

---

15. Darwin, *The Correspondence of Charles Darwin* (Cambridge: Cambridge University Press, 1983–2004), Vol 7, 345.

significant respects and that some humans will be significantly better than others. There is, of course, an elision in Darwin's thinking between better *in the struggle for existence* and more civilized. Bulgarian atrocities aside, there is no necessity here.

Indeed when we come to human affairs, the whole thing becomes rather ragged. We might indeed think that the Bulgarian atrocities are small compared to the atrocities produced by the "civilized" peoples of the twentieth century (or indeed to those perpetrated in the French Revolution and by Napoleon just a bit earlier). Is the society that produces reality television (or television at all) more civilized than that society which produced Chartres Cathedral and the Divine Comedy? Is there progress from Beethoven and Schubert to Stockhausen and Sir Harrison Birtwhistle (or even the Beatles)? For all our universal literacy have we produced any writers to compare with Aeschylus or Shakespeare, or thinkers to compare with Plato or Kant? These questions are, of course, not decidable, as is what lies behind them. It is impossible to see any general trend in human affairs towards progress or universal improvement, partly (but not only) because the terms in question are inherently vague, and where not vague are likely to be essentially contestable. What is, though, more clear to us than it may have been to Darwin is that in human affairs the struggle for existence is not in itself a guarantee of progress in any dimensions other than those of surviving and reproducing.

Darwinism and social policy

More clear, but Darwin was not entirely unworried in this area. For he did, like many of his contemporaries, notice a tendency in his time for the unfit, the inferior "in body or mind" and even the abject poor to breed, and, though he does not say this explicitly, possibly to outbreed the prudent and the strong. If mankind is to advance, we must uncover the laws of inheritance and then legislate against marriages among the inferior. We must encourage the poor not to marry (for abject poverty "tends to its own increase by leading to recklessness in marriage"), while at the same time urging the prudent and the most able to rear the largest number of offspring. (Maybe Darwin would have seen himself as suffering from a related dilemma had he not been personally so rich; at the time of his marriage he was wondering whether he would be able to have both books and children.) Above all we must ensure that the struggle for existence is not softened in its severity by laws and customs: "Otherwise (mankind) would sink into indolence, and the more gifted men would not be more successful in the battle of life than the less gifted."[16]

There is, in fact, a degree of tension in Darwin's own mind at this point, because as well as the struggle for existence, he wants our moral qualities to be developed (partly because he believes that a group with a strong communal morality based on mutual sympathy will do better than less coherent groups). But, might it not be just those moral qualities which recognize a common good, which protect the inferior and the poor against the most severe effects of the struggle for existence, which might then undermine human progress (in his view)? Indeed it is just so. "It is surprising," Darwin observed, "how soon a want of care . . . leads to the degeneration of a domestic race; but excepting in the case of man himself, hardly anyone is so ignorant as to allow his worst animals to breed." But in our own case, and for moral reasons, a degree of such "ignorance" must be tolerated. We must, Darwin admits, "therefore bear the undoubtedly bad effects of the weak surviving and propagating their kind." While at the same time doing what we can to ensure that "the weaker and inferior members of society do not marry so freely as the sound."[17] So the general import of his message is clear. We must take as much care in our own marriages as we take in the breeding and selection of our domestic animals, and we must also maintain social structures which allow untrammeled competition; both these injunctions follow pretty directly from applying the theory of natural selection to human society, as does the view that societies are to be ranked in degrees of success.

Evolution and the anthropic principle

We have been considering a number of aspects of Darwin's theory. In so doing we have found a tension between the theory of natural selection taken strictly and things which Darwin clearly holds strongly and wants to say. In particular we have found difficulties with his view of evolutionary progress, with his view of our own mental capacities, with his attempts to rank human societies, and also with what he considers desirable within

16. All quotes from Darwin, *The Descent of Man*, Vol II, 438–440.
17. *The Descent of Man*, Vol I, 206.

human societies. To put it bluntly, natural selection gives no warrant for any progressivism regarding evolution. It makes it hard to see what faith we should have in our scientific and philosophical speculations. It gives no warrant for associating success in evolutionary terms with a greater degree of civilization. At the same time the theory of natural selection seems to sanction a type of society which would run counter to many commonly held moral virtues and decencies. The interesting thing is that in each case Darwin himself gives signs of straining against the strict view of natural selection, and of wanting to promote a less austere view of things.

In a way, this connects with what we said at the beginning about moving away from a genocentric biology towards an approach which emphasized complexity and cooperation. If what is central to our study is not the gene or the organism, considered as discrete atomic individuals, but the complexes which they are and of which they form parts, we may begin to see existence in terms other than that of the survival of individuals and of what contributes to that.

In what we have come to see as the austere version of evolution, that delimited by Darwin's strict theory of natural selection, the picture which is given is of life being a desperate struggle by individuals to survive in an environment which if not actually hostile is largely indifferent to them. The key levers in this drama are random variations within the individuals and selective retention of a few of them by an environment that cares nothing for any of it. We are obviously a long distance from Darwin's own sense of natural selection carefully scrutinizing, selecting, preserving, ceaselessly and silently working for the good of all and each, and it is difficult to see where any such notion could gain a foothold. Nor is there any sense that the process as a whole is likely to move in a progressive direction, towards greater intelligence, complexity and morality. Rather to the contrary, the universe looks far more like that described by Jacques Monod in *Chance and Necessity*: "The universe was not pregnant with life, nor the biosphere with man."[18] We human beings are here by chance, in a universe which is not responsive to us at all, and within which our existence has no significance. For Monod, mankind is a gypsy, living in an alien world, which is deaf to his music. (He apparently saw no difficulty in having this alien world giving rise to creatures (us) who are able to conceive the world and their activity in terms of values.)

18. Jacques Monod, *Chance and Necessity* (New York: Knopf, 1971), 145.

In recent years, as is well known, the view that the universe was not pregnant with life and consciousness has been challenged by what has become
known as the anthropic principle. It is obviously true, tautologically so, that,
given that we are here, the universe must be such and must have been such
as to allow for the existence of intelligent knowers, such as ourselves. It
turns out, though, non-tautologically, that a very high degree of fine-tuning
even at the start of the universe, would have to have been in place in order
for intelligent life (us) to have been possible. Can anything be concluded
from the fine-tuning point?

At the very least, it suggests that Monod's basic stance needs qualification.
From the very beginning, the universe was, if not pregnant with life, certainly ready for the emergence of life. And the more precise the fine-tuning
and the more etched into the substance of things that fine-tuning is, given
the immense amounts of time and space involved for things to work themselves out, the closer readiness becomes to pregnancy. In a universe of the
extent of ours, it is not unrealistic to think that possibilities embedded in the
universe's basic structure are highly likely actually to occur. It is reasoning
of this sort which leads the adherents of the so-called "strong" anthropic
principle to conclude that life and mind do not have to be imported into
the universe from outside or by chance. They are, according to Paul Davies,
"etched deeply into the fabric of the cosmos, perhaps through a shadowy
half-glimpsed life principle."[19] Given the notorious problems in explaining
life and consciousness in purely physicalistic terms, such a view is not just
helpful in general terms. The difficulties themselves might actually open us
to the possibility that some such thing must be true, that life and mind are
there, embryonically, right from the start—otherwise it becomes well-nigh
impossible to see how they could have arisen.

At this point it is worth mentioning Christian de Duve's book *Vital
Dust*[20] in which the distinguished biologist (and, like Monod, a Nobel prize
winner) shows in great and sober detail, how, the importance of chance
events in the actual history notwithstanding, the development of life towards
human consciousness (and maybe beyond) is almost inevitable, once life in
its most basic form had emerged. (See especially his summary, 294–300.)
And he also argues, in line with proponents of the anthropic principle, that

19. Paul Davies, *The Goldilocks Enigma: Why Is the Universe Just Right for Life?* (London: Penguin
    Books, 2006), 302–3.
20. Christian de Duve, *Vital Dust* (New York: Basic Books, 1995).

given the physical conditions obtaining on the Earth 3.8 billion years ago, RNA-like molecules were bound to arise at some time or other. Further given the nature of the universe itself those conditions apt for the emergence of RNA were almost bound to arise not only on the Earth, but in many, many other planets. Hence de Duve's evocative title, *Vital Dust*, suggesting that the elementary particles of which the universe is composed have an inbuilt tendency to form themselves into life and mind-promoting complexes. In the letter to Lyell referred to earlier, Darwin had said that he "would give absolutely nothing for the theory of natural selection, if it requires miraculous additions at any one stage of descent." Consciousness and even life itself can look highly mysterious, if we are reductive physicalists, but not so miraculous if our perspective is that of de Duve. A de Duvian perspective, then, can help to smooth out the course of a theory of evolution in the way Darwin himself required.

We do not have to acquiesce in the more colorful conclusions drawn by advocates of anthropic thinking to see its basic orientation as suggestive in a number of ways. If the universe is disposed to produce life and mind right from the start, we will no longer see ourselves as tangential to it, a mere random accident in a fundamentally lifeless system, gaining whatever knowledge we have of it as a chance side effect of our striving to survive in it. If our mental faculties are rooted in the fabric of the universe, it will not be surprising or problematic if they do deliver knowledge of it way beyond the basics we need for survival. If the universe as a whole is evolving forms of life and mind, the progressive thrust of evolution in that direction will not be such a mystery. Also, if life and mind are themselves goods from the point of view of that evolution, we may well be led to value states of feeling and mind for their own sakes, and not simply as aids to survival and reproduction. Indeed something more than survival and reproduction may come to be seen as implicit in nature from the start; so our own tendencies to morality and cooperation (genuine altruism) will no longer seem the anomaly they will inevitably be if nature is conceived in strictly Darwinian terms. Finally, an approach to evolution and life which stresses complexity and mutual belonging will be far less concerned to emphasize struggle in the way Darwin does, which will obviously have ecological and ethical resonances.

It remains to be seen whether any of this would be helpful to religion, in restoring that sense of the Creator which Darwin found so hard to dispense with even in his agnosticism. On the positive side, a universe pregnant with life and a biosphere pregnant with mind would be far more congenial to religious understanding than the bleak cosmic landscape envisaged by Monod. And the idea of God or the divinity working through creative processes is one common to many religious traditions (and it would also pick up on Teilhardian ideas of the cosmos existing in order to know itself). On the other hand these ideas may in themselves do little to exorcise the weariness and despair many other than Darwin feel when confronted with all the apparent waste, prodigality and suffering inherent in creation. Without some revelation or gift of grace, the problems involved in reconciling ourselves to a God who chooses to work like that, or who can work in no other way (which may be even worse for the traditional notion of an intelligent designer) remain as intractable as ever.

FOUR

Evolutionary Emergence of Intentionality and Imagination

Dale Jacquette

Aesthetic object and subject

It is a frequent topic of philosophical discussion whether beauty is objective or purely subjective. There are dilemmas in aesthetics that duplicate the arguments on both sides of this perennial dispute in other areas of philosophy, in theory of knowledge and metaphysics, and in ethics as another branch of value theory.[1]

The ideological and methodological oppositions that divide philosophy generally into realisms and idealisms, objectivisms and subjectivisms, also pervade aesthetic theory. We can ask whether there was beauty in the world prior to the emergence of intelligent perceivers like ourselves, or whether beauty itself comes into existence only through the perceptual idiosyncrasies with which we happen to encounter the objects we happen to consider beautiful. It is a commonplace, bordering on cliché, that beauty is in the eye of the beholder—and not just of any beholder, but of beings who are not only capable of perception, but also appreciation in making value judgments, as well as interpretation, understanding, and a wide range of relatively sophisticated emotional responses. Or perhaps the right kind of emotional response alone is sufficient, so that some non-human animals might also be capable of appreciating beautiful scenery.

---

1. An extensive literature exists on this subject, primarily from the standpoint of objectivists criticizing subjectivists. Important discussions appear in I. C. Jarvie, "The Objectivity of Criticism of the Arts," *Ratio* 9 (1967): 67–83; D. W. Crawford, "Causes, Reasons, and Aesthetic Objectivity," *American Philosophical Quarterly* 8 (1971): 266–74.

The experience of beauty and its opposites under this description can easily seem to be an altogether subjective phenomenon, available at most only to a select subset of psychological subjects, for whom it resides ontically speaking exclusively in their thoughts. Or so subjectivists in philosophical aesthetics maintain. Objectivists at the other extreme in the ideological spectrum insist on the contrary that beauty exists already in nature independently of thought, waiting, so to speak, to be perceived if only an attentive observer of the appropriate kind should happen to arrive on the scene. The subjective side of aesthetics from such a perspective is only half of the story, incomplete in and of itself, in which the mind takes notice of a preexistent beauty that is not constituted or conditioned by the circumstances of the receptive perceiver, but exists as one of the perceivable properties of real physical things.[2]

The dispute about the ontology of beauty is an inexhaustible source of opposing, and for that reason, philosophically fruitful, arguments. What should not be in doubt is the manifest dependence of the existence of art on intelligent thinkers as makers of artworks. Art, beautiful or not, does not exist in nature, unless we suppose that the universe is the handiwork of a divine designer with a flair for the artistic. An artwork is something artificial and artifactual, as the etymology of these related terminologies unmistakably implies. Even if aesthetic objectivists are right to hold that beauty, at least in the form of natural beauty, obtains independently of thinking subjects objectively in the world, works of art are quite another thing. Although the point is obvious enough upon reflection, it bears repeating that without intelligent artists exercising judgment, taste, energy, and skill, there can be no such thing as art. Nor, from an empirical standpoint, as a matter of philosophical anthropology, can we attribute art as opposed to other kinds of artifacts, however this pre-analytically understood distinction is finally clarified, to any human-like animals we know of other than our own very recently evolved species.[3]

2. See e.g., Michael Scriven, "The Objectivity of Aesthetic Evaluation," *The Monist*, 50 (1966), 159–87. F. N. Sibley, "Objectivity and Aesthetics," *Proceedings of the Aristotelian Society, Supplement*, 42, (1968), 31–54. A. G. Pleydell-Pearce, "Objectivity and Value in Judgments of Aesthetics," *The British Journal of Aesthetics*, 10 (1970), 25–38. Michael A. Slote, "Rationality of Aesthetic Judgements," *The Journal of Philosophy*, 68 (1971), 821–39. I explain the subjective theory of aesthetic value developed by A. Meinong and S. Witasek in D. Jacquette, "Metaphysics of Meinongian Aesthetic Value," *Meinong Studies*, 4 (2010) special issue on The Aesthetics of the Graz School, ed. V. Raspa, 53–86.
3. One of the best recent sources is Erik Trinkhaus and Pat Shipman, *The Neandertals: Of Skeletons, Scientists, and Scandal* (New York: Random House, 1994), esp. chap. 1 and 10, 8–45, 384–410, and Epilogue, 411–19.

Wittgenstein, in *Tractatus Logico-Philosophicus* 2.1, says something profound for these purposes about the nature of humankind, when with remarkable insight introducing his afterward so-called picture theory of meaning, he flatly declares: "We make to ourselves pictures of facts."[4] We do indeed make to ourselves pictures of facts, and we have done so, as far as archaeology testifies, throughout our history. Modern human beings, since the evolution and global sprawl between the last two great ice ages of the first Cro-Magnon, have engaged in the production, use, and enjoyment of art. The historical record supports the anthropological claim that without art, whatever else we are, we are not modern humans. If we go back only as far as the Neandertals, with whom our remote ancestors coexisted for at least ten thousand years, we recognize a hominid species that was remarkably intelligent, social, and well adapted to its environment, whose members made tools, buried their dead ceremonially, made boats and navigated inland waters, as has recently been discovered, and were probably capable of some kind of speech, although, possibly, it is controversially believed by some researchers, with only two of the six vowel sounds which we modern humans command.[5]

Whether Neandertals are our progenitors or merely an evolutionary side-branch of the hominid family line, they were extraordinarily successful and exhibited many of the traits we associate with our own species. Whatever Neandertal humans accomplished, however, they did not, to the best of our historical knowledge, decorate their tools or dwellings, or make painted or carved images, icons, or representations of things in their world, nor, as Wittgenstein puts it, although they might have spoken, does it appear that they did not try extra-linguistically to make to themselves pictures of facts. The very moment modern human beings appeared, somewhere between 35,000 and 50,000 years ago, there, anthropologists tell us, we immediately find an abundance of art, decoration, images, totems, likenesses of animals and human beings, and in general pictures of facts. Unlike Neandertals, these people, our closest ancestors, genetically indistinguishable from ourselves, could not make a stone hammer, bone scraper, or flint knife without carving images on

---

4. Ludwig Wittgenstein, *Tractatus Logico-Philosophicus*, ed. C. K. Ogden (London: Routledge & Kegan Paul, 1922).
5. A scientifically accurate portrayal of interaction between Neandertals and modern Cro-Magnon humans in the ice age is given in B. Kurtén, *Dance of the Tiger: A Novel of the Ice Age* (Berkeley: University of California Press, 1995). On the limited vocal abilities of Neandertals, see P. Lieberman, *The Biology and Evolution of Language* (Cambridge, MA: Harvard University Press, 1984).

the handle; they could not long make use of a cave without painting the walls with bison and mammoths and their own handprints and even more meta-phorical or ceremonial mythological images. We marvel even today at the artistic quality of what our ice age forerunners accomplished whenever a new wall cavern site or anthropomorphic antler tool is unearthed.[6]

Among other conclusions to be drawn from the data of a scientific anthropology, accordingly, we may argue that Martin Heidegger in his influ-ential study of existential phenomenological ontology, *Being and Time*, has gotten things seriously wrong.[7] *Da-sein* or human being-in-the-world is not a matter of technology, of *Zuhandenheit*, or grasping of things, taking them to hand; not, at least if we mean modern human beings, our own spe-cies, Cro-Magnon men and women like ourselves, rather than hominids generally. For even Neandertals had a crude technology and grasped things and put them to use, and therefore must have taken care for themselves and things, and seen the world at least in part as a repository of raw materials for their use. What distinguishes modern human beings, as contemporary archaeology and anthropology indicates, is not technology, but art. We are not merely, to use the familiar gender-biased terminology, man the knower or man the tool-maker, but man the artist. Wittgenstein has it right where Heidegger goes astray (unless Heidegger is talking about hominids gener-ally), we are not just grabby tool users, but picture makers—we who Wittgenstein says make to ourselves pictures of facts.[8]

If so, then philosophy confronts the question of precisely how art is related to art-makers. What is required of a person in order to become an artist, or, better, to exercise the innate artistic potential that is our genetic birthright? The answer presumably must involve something that is immediately before us, something to which we need only pay proper attention in order to

6. An excellent account of ice age artworks and the imaginative thought processes of Cro-Magnon humans that they reflect is found in D. Lewis-Williams, *The Mind in the Cave: Consciousness and the Origins of Art* (London: Thames & Hudson, 2003). See R. J. Richards, "Darwin on Mind, Morals and Emotions," in *The Cambridge Companion to Darwin*, ed. J. Hodge and G. Radick. (Cambridge: Cambridge University Press, 2003), 92–115.

7. Martin Heidegger, *Being and Time, A Translation of Sein und Zeit* trans. J. Stambaugh (Albany: State University of New York Press, 1996), 132–7, 141–86, on disclosedness (*Erschlossenheit*), and 121–7, 171–230, on care (*Sorge*).

8. An insightful discussion of Heidegger's ontology in relation to Schopenhauer's theory of art is offered by Julian Young, "Schopenhauer, Heidegger, Art, and the Will," in Jacquette, ed., *Schopenhauer, Philosophy, and the Arts* (Cambridge: Cambridge University Press, 1996), 162–80. See also Jacquette, *The Philosophy of Schopenhauer* (Chesham: Acumen Publishing Limited, 2005), 244–9.

recognize it as the key to central problems in the philosophy of art. It must be there for us to see, given what we have already said, if it is true that compulsively and by nature we are all artists, to a greater or lesser degree, actively and competently, or only potentially and less competently, professionally or unprofessionally. Who, after all, has not at least as a child made pictures, who does not take pride in making photographs, entertaining oneself with singing or whistling, arranging flowers or furniture in a room in a pleasing way, decorating an object with respect to form and color according to a personally satisfying aesthetic? If we are all artists in one way or another, then we should be able to determine on reflection what is needed for art, why it is so essential for our humanity, and what is involved in becoming an artist; for in that case it is something that we cannot prevent ourselves from doing if we only follow what is deeply ingrained in our species heritage.

Evolution of intentionality and imagination

Imagination as we ordinarily think of it appears to be exercised only by the most highly developed consciousnesses. The concrete products of a fertile imagination are created only by those capable of art and literature, among other ways of simultaneously lying and telling the truth. It is conceivable that higher animals can imagine future states of affairs, when they engage deliberately and successfully with the causal properties of their environments. Their actions suggest that in some circumstances certain of them are expecting something to happen, which can be understood as imagining a state of affairs that does not yet exist but that is likely to occur in the future when they do something in order to produce a certain effect. If nothing else, non-human intelligent animals might be said to imagine the satisfaction of their desires upon causing something to happen. Why else does the chimp use a stick to get down the banana, rather than doing nothing at all? When we imagine something, we undoubtedly intend a nonexistent state of affairs. We must be capable in that case of intending nonexistent objects of imagination, a fact that must be acknowledged and given due importance in considering an intentional theory of imagination. Recognizing that only an intentional theory of imagination can account semantically for the differences between imagination episodes identical in every respect except the content of what exactly it is that is imagined, we are prepared to understand that whatever else is implied by the concept of imagination, an imaginative mental act is undoubtedly intentional. A phenomenology of imagination is therefore indispensable, and its first conclusion must be that imagination is intentional, an intentional phenomenon.

Intentionality is accordingly a necessary condition of imagination, although it is clearly not sufficient. Many thinking creatures capable of intentional states, of intending the objects of their psychologically primitive sensations and perceptions, and even of being conscious of their psychological states without yet being self-conscious, aware of themselves *as* thinking subjects, are not yet capable of the kind of intentionality required for what among our own species would be even the most elementary mental acts of imagination. Imagination intends complex experiential or propositional objects, as we find in imaginative art and literature, and in imagination as it functions in everyday applications in anticipating possible future outcomes of events, entertaining the mind and communicating valuable wisdom by telling stories and parables with a moral, however ambiguously expressed, in which nonexistent objects, facts and events are imaginatively projected for consideration and decision making, as a distraction, or for whatever other purposes such concentrated acts of imagination may find expression.

This is intentionality of a relatively high order when compared with that of an angelfish perceiving something moving in the water, which, lacking language, the fish obviously cannot describe. We encounter in such examples the philosophical problem of drawing even a very thick line between species that are capable and those that are incapable of imagination that still leaves many middle undecided grey area cases. Where would the angelfish that you buy in a pet shop fall on such a spectrum? Are fish clearly capable or clearly incapable of imagination, or are they somewhere in the grey area in between these extremes? The fact that angelfish do not linguistically describe what they experience does not necessarily mean that they do not think propositionally. If we agree that angelfish think at all, and if we think that there are innate languages by which some nonhuman animals are capable of humanlike imagination or imagination simulacra, then we cannot avoid the question of whether such lower animals as angelfish can also think imaginatively. Angelfish are relatively stupid animals, if we are being frank rather than kind, which by itself does not yet imply that angelfish are incapable of imagination. I strongly doubt that they are, although we might conjecture that free flights of imagination are precisely how angelfish cope with their otherwise intolerably droll existence in an aquarium with plastic plants and a florescent light overhead that stays on for hours at a time. In all likelihood, angelfish are capable at most of the intentionality of sensation and perception, but not of the intentionality of imagination. Angelfish presumably do not fantasize that they are red-tailed sharks or that they will return to a wild Amazon creek some day or that they might develop the power to fly outside of water in the aerosphere to escape to a new life in the brackish inland waters of the sunny Caribbean. Nor anything else in all likelihood do they imagine, at any possible level of simplicity or complexity. If this first intuition is correct, then imagination such as we find it expressed by our conspecifics in imaginative art and literature, as in decision making and expression of thought in any medium, in all action requiring deliberation, decision and intention, appears somewhere in the evolutionary tree among creatures capable of intentionality, of thought and hence of thinking in some sense about or intending objects as a distinctive psychological episode.

What we can infer from these facts is that intentionality in primitive form must have evolved as a property of living things, however cognitively basic, and that imagination as a particular type of intentional, minimally conscious if not fully self-conscious state, is a more highly refined, we might even say more highly evolved, type of intentionality. The present task is not to speculate about precisely when and how in the course of biological evolution intentionality and imagination may have emerged among living things, but rather to understand the metaphysics of such evolutionary emergence of unprecedented properties, and the general types of evolutionary pressures that might have given rise to these particular categories of mental states and cognitive capacities.

Human Beings (Cro-Magnon; Homo habilis, Homo erectus, Neandertal?)
——————————————|——————————————
IMAGINATION
Angelfish
——————————
INTENTIONALITY...

The immense survival advantage of collecting and processing information concerning both beneficial and hazardous factors makes it invaluable for the survival and reproductive fitness of living things to be able to perceive objects in their environments. Sensation and perception of even the most limited sort, such as the detection of motion or a change from light to dark or dark to light by a simple eyespot, would already confer on its possessor a significant advantage in the location of resources and avoidance of dangers.

Sensation and perception can be understood as purely causal occurrences at one level of description, accomplished by an otherwise undedicated neuronal cell mutated in function to become sensitive to changes in local ambient information-laden conditions. Information about the world is already available, on this model, awaiting only a receptor. It occurs as transmissions in sound and light waves within the electromagnetic spectrum, stimulating a modified nerve cell and transmitting a change of state in physically caused disturbances to the appropriate cognitive centers for processing. The animal's neurophysiology typically evolves corresponding mechanisms for engaging motor and muscular trains or similar locomotive routines to pursue or flee the respective information source, or to do nothing at all. Responding to environmental changes before they actually exert a direct physical impact can be vital to an organism's survival and reproductive success, especially once potential competitors evolve the ability.

The very instant perceptive faculties appear in the evolution of a species, and take their place among the capacities of living things, whose movements and activities are directed by such information processing, whenever that moment occurs, we can also say that intentionality of a corresponding primitive type will have also evolved. The reason is that for a living thing to sense or perceive is for it to sense or perceive *something*, to be directed in psychological occurrence toward the *object intended* by the sensation or perception, or by the creature's state of sensing or perceiving. And this is all that is required of intentionality in its most elementary manifestations. Sensation and perception involve the uptake of information, and are about whatever it is that is sensed or perceived, so that sensing and perceiving local environmental conditions, even among the most primitive organisms, is also literally intentional. We might imagine a mollusk on a primeval sea bottom snapping its shell shut when a potentially predatory shadow passes over and triggers a response mechanism beginning with a change of state in a motion or light detecting neuron or neuron cluster, surpassing a threshold value and activating an evolutionarily selected set of responses. The internal neuronal change triggered by environmental events will accordingly have an intended object, even in so simple an organism, as a proximate cause of the neuronal state change. The cause of the neuronal state change is in turn what the change intends or is *about*; the neural activation of an eyespot on the delicious and, unfortunately, except for its shell, defenseless bivalve *intends* whatever it is that has caused an abrupt change in the proximate light.

There is no question of consciousness let alone self-consciousness for such a simple entity. Primitive intentionality nevertheless exists whenever we can reasonably attribute the direction of a cognitive activity upon an object. We include thereby any change in the organism's internal state that is in some way directly conditional and contingent on the neuronal processing of information related to specific objects that are intended in the sense of being perceived at a neurologically and experientially very fundamental level. If we further think of the greatest flights of imagination of which we are aware, in our own conscious lives, and as expressed in imaginative works of art and literature, then, unless we are prepared to countenance explanations of empirical phenomena depending on supernatural entities or events, we must imagine that the intentionality present even in such simple creatures as angelfish and bottom-dwelling mollusks must have been refined and conditioned from a variety of directions under natural selection pressures to develop among other ways for evolved intelligences such as ourselves as a capacity for imagination. If we can imagine what might happen if we set a snare on a hare's trail, if we can imagine what might happen if we fail to store food and fuel for the winter, and if our intelligence is such that we can make provision for some of the most likely eventualities that we imagine in planning pragmatically a course of action over time, then we can pursue a more effective survival and reproduction strategy. If imagination, as appears obvious, has applications by which it confers genetic fitness advantages, then, other things being equal, it is certain to be preserved and refined both genetically and in the culturally evolving social order. At some point in this evolutionary process, from the light-sensitive hatch-hinge of the timid mollusk to the writing of *Anna Karenina*, the evolution of imagination among other powerful capabilities has permitted human beings to survive so well that we can afford to use imagination also for the evolutionary luxury enjoyed by few species of entertainment, invention, and fun. What, then, are some of the main features of the evolution of primitive intentionality into imagination as expressed in language, art, and artifacts, in planning, decision making, and human institutions, from an evolutionary and cultural perspective?

Art and language as the expression of ideas

When we consider the unprofessional art that most people make at some point or other during their lives, what do we learn? We may think of arts and crafts historically as they must have developed from an anthropological point of view, beginning with what seems to be an innate drive in human beings to make art and to make to ourselves pictures of facts, or other kinds of pictures or melodies or poems, leading by degrees to the most valued treasures of the fine arts among ancient civilizations to the present day, what can we say about the nature of art in relation to what it is that every person does in making an artwork?

Taking our cue from Wittgenstein's opening remark in explaining the *Tractatus* picture theory of meaning, it seems reasonable to begin at least with the hypothesis that art is somehow akin to language. It may be worthwhile first to review some of the positive analogies between linguistic and artistic practices. Both are apparently distinctively human activities, and in their developed forms more particularly they are activities unique to modern human beings. Although written languages do not appear in the cultural record until about five thousand years ago, we must assume that some forms of spoken languages were well established even among other hominids, and hence, that abstract symbolization in language as in the plastic arts and music characterized modern human life from its very inception. Like language, art is something requiring a certain amount of skill, that can be exercised more or less proficiently, and that permits in principle a wide range of individual expression. As Wittgenstein is aware, if language is a kind of picturing, then in a certain sense even our precursor hominid ancestors, insofar as they were capable of expressing themselves in language, were also in effect practicing art by making verbal pictures of facts. If this application seems too farfetched, we should nevertheless acknowledge the sense in which language can be poetic or prosaic, and in which written language can be as ornate in its calligraphy or pictographic and hieroglyphic styles as many other art forms. Until relatively recently, when reading and writing became democratized in literate societies, the ability to read and write was the jealously protected prerogative of a specially trained priesthood, as much involved in the ritual articulation of visual images as in inscribing court records, religious events, taxes, stores of goods, donations to the gods or the dead, and the important events of a people's history.

The concept is fueled by an obvious analogy. If we think of language as expressive, a public way of making ideas concrete to share with others, and if we think of language as sufficiently like art in certain ways, then it may be natural also to think of art as expressive of many kinds of things. At the very least, we can examine the hypothesis to see where, if anywhere, it leads. In language we use conventional sign systems to concretize our ideas in an almost endless variety of ways for as many kinds of ideas as thought is capable of considering. We can talk and write about the beliefs we accept and doubts we have, about our feelings and hopes and dreams and aspirations; we can preserve memories and advance hypotheses, issue commands, keep track of questions and problems, consider philosophical problems, and unlimitedly many other things besides, including the symbolic recording of thought as a relatively permanent *aide-de-mémoire*.

To a certain extent we can do the same kinds of things in artworks, although not always with the same degree of communicative success. By painting a caribou on a stretched skin we can express our desire for a bountiful hunt. By painting the so-called *Nightwatch* (*The Company of Frans Banning Cocq and Willem van Ruytenburgh*), Rembrandt, among other things, can express the prestige of a class of Amsterdam civil militia, the authority of office, implicit protection of the citizenry, the individual attitudes of the musketeers, and possibly the presence in absence of his beloved wife Saskia, if the woman dressed in white in a pool of illumination is her cameo portrait in the work. In painting *Guernica*, Piccasso can express his horror of war, disillusionment about the future of mankind, outrage at the first use of air weaponry against civilian noncombatants, and many other things besides. If all art expresses ideas, even if we must often guess and imperfectly try to interpret what those ideas might be, then it should be reasonable to define art as a kind of nonlinguistic expression. We understand different styles, genres and schools of art as different ways of expressing ideas or as concerned with particular kinds of ideas, devoted to religious concepts or to an ideal of harmony with nature or to an existential outlook about the human condition.

The theory of art as expression has a well established pedigree. It exists in a variety of guises that do not always expressly refer to themselves as expressivistic. The most conspicuous sources for this kind of aesthetic theory are John Dewey's *Art as Experience* and Arthur Berndtson's *Art, Expression, and Beauty*.[9] The same kind of theory is nevertheless to be found in any philosophical attempt to define art in terms of an artist's intentions in producing an artwork, such as Stephen Davies's proposal, in his more recent book *Definitions of Art*, to defend such a concept against William K. Wimsatt,

9. J. Dewey, *Art as Experience* (New York: Capricorn Books, 1958), chap. 4–5, 58–105. A. Berndtson, *Art, Expression, and Beauty* (New York: Holt, Rinehart and Winston, 1969), chap. 4, 8 and 9, 59–84, 144–92.

Jr. and Monroe C. Beardsley's assault against expressivism in their landmark essay, "The Intentional Fallacy."[10] Even Clive Bell's formalist theory of *Art*, justly famous and influential in Susanne K. Langer's formalist aesthetics in *Feeling and Form*, appears only superficially to characterize art exclusively in terms of its forms entirely at the expense of content, but defines the uniquely aesthetic quality of artworks more precisely as *significant* form.[11]

An intentionalist philosopher of language such as Roderick M. Chisholm, Joseph Margolis, or John R. Searle could hardly ask for a more suggestive parallel in the philosophy of art, depending, of course, on how *significance* is understood and what is packed into the concept.[12] The significantly formal aspects of language, from ordinary languages to symbolic logics and computer programming codes, testify in any case to the continuity rather than sharp division between art and language.

If we turn to Berndtson as a central figure in expressivist aesthetics, we find that he implausibly limits the expressive dimension of art exclusively to the expression of emotions. There is no reason to doubt that much of art is expressive in precisely this way, and, whereas Bell and Langer emphasize the formal aspects of art in the concept of significant form, Berndtson pays homage to Arthur Schopenhauer, George Santayana, Benedetto Croce, C. J. Ducasse, as well as Antonio Caso, Theodore M. Greene, Bell and Langer. The latter of whom speak especially of expressive form, but oddly in this context nowhere mentions Dewey's pragmatic theory of the emotively expressive act and emotively expressive object.[13] Berndtson writes:

> It is not sufficient... to think of expression as a relation of form and emotion, by virtue of which emotion or the self is clarified and made free and beauty is brought into being. It is necessary, among other matters, to consider how emotion is related to the expressing form, how clarity and freedom arise among other changes in emotion, and how beauty enters the expressive act. / The appropriate analysis may well start with a consideration of the unstudied range of meaning of the word *expression*. In the simplest context, the term can be applied to the act of squeezing water out of a sponge: the water literally is expressed from the sponge. An angry animal is said to express its emotion by growling and snapping. Concepts are expressed in words and sentences. And in the most complex context, emotion is expressed in a work of art.[14]

10. S. Davies, *Definitions of Art* (Ithaca: Cornell University Press, 1991), 181–221. W. K. Wimsatt, Jr. and M. C. Beardsley, "The Intentional Fallacy," *The Sewanee Review* 54 (1946): 468–88.
11. C. Bell, *Art* (New York: G. P. Putnam, 1981). S K. Langer, *Feeling and Form* (London: Routledge & Kegan Paul, 1953).
12. Bell, *Art*; Langer, *Feeling and Form*.   13. Berndtson 147, n. 1.   14. Ibid. 147.

What we must wonder is whether art is always and only emotionally expressive, or whether there are not other ways in which art expresses and things other than emotions it can also express. The problem is dramatized when neither artist nor critic can confidently identify a specific emotion as underlying the production of an artwork. Must we say even then that the art object nevertheless expresses an emotion, but one that, since we cannot find it, is perhaps in Freudian terms sublimated or subconscious, or that the artist in self-deception has hidden away behind a punishing super-ego? In any other field of inquiry, such desperate moves would rightly be regarded as unconscionable theory-saving. Berndstson is well aware of the need to support his concentration on the use of art to express emotion, when he later adds:

> The theory of art as expression accords to emotion the primary place in art, and devotes the greater part of its energy as theory to the description and understanding of the relations, transformation, and consequences of emotion in art. Here it stands in clear contrast to the theories of art as representation and as form, which find a secondary or incidental place for emotion in art, or deny it altogether. / The emphasis on emotion requires justification.... Apart from any theory of the essence of art, it was stated [in a previous chapter] that emotion has important relations to value, experience, and thought, which justify and even require its entry into the aesthetic experience. It was shown that aesthetic form implies emotion, whether in sensation, the choice and methods of representation, or in the diverse types of aesthetic structure.[15]

Part of the answer lies in Berndtson's definition of the concept of emotion, which he understands in this way:

> Emotion is the immediate awareness of value, and in expression that awareness achieves its most satisfying fulfillment. Emotion supplies to art an imposing matter and problem, and expression supplies a solution equal to the task. In this solution lies the only balance between life and art that aesthetic theory can discover: through emotion art draws without limit on life, and through expression it achieves a unique status and value that sets it apart from the rest of life.[16]

A similar commitment to art as specifically emotional expression by way of a necessary connection between emotion and expression and the view that all expression is emotional is found in Dewey's *Art as Experience*, when he argues:

---

15. Ibid. 150–1.   16. Ibid. 151.

Emotional discharge is a necessary but not a sufficient condition of expression. / There is no expression without excitement, without turmoil.[17]

It does not take a master of the counterexample method as subtle as Socrates to see that Dewey's or Berndtson's concept of emotion will hardly do on its own or in the context of his application in the theory of art as emotive expression. Without going so far as to accuse Berndtson of adjusting data to fit theory, it may still be cautioning to recall Wittgenstein's remark in *Philosophical Investigations* §593, where he refers to "A main cause of philosophical disease—a one-sided diet: one nourishes one's thinking with only one kind of example."[18] What excitement or turmoil, dramatic as it sounds to say so, do I require in order to express my belief that two plus two equals four or that Bern is the capital of Switzerland?

The value of emotion as it stands in immediate awareness according to Berndtson requires further clarification. It appears more consistent with the facts revealed by introspection that the immediate awareness of value is generally one thing, and the emotional overlay that sometimes accompanies such recognition is something else. I perceive the (negative) value of an insult or gross act of moral misconduct, and my anger about it, if I happen to experience any such emotion, is something else again that may not occur until later. If I am angry about paying my income taxes when I sign my check to the IRS with a violent sweep of the pen in recognition of the value of the money I am sending away, have I created a work of art? If I work for the Treasury Department and it is my daily job to sort through currency to distinguish legal tender from counterfeits, then in the course of a dull and often repeated routine, I might immediately recognize the monetary value of a bill as I place it on one pile rather than another, without feeling any particular emotion whatsoever, let alone an aesthetically relevant emotion, beyond the desire to do my work correctly or take an early lunch. On other occasions, I might experience a flood of emotion, say, of anxiety, without even knowing why. What if I am a production potter, engaged in a repetitious movement that I have mastered and executed many times as I make what is in fact an extraordinarily beautiful and valuable piece of pottery? In such circumstances, I may happen to experience no other emotion than boredom, or something quite aesthetically irrelevant as my mind drifts,

---

17. Dewey, *Art as Experience*, 61.
18. Wittgenstein, *Philosophical Investigations*. 3rd ed., trans. G. E. M. Anscombe (New York: Macmillan, 1968).

such as a feeling of regret for saying something impolite to a stranger many years ago. There may even be a complex causal connection, a feedback loop, between emotion and expression feeding and amplifying one another until some inhibiting threshold is surpassed.

Suppose that in answering a telephone call from the police I feel an intense emotion before I know whether the news is good, bad, or indifferent, possibly the result of nothing more portentious than a wrongly dialed number. If defending Berndtson in such cases requires us to say that any contact with the police is portent with some aesthetic value, then the thesis is threatened with triviality. In that case, whenever we are conscious we are constantly experiencing a significant immediate recognition of artistic value of stronger or weaker degree, at least of relief. If there is never a moment when we are not experiencing an emotion, then there is no contrast to be drawn between recognizing such a value and not doing so. In a related case, it appears that I can perceive the aesthetic value of a child's drawing, but without experiencing any particular emotion, until I realize as a matter of propositional knowledge that the drawing is something I made as a child, and I am suddenly transported back to a kindergarten classroom or a sunny patch of carpet at Grandma's house. Berndtson must say that recognizing the value of the drawing by definition is itself an emotion, regardless of whether it is experienced with anything remotely resembling the phenomenology of emotions as the concept of emotion is usually understood. As a final counterexample, consider the following dilemma. If I wake up with an unaccountable feeling of joy on a workday, must we say in order to accept Berndtson's thesis that this is my recognition of the positive value of work, even if at the time I loathe my job and refuse to assent to any such explanation? If, on the other hand I wake up on such a day with an otherwise unaccountable feeling of depression or dark despair, must we say in order to accept Berndtson's thesis that this is my recognition of the negative value of having to work for a living, even if at the time I refuse to assent to any such explanation?

If we are obligated to extend Berndtson's analysis to cover all situations as emotional in which an artist immediately values something enough to choose it as a subject for an artwork, then the same should be true of any choice of anything anyone does as an immediate recognition of the value of the thing as worth doing. Then, whatever anyone does in any walk of life must qualify as the expression of emotion and hence as art. It might be reasonable to treat absolutely everything a person does as an artwork of sorts, but Berndtson apparently does not want to collapse the distinction between artistic and non-artistic practices into art, and neither do most philosophers. The point is to identify what is distinctive about art and the making of art; otherwise, we can simply avoid talk of emotions altogether as epiphenomenal to aesthetics and define art more directly as whatever people do. This, interestingly, emphasizing the evolutionary approach to pragmatism that characterizes his thought, is more or less what Dewey bravely argues. His concept of the "impulses" to which all animals are subject and to which the motivation of human action is reduced suggests an unbroken line of continuity between animals and certainly in all actions of human agents as emotively expressive. The failure of a definition of art as the expression of emotion nevertheless need not entail the failure of a more general definition of art as a particular way of expressing ideas, among which emotions can be included as one category of thoughts among others.[19]

Perception and intentionality in the philosophy of art

The thesis that art is the expression of ideas seems right enough as far as it goes. Even if art is expression or if expression is indispensable to the concept of art, however, it remains equally true that art cannot adequately be explained as expression. The reason goes to the heart of an important division in art theory and aesthetic philosophy, between two ways of thinking about the nature of art, from the standpoint of production and consumption, and the complementary perspectives of artist and appreciator or audience. There is a synergy that exists between these two poles, involving both what goes into the making of art and the experience of art by perceivers other than the artist, without an adequate account of which the nature, meaning, and value of art cannot be fully understood.

We can divide many aesthetic theories into those that mistakenly focus exclusively or excessively on the manufacture of art from the artist's standpoint

---

19. Vincent Thomas, "The Concept of Expression in Art," in *Science, Language and Human Rights* (Philadelphia: University of Pennsylvania Press, 1952), 127–44. Alan Tormey, *The Concept of Expression: A Study in Philosophical Psychology and Aesthetics* (Princeton: Princeton University Press, 1971). Guy Sircello, *Mind and Art: An Essay on the Varieties of Expression* (Princeton: Princeton University Press, 1972). See also Paisley Livingston, *Art and Intention: A Philosophical Study* (Oxford: The Clarendon Press, 2005), 23, 141, 150, 177, 183.

to the neglect of the audience or spectator standpoint, and those that mistakenly focus exclusively or excessively on the experience of art from the audience or spectator standpoint to the neglect of the artist's standpoint. Art in its entirety is nevertheless the product of a cooperation between both its producers and consumers. This is true not only in the most abstract sense that such conspicuously important moments in the making, use, and enjoyment of art need to be included in a complete account simply because they are elements in the process by which art is made and the purpose for which it is made. We must include as well considerations of artistic success or failure both for and from the perspective of those who produce and those who consume artworks, because artists themselves judge their effects on audiences or spectators in a self-reflective process that includes criticism of many different kinds including immediate reactions on the part of those who experience and interact with art. The production of art can involve an artist's adoption of these distinct roles also at different times during the creative process.[20]

If we reconsider the analogy between expression in language and art, we discover remarkable continuities and even more significant disanalogies. We ordinarily expect that discursive language, verbal or written, is the expression of a thinker's ideas that are relatively easy for a listener or reader to correctly decipher. If I utter a simple declarative sentence, such as "Bern is the capital of Switzerland," I have expressed an idea, and might even do so with an accompanying state of emotion in recognition of the value of that fact or at least the truth value of the proposition. Whoever is linguistically competent in English will clearly understand what I have said and be able to gather from the sentence at least the denotation of the state of affairs I have expressed, if not absolutely all of the deeper subtleties, connotations, and psychological associations that the sentence might have for me in making the pronouncement. There is enough transparent communication of the idea I have expressed to make it possible for someone else to proceed with confidence, other things being equal, in knowing what I intend to say without confusion or misunderstanding.

---

20. Dewey is more sensitive than some emotive expressivists to the interrelation between the artist's expressive act and expressive object; see *Art as Experience*, 82–105. He writes, 82: "Expression, like construction, signifies both an action and its result. The last chapter considered it as an act. We are now concerned with the product, the object that is expressive, that says something to us." The problem in understanding art as emotional expression from the viewer or audience standpoint is that such meaning is often irrecoverable from a third-person perspective. A similar difficulty impedes intentionalist theories of expression in philosophical semantics and the philosophy of language.

As we move from the expression of categorical propositions or belief in simple states of affairs, things begin to get progressively more complicated and progressively more philosophically interesting. If I try to express an emotion or a state of mind more opaque to another person than a straight-forward statement of fact, then my use of language is equally expressive, but proportionately more difficult for another person to accurately interpret. The reason is that where first-person psychological occurrences are concerned, it can be challenging in the extreme to articulate the exact content of mental state even for one's own purposes, let alone in such a way that another person can take away from the linguistic expression a clear idea of what is being said. As we continue along the spectrum of expressive uses of language from beliefs in states of affairs to expressions of emotion and other psychological states toward more artistic uses of language in poetry, song lyrics and librettos and the like, we encounter linguistic expressions whose exact meaning can be increasingly difficult for persons other than the author to fully grasp.[21]

To focus for the moment on poetry, we can think of it as an activity or product of an activity involving the use of words and sentences that is equally both language and art. Poetry is undoubtedly expressive, but importantly for present purposes, the more artistic or art-like the use of language is in poetry, the more typically opaque its meanings and elusive its exact interpretation. If the standard of accuracy for understanding the content of poetry is supposed to be the recovery of the ideas an author intends and attempts to express in linguistic art or artistic language, then poetry is more like other kinds of art precisely in the obstacles it presents to the easy recovery of meaning when compared with descriptive scientific prose. It is a commonplace that the most intriguing poetry and the sort most often thought to succeed as art involves a kind of writing whose meaning does not immediately and univocally reveal itself, but that suggests multiple meanings and, unlike "Bern is the capital of Switzerland," may support a

---

21. The distinction between speaker meaning and hearer meaning is widely recognized in philo-sophical semantics and philosophy of language. Among the most discussed and nuanced treat-ments of the subject beyond those mentioned above are H. Paul Grice, "Meaning," *The Philosophical Review*, 66, 1957, 377–88; "Utterer's Meaning, Sentence-Meaning, and Word-Meaning," *Fundamentals of Language*, 4, 1968, 225–42. These and related essays are reprinted, some in updated form, in Grice, *Studies in the Way of Words* (Cambridge: Harvard University Press, 1989). Saul A. Kripke, "Speaker's Reference and Semantic Reference," *Midwest Studies in Philosophy*, 2, edited by Peter A. French, Theodore E. Uehling, Jr., and Howard K. Wettstein, (Malden, MA: Blackwell, 1977), 255–76.

different kind of interpretation every time we reflect on its content. Such poetry has depth and rewards frequent contemplation and rethinking, and captures in a word image a moment or scene that we appreciate more or less depending on the extent of our own personal experience to which we can relate in different ways at different times in our lives. Consider a few lines from Shakespeare's *Troilus and Cressida* that evoke a mood and convey a certain amount of information, but are not easily nailed down in terms of exact meaning, when Troilus speaks:

> And suddenly; where injury of chance
> Puts back leave-taking, justles roughly by
> All time of pause, rudely beguiles our lips
> Of all rejoindure, forcibly prevents
> Our lock'd embrasures, strangles our dear vows
> Even in the birth of our own labouring breath.
> We two, that with so many thousand sighs
> Did buy each other, must poorly sell ourselves
> With the rude brevity and discharge of one.
> Injurious time now with a robber's haste
> Crams his rich thievery up, he knows not how
> As many farewells as be stars in heaven,
> With distinct breath and consign'd kisses to them,
> He fumbles up into a loose adieu,
> And scants us with a single famish'd kiss,
> Distasted with the salt of broken tears.   (IV.4.32–47)

The Elizabethan theater was an artificial linguistic environment as well as a scene of plot and spectacle, action and humor. Its taste demanded an artful use of language, in which patrons delighted just as we do today in an author's poetic choice of language as a pleasing exercise in linguistically crafting comic and dramatic dialogue for its own sake as well as in support of the story with its moral and the play of emotions it occasions.

The language of the Elizabethan theater was very much a product of art catering to a desire for poetic fabrications interwoven with comic and dramatic effects. The audience in Shakespeare's time on the whole would have needed to puzzle over many passages of his beautiful and captivatingly dense verse, rhymed and blank, much as we still do today; that was and still remains a great part of its charm. Shakespeare undoubtedly expresses ideas, including emotions, his own and those of the characters whose situations he represents, in his writings and through the agency of the actors' voices and gestures when the plays are performed. The artistic purpose to which his language is put, in contrast with ordinary prose in the expression of belief in ordinary states of affairs, makes its artistic expression of ideas less accessible and easy to discern, more profound and resonant, and more variably recoverable, with greater potential for inaccuracy, and also for that reason more absorbing and stimulating of the imagination, than the use of language for the expression of simple states of affairs or belief in the existence of simple states of affairs. What Shakespeare says above, undoubtedly, cannot be taken literally but is rich in imagery, metaphor and simile.

What, exactly, did Piccasso mean to express by painting *Guernica*? What does Marcel Duchamp mean to express by exhibiting *Fountain*, a discarded porcelain urinal, as a readymade artwork? What does Vermeer mean to express by painting *De Keukenmeid*? Virtue? Domesticity? Loneliness? Social rank? Why not just the morning reverie of a pretty Dutch girl? In some cases, we may think we know what an artist intends, just as if the artist were to write out a series of simple declarative statements in ordinary language as a linguistic expression with easily literal discernible meaning. In other cases, we may find the meaning of an artwork endlessly ponderous, difficult or even impossible to decide. It is a familiar experience among persons who study an artwork whose meaning at first seems obvious that with time and greater maturity or different enhanced experiences they begin to discover new things that previously were concealed, and sometimes to reverse their judgment and appreciation of its meaning altogether, or at least to add to their sense of what an artist might be trying to express in what may have otherwise seemed to be an easily decipherable art object.[22]

---

22. To take just one example of a relatively recent, widely discussed and well-documented controversial artwork, consider Picasso's *Guernica*. Here are three reasonably authoritative interpretations of Picasso's large-scale 1937 canvas. Anthony Blunt, in *Picasso's Guernica* (New York: Oxford University Press, 1969), 56, summarizes the meaning of the painting in this way: "[Picasso's] aim in painting *Guernica* was the same as that of his predecessors: to give expression in visible form to his abhorrence of the evil which he saw in the world around him, and thereby, perhaps, to influence man, however slightly, toward better ways." Gertrude Stein, in contrast, who knew Picasso personally and had many opportunities to discuss his art with him, finds the main theme of the painting not to be as universal or its purpose one of the reform of mankind, but more momentary, nationalistic and nostalgic. In *Picasso* (Boston: Beacon Press, 1959), 47–8, Stein writes: "It was not the events themselves that were happening in Spain which awoke Picasso but the fact that they were happening in Spain, he had lost Spain and here was Spain not lost, she existed, the existence of Spain awakened Picasso, he too existed, everything that had been imposed upon him no longer existed, he and Spain, both of them existed, of course they existed, they exist, they are alive, Picasso commenced to work, he commenced to speak as he has spoken all his life, speaking with drawings and color, speaking with writing, the writing of Picasso." Picasso, himself, as quoted in Joaquin de la Puente's *Guernica: The Making of a Painting* (Monterreina: Silex, 1985), 122, had this to say: "This bull is a bull, this

The opacity of expression in nonlinguistic art from an audience point of view is so pronounced that philosophers have described the effort to interpret art in terms of an artist's intentions as a kind of fallacy. The "intentional fallacy," a term coined by Wimsatt and Beardsley in their much-discussed essay in the philosophy of art, indicates the authors' despair at being able to judge an artwork's meaning or value from the perspective of what the artist intends. To such an extent do Wimsatt and Beardsley regard artistic intentions as an explanatory dead-end in aesthetics and art criticism that they not only recommend abandoning the effort to understand art from the standpoint of the artist's intentions, but argue that it is always a mistake to try to bring an artist's intentions to bear on the interpretation of art.[23] This is a problem of perception, a problem for consumers of art who must try to interpret, assess and evaluate an artwork's meaning and merits. Insofar as artists in the complex interplay of roles in which they engage as both producer and critic of their own work are also perceivers of their productions, and insofar as artists may sometimes be unclear about their own intentions and exactly what it is they mean to express, insofar as the act of making art can be understood in turn as a method of clarifying what an artist wants to say, of physically thinking through a problem of expression in concrete terms as a process taking place over time, to that extent the problem of perceiving intention and discerning what is being expressed in art blurs the theoretical distinction between artist and audience, producer and consumer, active maker and passive perceiver of art.

There is a balanced commonsense point of view about interpreting art in relation to what an artist intends to express in a given artwork. We should not expect to have access to an artist's intentions in every case, and therefore we

horse is a horse. There is also a sort of bird, a chicken or pigeon, I can't remember which, on the table. This chicken is a chicken. Yes, of course, the *symbols...But the painter does not need to create those symbols.* Otherwise, it would be better to write once and for all what one wants to write instead of painting it. *The public, the spectators, must see in the horse or in the bull symbols* (then the painter had created them!) *which they should interpret as they wish...* That is, 'let the public see what it wants'."

23. There is a sense in which Wimsatt and Beardsley's attack on the intentional fallacy fits into a tendency toward extensionalism and against "psychologism" in philosophical semantics, epistemology, metaphysics and the philosophy of logic, mathematics, and language, and in support of behaviorism and other types of mind-body reductivisms in philosophical psychology. Efforts to do away with first-person introspection and phenomenological inquiry or descriptive psychology as methodologically and ideologically suspect in favor of public, externalist or third-person perceivable properties of psychological subjects are among the after-effects of the heyday of logical positivism, which, oddly, have not suffered the same popular disavowal as positivism itself in the philosophy of science.

should not suppose that we can only understand an artwork when we can be sure that an artist means thereby to express a certain imaginative set of ideas. In those instances where we happen to have insight into what an artist intends, such as a reliable verbal description in a letter or diary, or that can be inferred circumstantially, it seems only reasonable to take advantage of the information in building up a reasonable hypothesis of how an artwork might best be interpreted. Why should we deliberately overlook such facts if they contribute to understanding what an artist means to express in producing a certain artwork merely in order to avoid what is supposed to be the intentional fallacy? If we agree that art is an expression of ideas, how can we afford to ignore whatever facts might be relevant in trying to uncover an artist's intentions and the particular ideas an artist may have wanted to express? The information can offer at least some insight into the artist's imagination.

If we agree with Wimsatt and Beardsley that it is always a logical mistake to consult an artist's intentions in order to interpret and understand an artwork, then, given the continuity between linguistic and artistic expression mediated by poetry, it should follow that we must also adopt the same attitude toward understanding meaning in ordinary language, refusing on every occasion to consider an author's intentions as irrelevant to his or her meaning in linguistic expression. If that kind of limitation does not seem reasonable in the task of understanding expression in language, then it should be equally ill-advised to renounce information about an artist's intentions in interpreting and trying to understanding the meaning of art. The same is true beginning with linguistic art forms like poetry and literature, novels, plays and librettos, and including, in lieu of any reasonable cut-off principle, works that grade off imperceptibly into grey zones between clearly linguistic and clearly nonlinguistic expressions of imagination in painting, drawing, etching, printmaking, sculpture, music, and architecture.[24]

Perception, intentionality and expression in the aesthetics of art and nature

We have identified several ways in which perception is involved in the creative act of making and appreciating art. Without paying due attention to both the producer and consumer ends of artworks, we cannot hope to fully

24. For additional discussions of the intentional fallacy, see also Isabel Hungerland, "The Concept of Intention in Art Criticism," *The Journal of Philosophy* 52 (1955): 733–42. Henry Aiken, "The

understand the dynamics of art. When we consider what is involved in producing and enjoying art, we find the concepts of perception, intentionality,
and expression tightly intertwined.

Art, like other forms of expression, begins with perception. We are
inspired by the things we experience in sensation. We recognize beauty or
we are otherwise moved to express what we perceive or how we feel about
what we perceive. We can express such ideas in a variety of ways, in language, art, and in other ways, including such simple acts as smiling or frown-
ing, hugging or fleeing the presence of another person. These latter modes
of expressing our thoughts are neither linguistic nor artistic, but are continuous with speech acts and art-making as outlets for the need we have to
make our thoughts perceptible to ourselves and others in communication.
We use language and make art as we engage imaginatively in other activities
in order to express ourselves, to produce something tangible and hence
perceivable for the sake of leaving a more or less permanent record of our
ideas, of sharing them with others, or interacting with them at a number of
perceptual and cognitive levels and testing their reactions to what we think,
helping all the while to clarify for our own purposes what it is we believe
and how we feel.

We often assume that the first neolithic artists were moved by the appreciation of the aesthetics of the natural world to try to imitate such qualities
on a lesser scale in representational art. From such a perspective the idea that
the beauty of art comes first and then we learn to see the world as a kind of
artwork seems to have things upside-down. The impression, while compelling in its way, need not be correct. We can resist the overly simplistic picture
of natural beauty taking priority over artistic beauty if we recognize that an
artwork of something non-beautiful can itself be beautiful, brilliantly executed and demonstrating skillful control and attention to detail. The expressive object of imaginative art as a derivatively intentional expression of an
artist's ideas can be beautiful even when what it represents has no special
aesthetic qualities of its own. We do not know nor do we have any special
reason to think that early modern human artists thought that bison were

Aesthetic Relevance of Artists' Intentions," *The Journal of Philosophy* 52 (1955): 742–53. Richard
Kuhns, "Criticism and the Problem of Intention," *The Journal of Philosophy* 57 (1960): 5–23.
Frank Cioffi, "Intention and Interpretation in Criticism," *Proceedings of the Aristotelian Society*
64 (1963–1964): 85–106. J. Kemp, "The Work of Art and the Artist's Intentions," *The British
Journal of Aesthetics* 4 (1964): 150–1. Berel Lang, "The Intentional Fallacy Revisited," *The British
Journal of Aesthetics* 14 (1974): 306–14. Anthony Savile, "The Place of Intention in the Concept
of Art," *Proceedings of the Aristotelian Society* 69 (1968–1969): 101–24.

beautiful as opposed to totemic, powerful, or nourishing; even if they found their paintings and carvings of them on cave interiors or spear handles beautiful. It is perfectly possible from everything we currently know about early art-making that the first artists developed the concept of beauty and related aesthetic values from their own standards of pleasure in the imaginative work of their own hands and only afterward applied them by analogy to some but not all of the things around them in the world of nature. There may also be more purely utilitarian motivations. If you carve your distinctive totem in your distinctive style on the handle of a fishing spear, no one will be able to steal it and claim afterwards that it was theirs or that they did the carving. With art we can literally put our mark on things.

Does this conclusion also answer our first question, whether beauty is objective or subjective? The right solution might be to refine and re-qualify the question. For all that this approach has to say, all the elements that enter into judgments of beauty might exist objectively in nature. If the concept of beauty originates with a human appreciation for the qualities of human art carried over thereafter into the perception of the natural world, then beauty in one sense is undoubtedly subjective. If what we mean by an aesthetic quality is a property first and foremost of artworks, then there may be an objective answer to the question whether this or that object in art or nature is beautiful, depending on whether or not it conforms to the standards set by an appreciation for the beauty in art with which the concept originates. This is slender consolation, unfortunately, since these standards are not only lost in time, but most probably incorporated from the very beginning a wide range of differing opinions about what constitutes positive aesthetic value. The category of beauty and aesthetic appreciation might have begun historically from the standpoint of philosophical anthropology with human-made art, which was only later extended or projected onto nature. If our species originally came to appreciate a sunset because it is like a watercolor, we are by no means prevented from admiring a watercolor because it is so like a sunset.

FIVE

Naturalism, Imagination, and the Scientific Worldview

E. J. Lowe

Even the most austerely scientific conception of the physical world inevitably draws for its intelligibility upon features of human perceptual and imaginative sensibility which appear to defy explanation in terms of the scientific worldview itself, thereby creating a tension for any account of reality that aspires to be wholly naturalistic. So, at least, I contend. However, because a direct argument for this thesis from general first principles would be impossible in as short a space as I now have available, I shall try instead to demonstrate its plausibility through a critique of specific naturalistic proposals—in particular, two such proposals advanced independently by the philosopher David Chalmers and the evolutionary anthropologist Merlin Donald. Against both of these proposals I shall argue that they neglect certain crucial insights into the character of the human mind that we owe, ultimately, to Kant. These insights concern the intimate relationship between human perception and imagination and the indispensable role that they play in engendering the very possibility of conceptual thought and understanding that human beings characteristically and—as far as we know—uniquely possess.

I

The first object of my critique is a well-known division of the problems of consciousness into the "easy" ones and the "hard" one, proposed by David Chalmers. According to Chalmers, the easy problems are all susceptible to resolution in terms of computational or neural mechanisms, while the hard problem arises from the fact that the so-called "qualia" of sensory experience resist any sort of functional definition or reduction. This purported division, I maintain, rests upon a fundamental misconception of the nature of human cognition and experience—one which neglects a vitally important insight of Kant's. From a Kantian perspective, our capacity for conceptual thought is so inextricably bound up with the nature of our phenomenal consciousness that it must be an error to suppose that there are any easy problems of consciousness, resolvable in computational or neural terms. Chalmers is to be commended for challenging the complacent assumptions of many physicalists regarding the tractability of the problems of consciousness, but he concedes too much in allowing that most of these problems— the allegedly easy ones—will fall prey to their favored methods. His contention that there remains just one hard problem plays into the hands of physicalists by implying that their only difficulty lies in accommodating qualia. Faced with this objection, strong-minded physicalists are, unsurprisingly, happy simply to deny that qualia exist at all, dismissing belief in them as an illusory by-product of the way in which the brain represents information about itself to itself.

It will be helpful, at this point, to identify more precisely some of the problems of consciousness which Chalmers considers to be easy. These are the ones which, in his view, "seem directly susceptible to the standard methods of cognitive science, whereby a phenomenon is explained in terms of computational or neural mechanisms."[1] These problems allegedly include the ability to discriminate, categorize, and react to environmental stimuli; the integration of information by a cognitive system; the reportability of mental states; and the deliberate control of behavior. Chalmers remarks that "[all] of these phenomena are associated with the notion of consciousness" and confidently asserts that "[all] of them are straightforwardly vulnerable to explanation in terms of computational or neural mechanisms."[2] But it should be pointed out at once that the terms which Chalmers employs in describing these problems—terms such as "discrimination," "information," "report," and "control"—are highly ambiguous ones. We use them both in a "high-level" way to describe the conscious, intelligent activity of genuinely thoughtful creatures like ourselves, but also in a "low-level" way— which may in fact be no more than a metaphorical way—to describe the

1. David Chalmers, "Facing up to the Problem of Consciousness," *Journal of Consciousness Studies* 2 (1995): 200.
2. Ibid. 200–1.

"programmed" behavior of mindless machines and various primitive forms of life. For example, we may speak of a thermostat as "discriminating" between ambient temperatures and as "controlling" a switch, or of a computer as "storing information" and "reporting" on the contents of its "memory." But there is no reason whatever to believe that the activities thus described really have much in common with those activities of thoughtful human beings that we would customarily describe in these same terms. It is true enough that the activities of thermostats and computers which we describe in such terms can indeed be explained in the ways Chalmers suggests, but it is far from evident that those of human beings can. Indeed, I shall try to make it evident in what follows that the latter activities can certainly not be explained in these ways and that the reason for this lies in the very nature of human consciousness and its involvement in our capacities for imagination, thought, and concept-formation.

To begin with, I want to say something more about Chalmers' notions of experience and consciousness, which in my view are deeply problematic. As for the notion of experience, I consider that he seriously distorts it by focusing exclusively upon the sensuous, phenomenal, or qualitative character of experience—the "what it is like" aspect of experience, to use Thomas Nagel's well-known phrase.[3] This distortion serves to obscure the intimate relation between experience and thought. Some experiences—bodily pains provide a possible example—may indeed be almost purely sensational in character. But experiences of the kind most relevant to our cognitive capacities—namely, perceptual experiences—are certainly not. Perceptual experiences—such as, for example, the visual experience of seeing a green book lying on top of a round wooden table—possess not only qualitative or phenomenal characteristics but also, most importantly, intentional or representational content. It is indeed "like something" to enjoy such an experience, because in having it the phenomenal character of various sensed colors and shapes vividly impresses itself upon our visual awareness. However, such an experience evidently also represents—or, better, presents—our immediate physical environment as being some way: in this case, as containing in front of us a green book lying on top of a round wooden table. Moreover, and quite crucially, the intentional content of such an experience stands in an especially intimate relation to its qualitative or phenomenal character; the two aspects of the experience are not simply independent of one another.

---

3. Thomas Nagel, "What is it Like to be a Bat?" *The Philosophical Review* 83 (1974): 435–50.

It is conceivable, perhaps, that a creature might enjoy a visual experience which had all the phenomenal characteristics of the one just described, and yet which lacked any intentional or representational content. But it is impossible to envisage enjoying a perceptual experience which possessed intentional content despite completely lacking any phenomenal character.

The key lesson of these observations is that the intentional content of any perceptual experience is always, at least partly, grounded in its phenomenal character. The ultimate reason for this lies in the way in which we human beings gain knowledge from experience. One of the most important things that we learn through perception is what various kinds of physical objects look, sound and feel like—in short, how they appear to our senses—in a wide variety of circumstances. It is only because we learn this that we are subsequently able to imagine these objects in many possible circumstances in which we have never actually encountered them before. But how objects appear to us is, at least in part, a matter of how they affect the phenomenal or qualitative character of our perceptual experience. As a consequence, the very way in which we conceive of physical objects is inextricably bound up both with how they appear to us in experience and what we can imagine in regard to them. Thus, although conscious thought is importantly different from perceptual experience, the conceptual content of thought is intimately related to the nature, both phenomenal and intentional, of perceptual experience. Thoughts differ from perceptual experiences in possessing only an intentional and not sensuous nature. Yet even so, the intentional content of our thought depends inescapably, by way of its conceptual ingredients, upon our capacity to enjoy perceptual experiences with various sensuous or phenomenal characteristics. At the same time, our perceptual experiences possess an intentional and not merely a sensuous nature because we are able to bring concepts to bear upon the deliverances of our senses, thereby giving them a cognitive character without which the very distinction between veridical and non-veridical perception would be inapplicable.

The foregoing points can be summarized in terms of Kant's famous dictum that "Thoughts without content are empty, intuitions without concepts are blind."[4] The upshot is that it is erroneous to suppose that we can ascribe genuine thoughts, with conceptually articulated structure, to creatures or machines altogether lacking the capacity to enjoy conscious experiences with phenomenal or qualitative character. Whatever a computer can

4. Immanuel Kant, *Critique of Pure Reason*, trans. N. Kemp Smith (London: Macmillan, 1929), 93.

do by way of information-processing, storage and retrieval is not by any means to be confused with what a thinking human being does by reasoning, remembering, and recalling. Here I note a particularly serious inadequacy in the notion of information which philosophers like Chalmers deploy in attempting to characterize various aspects of human cognition. This notion of information, which we owe ultimately to Claude Shannon,[5] may be appropriate enough for describing the activities of computing machines, but it is wholly inappropriate for characterizing the cognitive states—beliefs, thoughts, and judgments—of human beings. The reason, once again, has to do with conceptual content. An informational state in this impoverished sense is not, essentially, a state possessing conceptually articulated content, but the beliefs, thoughts and judgments of human beings most certainly do possess such content essentially. A simple example will serve to bring out this distinction. Consider the pattern of rings exposed by a horizontal cut through a tree's trunk. Such a ring-pattern is, in the sense of "information" now at issue, an informational state of the tree—for example, it carries "information" about the tree's age, among other things. Clearly, though, it is not a state with conceptual content: it would be ludicrous to suggest that the ring-pattern somehow embodies the concepts of number and time. By contrast, one cannot properly ascribe to a person a belief that a certain tree is so-and-so many years old without simultaneously ascribing to that person the concepts of number and time. The reason, once again, lies in the Kantian principle that our conceptual capacities—even where they concern such abstract concepts as those of number and time—are intimately related to our rich capacities for perceptual experience. That a tree can merely carry Shannonian information about its age, whereas a human being can believe or think that it has a certain age, is intimately related to the fact that human beings can, whereas trees cannot, enjoy conscious perceptual experiences with phenomenal character. Shannon and Weaver themselves, it should be noted, expressly caution us that "The word information, in [their] theory, is used in a special sense" and that "In particular, information [in their sense] must not be confused with meaning."[6]

So far I have criticized the notions of experience and information deployed by philosophers like Chalmers, but there is a related criticism

5. C. E. Shannon and W. Weaver, *The Mathematical Theory of Communication* (Urbana and Chicago, IL: University of Illinois Press, 1949).
6. Shannon and Weaver, *The Mathematical Theory of Communication*, 8.

I have to make which goes to the heart of his attempted distinction between the easy problems of consciousness and the hard problem. This concerns his terminological proposal regarding the use of the words "consciousness" and "awareness." Chalmers suggests that we "reserve the term 'consciousness' for the phenomena of experience, using the less loaded term 'awareness' for the more straightforward phenomena described earlier."[7] But given that I dispute Chalmers' claim that the latter phenomena are indeed "more straightforward" in the sense of being amenable to computational or neural explanation, I cannot acquiesce in this terminological proposal. To do so would be to concede implicitly far too much to physicalism and at the same time would be to gainsay all I have just said concerning the intimate relationship between phenomenal consciousness and the intelligent thought of human beings. In Chalmers' proposed sense of awareness, it seems fair to say, there could be nothing in principle wrong in speaking of a computer, or even a thermostat, as being aware, but then to suggest that human beings are often only aware in this attenuated sense is completely to misrepresent the capacities involved in our being aware of ourselves and of our own thoughts and experiences. Such a misrepresentation is extremely damaging, not least because it encourages in the advocates of physicalism altogether false hopes about the extent to which their methods can succeed in explaining the nature of human awareness. It serves only to distract scientists from pursuing the real problem, with all its profound difficulties, by holding up an easy target which it misleadingly labels with the same name.

My preceding criticisms of Chalmers bear directly upon his attempt to explain why the supposedly easy problems are easy and the supposedly hard problem is hard. He asserts that "The easy problems are easy precisely because they concern the explanation of cognitive abilities and functions [and] to explain a cognitive function, we need only specify a mechanism that can perform the function."[8] He gives the following example: "To explain reportability...is just to explain how a system could perform the function of producing reports on internal states."[9] But of course, I must immediately protest that if by "producing a report on an internal state" Chalmers just means generating a second-order informational state—in the Shannonian sense of information—then although this is something which

7. Chalmers, "Facing up to the Problem of Consciousness," 201–2.
8. Chalmers, "Facing up to the Problem of Consciousness," 202.
9. Ibid.

can indeed be perfectly well explained in a mechanistic way, it is not the sort of thing that needs to be explained when we are talking about the ability of human subjects to express in words their knowledge of the contents of their own thoughts and experiences. For such an ability demands the possession of genuine concepts—not only concepts of the things those thoughts and experiences are about but also the very concepts of thought and experience themselves. The truth is that we have not the slightest reason to believe that a mechanistic explanation is available, even in principle, for the capacity of creatures like ourselves to deploy the concepts of thought and experience and to ascribe the possession of such concepts to ourselves. Only by trading upon a thoroughly jejune sense of reportability can Chalmers make out even the semblance of a case for saying that such a capacity, as exercised by human beings, is easy to explain as being a function performed by a computational or neural mechanism.

The key point here is that a function, in Chalmers' sense, is specified in terms of certain behavior which a system subserving that function produces. As Chalmers himself puts it: "Here 'function' is...used...in the...sense of any causal role in the production of behavior that a system might perform."[10] But then everything turns on how we characterize the behavior in question. In the example just discussed, the behavior in question was described by Chalmers as that of "producing reports on internal states." But only if such behavior is interpreted in a narrowly physicalistic way—for example, in terms of the generation of a second-order Shannonian informational state—is a mechanistic explanation of the corresponding function going to be straightforwardly available. If, by contrast, we understand "producing reports on internal states" to embrace such genuinely intelligent, thoughtful activities as a human being's use of language to express his or her knowledge of the contents of his or her own thoughts and experiences, then there is not the slightest reason to suppose that a mechanistic explanation of this capacity is possible. Mechanistically characterized behavior is, quite unsurprisingly, amenable to mechanistic explanation. Indeed, this is what underlies Chalmers' own acknowledgement that "In a way, the point is trivial"—the point being that you can always explain the performance of a function by "specifying a mechanism that performs the function."[11] Chalmers' mistake is that he begs the real question at issue in supposing that the sort of performance we have to do with in cases of thoughtful human

10. Ibid.   11. Ibid.

activity is something that can be characterized in a mechanistic way and which, consequently, a mechanism can uncontroversially be supposed capable of engaging in. We trivialize and misrepresent such thoughtful human activity if we describe it purely in physicalistically acceptable terms, as the generation of various information-bearing states and the like.

Because Chalmers misconstrues what he sees as being the easy problems of consciousness, he also misrepresents what he calls the hard problem. According to Chalmers, the hard problem is this: "Why doesn't all this information-processing go on 'in the dark,' free of any inner feel?"[12] Believing as he does that human thought and cognition in general are just a matter of "information-processing," of a sort which could, in principle, go on in a mindless computer, he is left with the idea that all that is really distinctive about consciousness is its qualitative or phenomenal aspects—the "what it is like" or "inner feel." Then it begins to look like a strange mystery or quirk of evolution that creatures like us should possess this sort of consciousness in addition to all our capacities for thought and understanding— these capacities being, for Chalmers, simply capacities for certain sorts of information-processing and storage. My response is that consciousness has only been put in this invidious position by Chalmers—and, to be fair, by many others—because he has mistakenly denied it any role in his account of the nature of human thought and understanding. In short, it is the reductive and wholly inadequate information-processing conception of human cognition which is responsible for the misperception that "consciousness" (in the form of qualia and the like) occupies what threatens to be a merely epiphenomenal role as a peculiar additional feature of human mentality which is in no way essential to our basic intellectual capacities. Once we appreciate the Kantian point that genuine thought, with real conceptual structure, is only available to creatures having a capacity for perceptual experiences with a properly integrated intentional and phenomenal nature, we can see that the sort of phenomenal consciousness which we humans enjoy but which computers and trees do not, far from being an epiphenomenon of information processing in our brains, is an absolutely indispensable element in our cognitive make-up, without which we could not properly be described as thinking beings at all. Ultimately, Chalmers' error lies in a failure to recognize that human cognition is not a matter of abstract computation but is, on the contrary, thoroughly integrated with our sensitive nature as embodied

12. Chalmers, "Facing up to the Problem of Consciousness," 203.

creatures acted upon by and ourselves acting on our physical and social environment. There is irony, then, in Chalmers' belated concession that "Perhaps [experience] will turn out to play an important cognitive role."[13] If Kant is right, no one who is in any doubt about this has even begun to grasp the true nature of human experience and cognition.

If what I have said so far is correct and our capacity for genuine thought and understanding is quite inseparable from our capacity for phenomenal consciousness, then—to the extent that Chalmers himself is correct in contending that physicalism offers no prospect for an explanation of phenomenal consciousness—the conclusion ought to be that physicalism, far from being equipped to solve the so-called easy problems of consciousness, has in fact nothing very useful to say about any aspect of consciousness. This indeed is my own conclusion. But Chalmers, by contrast, occupies an unstable middle ground, precisely because he has already conceded so much to physicalism. Effectively, he subscribes to a position which we might call "functionalism plus qualia," or "FPQ." According to FPQ, everything about human mentality except for the fact of qualia can be explained in reductive—that is, in computational or neural—terms. But how, then, can qualia be anything but epiphenomenal—and in that case, why should they exist at all? FPQ is unstable because there is intense pressure on it either to give qualia some more substantive causal role—and this would be to challenge the physicalist's account of the rest of human mentality—or to eliminate qualia altogether, as Daniel Dennett[14] and others have tried to do. The awkwardness of Chalmers' position is, I think, clearly brought out by his allegiance to what he calls the "principle of organizational invariance."[15] According to this principle, "any two systems with the same fine-grained functional organization will have qualitatively identical experiences."[16] As he himself points out, this means that the "philosophical hypotheses of 'absent qualia' and 'inverted qualia,' while logically possible, are empirically and nomologically impossible."[17] But this is, in effect, finally to concede the whole game to functionalism. For once one has adopted what I am now calling FPQ, the only reason for holding on to a special, physicalistically irreducible notion of phenomenal consciousness

13. Ibid.
14. Daniel Dennett, "Quining Qualia" in *Consciousness and Contemporary Science,* ed. A. J. Marcel and E. Bisiach (Oxford: Oxford University Press, 1988).
15. Chalmers, "Facing up to the Problem of Consciousness," 214.
16. Ibid.   17. Chalmers, "Facing up to the Problem of Consciousness," 215.

is that possibilities like those of absent and inverted qualia apparently escape any attempt at functionalist reduction or explanation. But now that these possibilities are denied to be anything more than merely logical possibilities, there is nothing substantive left that functionalism is allegedly incapable of explaining about human mentality. One can perfectly well see why Chalmers is attracted to his "principle of organizational invariance," given how much ground he has already conceded to functionalism and given the correspondingly nugatory role he accords to phenomenal consciousness in an account of the nature of human cognition. What he doesn't seem to appreciate is that, having conceded this much, to adopt this principle as well is effectively to cede victory completely to functionalism.

At the end of his account, Chalmers becomes more speculative, suggesting that the most fundamental notion of all, both as regards the physical world and as regards conscious experience, is that of information—again, quite explicitly in Shannon and Weaver's technical sense of this ambiguous term. He even offers a "double-aspect" hypothesis, whereby one and the same "information space" is both physically and phenomenally embodied. Noting that physics only characterizes its basic entities extrinsically, he even goes so far as to speculate, in what seems to be a quasi-idealistic vein, that "the intrinsic properties of the physical . . . are themselves phenomenal properties."[18] Such a proposal to some extent offsets the earlier concessions that Chalmers has made to physicalism. But this sort of challenge to physicalism comes too late, operating as it does only at the level of speculative metaphysics. By this account, physicalism is still left unchallenged as a scientific doctrine. My own view, as I hope I have made plain, is that the challenge to a physicalist account of the human mind has to be mounted much earlier than this and that in mounting such a challenge one of the first things to appreciate is that the Shannonian notion of information is too impoverished to be of use in characterizing the conceptually articulated structure of human thought and its intimate relation to our capacity for phenomenal consciousness. We human beings are creatures capable of both thought and perceptual experience, but these capacities are inextricably interrelated. Thought is more than just information-processing, and perceptual experience is more than just the having of qualia: both are states which are essentially infused with concepts and each depends for its very possibility upon the other.

18. Chalmers, "Facing up to the Problem of Consciousness," 217.

II

My second case study in the deficiencies of a purely naturalistic approach to the human mind focuses on a proposal advanced by Merlin Donald in his *Origins of the Modern Mind*, a book in which he argues that human culture and cognition have passed through three distinct evolutionary stages to produce the modern human mind.[19] According to Donald, the first transition, from the level of culture of apes and australopithecines to that of Homo erectus, involved "the emergence of the most basic level of human representation, the ability to mime, or re-enact, events."[20] The second transition, from the culture of Homo erectus to that of Homo sapiens, in which the biological evolution of modern humans was completed, involved "the emergence of the human speech system, including a completely new cognitive capacity for constructing and decoding narrative."[21] The third and final transition, he believes, was much more recent and non-biological in nature, involving "the emergence of visual symbolism and external memory as major factors in cognitive architecture."[22] Inevitably, these claims are somewhat speculative, in view of the absence of any physical remains which could point conclusively to the separate occurrence of the first two transitions, each involving changes in forms of behavior alone—the emergence of "mimetic" activity and the emergence of speech activity, respectively. (There is, of course, physical evidence of changes in the structure of the human vocal tract, preserved in the fossil record[23], but the mere capacity to vocalize in a modern human way by no means points conclusively to a modern human capacity for spoken language.) In the nature of the case, only the third transition can have left physical remains as clear evidence of its occurrence, in the form of human artifacts with an obvious symbolic or representational function.

Accepting that this third transition occurred—and leaving aside the altogether more contentious claim that it was indeed the last of three equally momentous but distinct transitions, as characterized by Donald—we may

---

19. Merlin Donald, *Origins of the Modern Mind: Three Stages in the Evolution of Culture and Cognition* (Cambridge, MA: Harvard University Press, 1991).
20. Donald, *Origins of the Modern Mind*, 16.
21. Donald, *Origins of the Modern Mind*, 16.
22. Donald, *Origins of the Modern Mind*, 17.
23. See P. Lieberman, *The Biology and Evolution of Language* (Cambridge, MA: Harvard University Press, 1984) and *Uniquely Human: The Evolution of Speech, Thought, and Selfless Behavior* (Cambridge, MA: Harvard University Press, 1991).

ask the following question: What exactly is the significance for modern human cognition of the emergence of systems of "external symbolic storage" (ESS), in the form of visual symbolism, pictorial and written? One view—which I think is broadly Donald's own—is that the chief cognitive significance of this evolutionary development, which seems to have begun some thirty to forty thousand years ago, is that it freed human memory (both working memory and long-term memory) from the severe limitations imposed by the biology of the brain, as an information-processing system. Information could now be stored outside the individual brain, processed there—for instance, by using written mathematical symbolism for numerical calculation—and transmitted and accumulated in robust and reliable forms. Collective human knowledge, embodied in the world's libraries and more recently in computer databases, now far transcends the memory capacity of any single human brain. Without written symbolism, it may be urged, most of modern scientific knowledge would simply be impossible: such symbolism, it may be said, is essential for the very construction of scientific knowledge, as well as for its storage and transmission.

I am not entirely convinced by such claims, even though they do clearly contain a measure of truth. I believe that the emergence of ESS was a highly significant development for human cognition—but more on account of what it was symptomatic of than purely on account of any efficiency and capacity gains it incurred for human information-processing and data-accumulation.[24] It is possible to exaggerate the degree to which ESS is essential for the emergence of anything like modern scientific knowledge. Even as recently as the Renaissance, it was probably possible for a single human individual to assimilate a sizeable fraction of the collective knowledge embodied in the books then in existence—not in the sense of being able to recite all of these books by heart, but in the sense of understanding and retaining much of their significant content. The sheer preservation of such written knowledge could, moreover, in principle be achieved by a sufficiently well-organized oral tradition of the kind which, it seems, may initially have preserved such large-scale poetic works as Homer's Iliad and Odyssey. A nice illustration of this possibility is provided by Ray Bradbury's futuristic novel *Fahrenheit 451*, which envisages a state in which books have been banned, but in which dedicated members of a dissident group take it

24. Cf. D. R. Olson, *The World on Paper: The Conceptual and Cognitive Implications of Writing and Reading* (Cambridge: Cambridge University Press, 1994).

upon themselves to memorize the last copies of whatever books they can lay their hands on before these are committed to the flames. Undoubtedly, ESS makes life much easier and the transmission and accumulation of collective knowledge much more secure, but it is not clear that it is absolutely indispensable in order for such transmission and accumulation to occur in anything like the way in which it has within historical time.

An alternative view of the cognitive significance of ESS, and one which I shall expand upon and defend, sees it as lying in the fact that the ability to use one physical object explicitly as a symbol for, or representation of, another physical object is indicative of—because it demands—a capacity for conceptually structured thought. Here it may be objected that an ability to use spoken language is itself precisely such an ability to use symbols or representations, so that this account of the cognitive significance of ESS fails to distinguish the significance of ESS from the significance of human systems of symbolism or representation in general. To this objection there are several possible replies. On the one hand it may be urged by psycholinguists, such as Jerry Fodor and Noam Chomsky, that human linguistic capacity is innate, "hard-wired" and modular, involving only a tacit knowledge of phonetic, syntactic and semantic principles,[25] and accordingly that it does not demand, at root, an explicit recognition of certain physical objects (spoken words and sentences) as having a symbolic role. In this view, the human capacity for spoken language no more indicates a capacity explicitly to recognize one physical object as symbolizing or representing another than does the so-called "language" of the bees. On the other hand, if it is held, as Donald Davidson holds, that a capacity for conceptual thought itself demands a capacity for language, and moreover that a language-user must be able to recognize both others and him or herself as being a language-user, then it will follow that it is correct, after all, to see a capacity for ESS and a capacity for language as being all of a piece as regards the cognitive demands which they impose upon those possessing them.[26] Moreover, in this view of language, it would be proper to see spoken language itself as being, effectively, a resource for ESS no different in principle from the resources provided by visual symbolism. Sounds are, indeed, short-lived in comparison with pictures and inscriptions, but they do provide a means both for reducing the

25. Jerry Fodor, *The Modularity of Mind* (Cambridge, MA: MIT Press, 1983).
26. Donald Davidson, "Thought and Talk," in *Inquiries into Truth and Interpretation* (Oxford: Oxford University Press, 1984).

burden on the working memory and for storing collective knowledge. On the first point, it is a familiar fact that "thinking out loud" (that is, in spoken words) facilitates processes of comprehension and reasoning. On the second point, as already alluded to above, mnemonic techniques such as those embodied in rhyme and meter enable complicated bodies of information to be preserved accurately through oral tradition. It is true, of course, that memorizing a poem or recipe does utilize biological memory—but it greatly eases the burden on biological memory by reducing the require-ment on semantic memory. In short, rote learning enables one to preserve detailed information much more accurately than does learning which requires a grasp of semantic content—think, for example, of how we learned our multiplication tables at school.

The next thing that I need to explain is why it is that the ability to use one physical object explicitly as a symbol for, or representation of, another physical object demands a capacity for conceptually structured thought. The reason is that only a creature which perceives objects as falling under concepts can be in a position to recognize objects as standing in symbolic or representational relationships to one another. In order to see a visual mark—such as a pattern of lines scratched on a stone—as a symbol for or representation of, say, a tiger, I must first of all possess the concept of a tiger. That is, I must be able to think of certain objects, even in their absence, as being things of a certain kind—in this case, things of a ferocious, flesh-eating, four-legged, furry kind. In addi-tion, and even more importantly, I must recognize the visual mark itself as falling under the concept of a symbol (even if I have no word for that con-cept) and thereby likewise as being something of a certain kind—namely, something intentionally produced by a thinking being with a view to repre-senting an object of another kind (in this case, a tiger). The very concept of a symbol is the concept of something designed to represent something of some kind, and thus something falling under a concept—so that any creature possessing the concept of a symbol must thereby possess the concept of a concept too, and indeed must conceive of itself and others with whom it communicates by means of symbols as being concept-users. In short, a sym-bol-producing creature must have something like a "theory of mind," by which it interprets the behavior of other such creatures as being expres-sive of inner thoughts and feelings.[27] Here it is worth noting that even

27. See further A. Whiten, ed. *Natural Theories of Mind: Evolution, Development, and Simulation of Everyday Mindreading* (Oxford: Blackwell, 1991).

primatologists who are much more ready than I am to attribute conceptual abilities to monkeys and apes are hesitant about crediting them with anything like a fully-fledged "theory of mind."[28]

At this point we need to appreciate how very different is the perceptual world of a concept-user from that of an animal incapable of conceptual thought. We are apt to underrate or overlook this difference, partly because it is very difficult for the mature concept-user to imagine what naïve, conceptually uninformed perception must be like—and therefore difficult to imagine how different animal perception must be from our own. As we survey our perceived environment, we unavoidably see it as populated by objects falling under concepts, that is, by objects of certain recognizable kinds.[29] Here a wall, there a tree, beyond that a cow standing by a gate, and so on. Sometimes, of course, we notice objects which we cannot easily classify in familiar terms, apart from very general and vague ones. I might ask someone in a house strange to me, "What is that large, shiny cylindrical object in the corner of the room?" and perhaps be informed that it is an old artillery shell-case which is now being used as an umbrella stand. Undoubtedly, language facilitates such conceptually informed perceptual recognition, though it seems highly unlikely that such recognition is impossible without the aid of language. On the contrary, it seems likely that true language— understood as a means for communicating conceptual thought from one thinking creature to another—could only have emerged amongst creatures antecedently capable of conceptually informed perceptual recognition.

What, then, of conceptually uninformed—what I have called "animal"— perception? What does an animal see, if it doesn't see its environment as populated by objects of recognizable kinds? On what grounds can we deny that animal perception is conceptually informed in the way that human perception is? Here we need to appreciate that to recognize an object as falling under a concept—that is, as being something of a certain kind— involves a grasp of certain general and conditional truths, including a criterion of identity for objects of this kind. Such a grasp involves far more than a mere ability to discriminate perceptually between presented objects of that kind and presented objects of other kinds, an ability which many lower

28. See D. L Cheney and R. M. Seyfarth, *How Monkeys See the World: Inside the Mind of Another Species* (Chicago: University of Chicago Press, 1990).
29. See E. J. Lowe, *Kinds of Being: A Study of Individuation, Identity, and the Logic of Sortal Terms* (Oxford: Blackwell, 1989) and *More Kinds of Being: A Further Study of Individuation, Identity, and the Logic of Sortal Terms* (Oxford: Wiley-Blackwell, 2009).

forms of animal life possess (and one which ethologists sometimes extravagantly take to be indicative of concept-possession). Thus, to know that a certain object is a tree, say, is to know, among other things, that it is a living thing, a plant, that it has leaves and roots, that it is not capable of self-motion, that if it is cut down it will die . . . the list is long and open-ended. Because these general and conditional truths involve the concepts of many other kinds of thing, a creature can only recognize an object as falling under a concept if it possesses a whole system of interlocking concepts, linked by general and conditional truths which that creature grasps. (By a "conditional" truth, I mean one that requires the use of the word "if" for its natural expression in English, such as "If a tree is cut down, it will die.") There is no clear reason to suppose that any non-human animal possesses a sophisticated system of concepts like this. Apart from anything else, there is no clear reason to suppose that any non-human animal genuinely possesses general or conditional knowledge or beliefs.[30]

So, in answer to the question, "What does an animal see?" we must be careful not to say that it sees the objects which we see as we see them, that is, as falling under concepts. Of course, an animal may be visually sensitive to the presence of a certain object and may on that account react appropriately (that is, "adaptively") to it—for instance, by walking around it, sniffing it, chasing it, or running away from it. This requires, among other things, that an animal be visually sensitive to (though not that it be conceptually cognizant of) the spatial properties of an object, such as its distance, size, shape and texture, and likewise to its dynamic properties, such as its velocity and momentum. Thus the animal's visual experience must, in some sense, correctly represent to it the general spatial layout of its environment as it changes over time, segmenting that environment into distinct parts with respect to which different behaviors are mandated—and these different behaviors, we may suppose, are some of them innate, while others are learned inductively, being reinforced by nature's regime of punishment and reward. But none of this requires us to think of the animal as recognizing objects in its environment, in the distinctively human sense of seeing its environment as composed of things falling under various concepts, linked by a system of general and conditional beliefs.

30. For another skeptical assessment of the suggestion that non-human animals possess concepts, in anything like the human sense, see N. Chater and C. Heyes, "Animal Concepts: Content and Discontent" in *Mind and Language* 9 (1994): 209–46.

Symbols are, of course, a species of artifact. But the production of artifacts as such is not a distinctively human activity, nor one which demands high-level, conceptually informed cognition. Animal artifacts are commonplace: the beaver's dam, the honey bee's comb, and the spider's web are just three of the more familiar examples. As Richard Dawkins has urged, we should think of animal life forms as exhibiting "extended phenotypes," which include not just bodily morphology but also effects on the wider environment which an animal partially shapes to its own ends.[31] When it is alleged, as it sometimes carelessly is, that apart from human beings only some of the other higher primates are "tool makers," it should be acknowledged that this assertion requires qualification in the light of the widespread existence of animal arti-facts even amongst much lower life forms. Probably what is intended by this sort of allegation is that only human beings and, perhaps, chimpanzees inten-tionally produce artifacts, designing them deliberately with a specific pur-pose in view. That human beings do this is evidently true, though whether chimpanzees ever do is more difficult to assess. But then we see that what is cognitively significant about human artifact production is, once again, that it is indicative of—because it demands—a capacity for conceptually structured thought. In order for a creature to design and produce an artifact intention-ally, with a specific purpose in view, it must be able to think of objects as falling under concepts. For instance, deliberately to create something with the function of an axe, designed to cut certain kinds of things such as trees, one must conceptualize the objects to be acted upon as objects of a kind suited to the sort of action for which an axe is designed, and this will require the designer to have a complex body of general and conditional beliefs about the objects to be acted upon, as well as about the materials from which something with the properties of an axe can be produced. Likewise with symbols, which are just artifacts with a special kind of purpose. What is espe-cially significant, cognitively speaking, about a creature capable of designing symbols, is not just that it must be a concept-user—any creature capable of designing an artifact must be that—but that it must possess the very concept of a concept, because it must recognize both itself and others in its commu-nity as concept-users, inasmuch as the concept of a concept-user is involved in a specification of the very purpose for which a symbol is designed.

What is beginning to emerge, I hope, from these reflections is that the most significant cognitive transition involved in the evolution of the human

31. Richard Dawkins, *The Extended Phenotype* (Oxford: Oxford University Press, 1982).

mind was the transition to conceptual thinking. This transition could not, in my view, have been a multi-staged process: a creature is either capable of thinking in concepts or it is not—there is no halfway house. (This is also plausibly true of the transition to syntactically organized language—which may, of course, be in effect the same transition.[32]) Different creatures may have different conceptual repertoires—some, for instance, may have and some may lack the concept of a concept, or that of a concept-user. But between true conceptual thinking and an animal's mere sensitivity to features of its environment, coupled with innate and acquired behavioral responses to those features, there is a cognitive gulf of enormous magnitude—a qualitative rather than a merely quantitative difference. Here I once more take my lead from Kant, whose profound insights into the structure of the human mind have still not been adequately absorbed either by philosophers or by psychologists and ethologists. The distinctive feature of human cognition lies in its synthesis of the elements of sensory awareness through the application of concepts, thereby at once providing the human mind with objects of thought and thought itself with logical structure, apt for the deployment of processes of theoretical and practical reasoning. When a human being thinks, he or she has thoughts of objects with properties, or standing in relation to one another, these thoughts often being of a general or conditional form—to use again a now familiar example, one may have the thought, at once general and conditional in form, that "any tree, if it is cut down, will die." If one then adds to this general thought the singular thought that this object now before me is a tree, one may infer, logically, that this object will die if it is cut down. However, there is no clear evidence, I believe, that any creature other than a human being is capable of conceptualized, logical thinking of this order.

On this question of animal inference, chimpanzees are indeed sometimes held to be capable of elementary practical reasoning, appeal being made to examples like that of Wolfgang Köhler's famous chimpanzees, who joined sticks together and used them to rake bananas towards themselves through the bars of their cage, or stacked boxes on top of one another and climbed up them to obtain bananas which were previously out of their reach.[33] However, it is by no means evident that one need ascribe a capacity for general or conditional thoughts to a chimpanzee—nor, hence, a capacity

32. See D. Bickerton, *Language and Species* (Chicago: University of Chicago Press, 1990).
33. Wolfgang Köhler, *The Mentality of Apes* 2nd ed. (New York: Viking, 1959).

for genuine reasoning—in order to explain such behavior. We are, regrettably but understandably, apt to anthropomorphize when attempting to explain the apparently intelligent behavior of animals—saying, for instance, that our pet dog approaches its feeding bowl because it sees food there, feels hungry, and knows that by approaching the bowl it can obtain the food and thereby satisfy its hunger. This rationalistic interpretation of such animal behavior does not, however, easily survive the results of careful empirical inquiry. In one ingenious experiment, for example, a feeding bowl was attached to a mechanism designed to move the bowl away from an animal if the animal approached and towards it if the animal retreated. The animals that were tested consistently failed to make the appropriate adjustment to their behavior in order to secure the food, putting in doubt the initial appearance of their having a capacity for practical reasoning.[34] This finding is reminiscent of one of Köhler's less well-known observations: that when one of his chimpanzees was presented with a banana outside its cage, but so situated that the chimpanzee would have to push the banana away from itself before raking it in, the animal proved to be unequal to the task.[35]

I should explain that when I speak of objects falling under concepts or belonging to kinds, I am speaking of things which we think of as being identifiable and, indeed, re-identifiable as "the same thing again"—things such as tables, trees, mountains, and people.[36] A creature lacking the concept of numerical identity could not think of or perceive its world as being populated by objects in this sense—nor, of course, could it think of itself as a subject of experience within that world.[37] (It is important to distinguish here between numerical identity and mere qualitative identity, or exact similarity: even pigeons can be trained to discriminate perceptually between qualitatively different shapes, such as triangles and rectangles—although, as mentioned above, this by no means implies that they possess the concepts of triangularity and rectangularity.)[38] To see something as a tree, say, is to see it as a thing with a past and a potential future, that is, as something which can persist identically through time despite undergoing qualitative changes of various sorts, appropriate to the kind of thing that it is. Thus we do not see

34. See C. Heyes and A. Dickinson, "The Intentionality of Animal Action" in *Mind and Language* 5 (1990): 87–104, and "Folk Psychology Won't Go Away: Response to Allen and Bekoff" in *Mind and Language* 10 (1995): 329–32.
35. Cheney and Seyfarth, *How Monkeys See the World*, 276.
36. See Lowe, *Kinds of Being* and *More Kinds of Being*.
37. See E. J. Lowe, *Subjects of Experience* (Cambridge: Cambridge University Press, 1996).
38. See Chater and Heyes, "Animal Concepts."

the loss of its leaves as being inimical to the identity, or continuing existence, of a tree because we conceive of trees as being things of a kind for which such a change is natural. From the fact that human beings perceive their world as being populated by objects, capable of persistence through changes of shape and position, it follows too that they see that world as existing within a unified framework of space and time (another Kantian insight). Thus humans perceive their immediate environment as forming just a small part of a wider framework of interrelated objects, spread out in space and time beyond the "horizon" of present perception—a feature of human understanding vastly more sophisticated than the sort of locational recognition capacities attributed (in the form of "cognitive maps") to pigeons and rats in order to explain their ability to find their way home or to relocate a food source.[39] Hence humans can form expectations with regard to the future and reflect on past happenings: they can make provision today for tomorrow's needs, and try to make amends today for yesterday's failures. None of this is really possible in full measure for animals, for whom perception is merely a registering of repeatable features (including, no doubt, geographical ones), followed by habituated action. When there is rain, the animal may take shelter. When there is danger, it may flee. But it can have no conception of there being some one persisting object which it now sees and may encounter again, perhaps in a changed condition, after an indefinitely long period of absence.

All of these remarks are intended to emphasize how truly vast is the gap between animal and human cognition. Donald, to his credit, at least to some extent recognizes the size of that gap and therefore attempts to show how it can have been bridged, not in one fell swoop—for this would be difficult to reconcile with an evolutionary perspective on human cognition—but rather through three successive transitions. However, as I have already remarked, I think that what is truly distinctive of human cognition—our capacity for conceptual thinking—is an all-or-nothing affair: either a creature has it in full measure, allowing for differences in conceptual repertoire, or else it lacks it altogether. The conceptual capacity which is required for a mastery of true language—understood as a means of communicating conceptual thoughts—is one and the same as that required for the intentional production of visual symbolism, whether in the form of pictorial representations or in the form of writing. To the extent that

39. See John Campbell. *Past, Space, and Self* (Cambridge, MA: MIT Press, 1994).

"mimesis" is understood as the intentional re-enactment of events for purposes of communication (as opposed merely to imitative behavior, of a sort exhibited by many lower animals), then it, too, demands precisely the same conceptual capacity for object recognition and so forth. It is unsurprising, then, that no human or animal community has ever been discovered clearly to possess one of these behavioral traits—mimesis, language and the production of visual symbolism—without the others.

One thing which, I strongly suspect, blinds modern cognitive scientists to Kant's insights about the structure of the human mind—and which may in consequence deceive them into imagining that the problem of explaining the evolution of the human mind is easier than it really is—is the current fashion for information-processing or computational models of human cognition. As I suggested in the first part of this essay, so long as the human mind–brain is thought of as merely an information-processing device, analogous to a digital electronic computer, Kant's insights about the conceptual structure of human thought threaten to go unheeded. A computer can process vast amounts of information, but it clearly doesn't need to possess concepts in order to do this. The computer's designer and programmer must possess them, of course, if their work is to be the product of deliberate thought and planning, and the computer's output is only of use to someone who can interpret its computations by means of conceptually informed thought. If one regards the human brain merely as a highly complex biological computer, however, one will be apt to see differences between it and animal brains as residing merely in such factors as speed of information-processing and storage capacity. The qualitative difference between animal cognition and the sort of conceptual thinking engaged in by humans will be entirely lost to view. For, once again, the technical, Shannonian notion of "information," as deployed in computer science, is entirely insensitive to issues concerning concept possession and conceptual structure. What is stored on the hard disk of a computer, in the form of patterns of magnetized particles, is indeed information in this technical sense. Human belief, however, is a conceptually structured state of mind, not merely a state of information storage.

These remarks have implications for the very idea of external symbolic storage, or ESS, for that idea is evidently closely related to the computational notion of information storage. Precisely because a page of a book, like the hard drive of a computer, stores information in a sense which is radically different from the sense in which human beings possess knowledge or beliefs, we should be careful not to take too literally the notion of ESS as being some sort of adjunct to, or extension of, the human mind. In short, we should be extremely wary of Donald's inflated talk of "the emergence of visual symbolism and external memory as major factors in cognitive architecture."[40] The notions of "external memory" and "cognitive architecture" that are being invoked here are clearly ones drawn from computer science and the related computational conception of the mind. If the human mind or brain could be adequately described merely as an information-processing device, then indeed it would make perfect sense to think of that device as being capable of having its computational capacities "upgraded" by "connecting it up" to external devices of various sorts, such as an abacus or, more ambitiously, an electronic computer. But I want to resist—once more for basically Kantian reasons—the very metaphor of the human mind or brain as being a computational or information-processing device. A book, an abacus, an electronic computer—all of these human inventions are certainly aids to cognition. But that is all they are—aids—not extensions. The difference is the difference between a walking stick and an automobile: the stick aids us in walking, whereas the automobile extends our ability to move by providing us with a new means of locomotion. The book, abacus, or computer may help us to think more efficiently, but using it doesn't constitute a mode of thinking unavailable to us without it, in the way that using an automobile constitutes a hitherto unavailable mode of locomotion. The reason for this is that genuinely conceptual thinking is required to interpret the very "input" and "output" of a book, abacus, or computer. Nothing that resides in the structures of these devices themselves bears any relation to genuine thought, save through the interpretative efforts of a thinking human user of them.[41]

The final question that may now be posed is this: if the gulf between human conceptual thinking and animal cognition is as great as I have been suggesting, how can the bridging of that gap in human prehistory be explained in evolutionary terms? My response is that I simply do not know. It may even be that we are constitutionally incapable of answering a question like this: it might be a case of what has sometimes been called "cognitive closure."[42] Human thought is conceptually structured. We think of the

40. Donald, *Origins of the Mind*, 17.
41. Cf. John Searle, *The Rediscovery of the Mind* (Cambridge, MA: MIT Press, 2002).
42. See, for example, Colin McGinn, *The Problem of Consciousness: Essays Towards a Resolution* (Oxford: Blackwell, 1991).

world as being populated by objects falling under concepts. Accordingly, our scientific theories, including the theory of evolution itself, are themselves conceptual structures. (I do not in the least mean to call into question their truth on this account—on the contrary, a scientific theory can only be true because it is a logical structure of concepts, since truth and falsehood are predicated precisely of such structures.) But now we want to know how the emergence of conceptual thinking itself can be explained, scientifically, that is, in terms which unavoidably presuppose the very structure of conceptual thought whose origins are now in question. This looks suspiciously like trying to pull ourselves up by our own bootstraps and it should not surprise us if the task should prove to be beyond our ability. In fact, I strongly suspect that the question that it raises does not ultimately even make sense.

SIX

Homo Imaginans
and the Concursus Divinus

Douglas Hedley

> The word "Imagination" has been overstrained, from impulses honorable
> to mankind, to meet the demands of the faculty which is perhaps the
> noblest of our nature. (Wordsworth)

Man is amphibious. In my book, *Living Forms of the Imagination*, I argue
that the imagination is best thought of as the capacity to exist both
in the immediate and imagined reality. This feature of *homo imaginans* (man
imagining) should not be confused with fantasy or delusion. Imagination
has etymological links with *imaginari* (to imagine, conceive, or picture men-
tally) and *imago* (likeness). Given this etymological history, it is natural to
think of imagination in terms of a capacity for analogy. As such, it is the basis
for thinking about absent or occluded realities. Analogy operates by employing some likeness between two items, events or situations. Indeed, the failure to employ imagination on the basis of perceived likeness is often the
basis of cruelty and injustice. The incapacity to imagine genuine likenesses
between perceived and unperceived instances in the case of inductive reasoning would lead to rational collapse.

Fantasy, by way of contrast with imagination, is often considered the
capacity merely to entertain or, more particularly, to confuse appearances
with reality. Fantasy is rooted in the Greek *phantasia*, and cognates with
verbs of appearance (*phainesthai*—to appear) or appearing (*phainein*—to
show). This etymological sense of fantasy as linked to appearance rather
than reality, with deception or illusion, is captured neatly by the Renaissance

humanist Shakespeare. In the first scene of Hamlet, Marcellus the guard asks whether the ghost has appeared and Horatio says "'tis but our fantasy." Superstition and fanaticism are often the fruits of fantasy. Emerson is characteristically eloquent on the point:

> It is a problem of metaphysics to define the province of Fancy and Imagination. The words are often used, and the things confounded. Imagination respects the cause. It is the vision of an inspired soul reading arguments and affirmations in all Nature. Of that which it is driven to say. But as soon as this soul is released a little from its passion, and at leisure plays with resemblances and types, for amusement and not for its moral end, we call its action Fancy... Fancy amuses; Imagination expands and exalts us.[1]

To "see" a tree is also to imagine its three dimensional nature, including those parts phenomenologically hidden to the specific observer. To observe an artifact, say a building like a Gothic cathedral, is to engage, perhaps unconsciously, with the "world" embodied by the building, for example, gargoyles, saints, and angels. The world that we in fact experience includes many imaginative constructs—elements of myth, legend, and fiction, as well as theories provided by scientific thought that pervade our experience of the phenomenal world. Consider a walk on the Cornish coastline. Who cannot think of Arthur and Merlin, Tristan and Isult, pirates and smugglers, while contemplating the lush vegetation and the company of sea birds visiting the Cornish coasts? We are also used to accepting the powerful sway of the imagination over our minds. Indeed, a foreign traveler with an appetite for light opera on such a Cornish sojourn might be pleasantly surprised to discover that Penzance is a real place and not merely the imaginary abode of the fantastical pirates of Gilbert and Sullivan!

Imagination is a dimension of human thinking that is often defined in terms of the analogous employment of images or concepts in terms of memories, possibilities, or plans. These need not be images as such; they can be touches, tastes, or smells. Yet the paradigm of an image that can be drawn from memory or projected into the future in daydreams or plans can serve as a useful starting point. The practical employment of such imaginative powers in remembering incidents or planning actions, and of course creative work in literature, the arts and natural science depend upon the use of such uniquely human powers. Socrates was a thinker who demanded strict definitions, if not rigid formulas, from his interlocutors. Yet, Plato presents

---

1. Emerson, *Works: The Harvard Edition*, viii (Boston and New York: Houghton Mifflin, 1929), 26.

Socrates contemplating the nature of morality and justice and producing a picture of the righteous man in the well-ordered state. Indeed, he contrasts this picture with its opposite image—that of the tyrant. Socrates' greatest pupil was a rationalist, and yet one who used "likely tales" or myths at the most decisive points of his dialogues, such as the analogy of the cave in the *Republic* or the myth of the chariot in the *Phaedrus*. These imaginative stories are not fantasies. In Plato's writings, they are governed by *logos* or reason and are necessary when we attempt to climb out of the cave that is the realm of appearances. Various philosophers from Meinong to David Lewis have developed theories of imaginary worlds. Russell's Theory of Descriptions is an explicit attempt to raze such ontological extravagances. The imaginary is the counterpart to the "real" and as such is as an essential part of human experience. An imagined item does not have to be at hand to be a forceful presence. But imagination, like memory, vastly increases the scope of human experience. Lacking imagination and memory, mankind would dwell in a constricted *hic et nunc*. Not only would poetry or history be unlikely without imagination, experimental science would be impossible as it extends decisively beyond the immediate scope of the senses.

As we have insisted, imagination is not necessarily a creative or cognitive process. Indeed, sometimes imagination is thought of primarily in terms of hallucination. The ability of the human mind to employ creative images copied or derived from sensible experience in memory, to entertain suppositions or projections, or to make hypotheses and imaginative plans has long intrigued philosophers. Yet is not philosophical speculation about the imagination an outrageous instance of piling Pelion on Ossa? The emphasis upon lucid and rigorous argument, and perhaps less admirably the scrupulously "everyday" style of analytic philosophy, marks a conscious aversion to any literary or imaginative mode in philosophy. However, this is somewhat paradoxical—philosophy involves a creative employment of words to explore the relation between the self-conscious mind and the phenomena that it encounters. Bacon's fine definition of allegorical poetry as that "which represents intellectual things to the senses"[2] can be expanded to express the general significance of the imagination in religion and science. Much of the Enlightenment critique of religion is a critique of the misuse of imagination. Against a host of contemporary, cultured despisers of religion, reason must be employed to expunge dangerous fantasy. I would wish to argue for the

2. Bacon, *Advancement of Learning*, book 2, (1605) chap. 13.

constructive use of, in Baudelaire's apposite phrase, *la reine des facultés*. I will not try to offer a definition of this phrase, but will mention that I will conform to conventional usage. Perhaps in philosophical reflection there is a proper place for scouring an idea within the tradition of thought; sometimes that idea has been variously named. Especially since the idea of imagination has generally lost much of its prestige and currency. Heidegger pointedly refuses to use the term imagination (*Einbildungskraft*) in his theory of art.[3] Ryle, in his *The Concept of Mind*, devotes a chapter to the idea, but only to demolish the notion of a "special Faculty of Imagination, occupying itself single-mindedly in fancied viewings and hearings."[4] The post-structuralists, notwithstanding their post-Heideggerian critiques of truth as *adaequatio rei et intellectus*, do not appeal to imagination.

Given the paucity of material in more contemporary discussions, it is necessary to consider some of the ideas and assumptions of past thinkers. In our thoughts about the idea of imagination we shall operate like Isis in the story of Isis and Osiris, where the goddess collects the scattered parts of her husband. We are compelled to draw upon the rich tradition of philosophical reflection about this remarkable dimension of the human mind from Plato to Nicholas of Cusa, Vico to the Romantics.

History, imagines, and human agency

Ancient and primordial images suffuse the modern mind, whether it is aware of these or not.[5] Though contemporary culture tends to diminish the significance of the historical, one philosopher in the modern period who resolutely challenged this ahistorical dimension of modern thought, and who identified it with the legacy of Descartes, was Giambatista Vico (1668–1744). One must consider the role of Vico in challenging the idea of a knowledge that comprises of clear and distinct ideas, *l'esprit de géométrie*. Vico's critique of Cartesianism requires a strong philosophical theory of tradition. Vico's view of history is dominated by the concept of the *ricorsi*, the cycles of history, the view of history that we tend to associate with disreputable historians like Spengler and Toynbee. But the salient point is

---

3. Heidegger, *Holzwege* (Frankfurt: Klosterman, 1950), 60.
4. Ryle, *The Concept of Mind* (Harmondsworth: Penguin, 1949), 244.
5. Mali, *The Rehabilitation of Myth: Vico's New Science* (Cambridge: Cambridge University Press, 1992).

made by Vico. Through the idea of *ricorsi*, we can see Vico interpreting historical events through poetic archetypes and seeing the facts of history as part of an intelligible structure:

> The poetic speech which our poetic logic has helped us to understand continued for a long time into the historical period, much as great and rapid rivers continue far into the sea keeping sweet the waters borne on by the force of their flow.[6]

For Vico, understanding agency in the present must involve an awareness of the continuing significance of the past. Donald Phillip Verene has laid great emphasis upon imagination in Vico, particularly the idea of *universali fantastici* or imaginative universals.[7] Vico also uses the terms *caratteri poetici* and *generi fantastici*. These several formulations of the same idea constitute a key element in Vico's thought: how human beings create society and thereby move from the stage of beasts to men. It is, for Vico, through imagination that we can appreciate how we can understand even the most alien of societies. Hence amid the apparently "deplorable obscurity" of the ancient nations, we can find intelligible patterns. Among the very muddle of history, we can find materials for metaphysics. From the vantage point of a perspective like that of Vico, we can turn to reflect upon the impact of the imaginary upon actions and events in history. Take, for example, the impact of atheism on human history. The first great high point of atheism in modern culture was the French Revolution, a development deeply influenced and shaped by philosophical ideas. Indeed, we might consider not just the atheism of the French Revolution but its other related ideas. The year 1789 is a nodal point for Western culture as the ideas of the French Enlightenment were put into practice in France and throughout much of Europe in the wake of the revolutionary wars. Many of the conflicts about religion in particular in contemporary states can be traced back to ideas of the French Revolution and the establishment of a secular state in France. The French Revolution inaugurated an enduring battle within our culture concerning the role of religion in public life. Europe is divided between those cultures that have retained the monarchy and an established form of Christianity like Great Britain, the Netherlands, or Scandinavia (with the recent exception of Sweden) and secular states like France. Paradoxes abound here. The United States, notwithstanding its strict division of church and state, is more

6. Vico, *New Science*, trans. D. Marsh (Harmondsworth: Penguin, 1999), §412, 163.
7. D.P. Verene, *Vico's Science of Imagination* (Ithaca: Cornell University Press, 1981).

outwardly religious than officially "religious" states like Britain or Norway. This can lead to practical problems, particularly the idea that only the secular state can guarantee rights and liberties. The question of the Muslim veil is a typical example. In a self-proclaimed secular state such as France, "freedom" is considered to be the freedom from religious tyranny and thus those public symbols are viewed as subversive. From another historical perspective, for example, that of the United States where freedom is often perceived as the freedom to practice one's religion, actions such as the ban on the scarf seem draconian.

The great sterile beauty of Versailles became a mausoleum of the grandeur and futility of the *Ancien Régime*, yet it exerted a symbolic power. Napoleon and the Bourbons refused to return there. After the collapse of the second French Empire and the capture of Louis Napoleon, King Wilhelm I of Prussia was declared Emperor of Germany in the Hall of Mirrors in the Palace of Versailles. This makes no sense apart from the German sense of humiliation throughout the seventeenth century and the Prussian revenge for perceived servitude under French domination.

Homo imaginans and the self imagined

Such reflections about the *universali fantastici* (imaginative universals) of Vico raise questions about the identity of self in relation to the imagination. Imagination enables the individual mind to relate to objects and thus investigate nature, whether in the limited sense of Hume or the stronger transcendental sense of Kant. It also generates the space, as it were, of selfhood. The self can distinguish itself from other agents and thus develop a domain of interiority through the employment of the "mind's eye." Self-consciousness relies upon imaginative powers, those that create a theater of consciousness. Daniel Dennett is scathing about this idea as the "Cartesian Theater," a temper of mind that he associates with residual dualism even for physicalist philosophers:

> Cartesian materialism is the view that there is a crucial finish line or boundary somewhere in the brain, marking a place where the order of arrival equals the order of "presentation" in experience because *what happens there is what you are conscious of*.... Many theorists would insist that they have explicitly rejected such an obviously bad idea. But... the persuasive imagery of the Cartesian Theater keeps coming back to haunt us—laypeople and

scientists alike—even after its ghostly dualism has been denounced and exorcized.[8]

Dennett's argument is called into question by the empirical evidence of child development. Imagination plays a powerful role in childhood. This capacity seems to play an important role in the healthy psychological development of the child. The distinction between fantasy and reality, which is so important for adults, requires the imaginative play of childhood. Autism seems to be grounded in a physiological infirmity of the brain that produces instances of a failure to engage in imaginative play during childhood, a state that seriously inhibits the psychological capacity of agents to engage in the minds, intentions, and concerns of others. At the age of two years, children are involved in make-believe activities, which can be distinguished from the straightforward sensory and motor actions of the earlier stage from birth. From three to five years of age this use of imaginative play develops with a narrative component, and in early school years the imaginative play of the child becomes increasingly internalized and helps to create and reinforce the sense of identity in the child. In this context the child can conform to the conventions and rules of the classroom while fantasizing about parallel universes. This ability to be amphibious, to dwell in both the present and absent—through memories, imagined worlds, and fantasies—is an important component in the development of the sense of an abiding self that can straddle different slices of time and space. However, this presupposes the contrast between the finite solidness of the world of discrete physical objects and the infinite world of "personal inwardness." Dreaming is a philosophically intriguing instance of this interior world at work, but without the controlling force of reason. Dreaming is a very interesting instance of the imagination released from conscious control, and for just that reason is employed by psychologists as an indication of the contents and tendencies of the subconscious mind. Fears and aggressions can be revealed through dreams, and for such reasons psychoanalysts in the wake of Freud have viewed dreams as a high road to the subconscious.

But philosophers from Plato to Descartes thought about these issues before the psychologists. Consider the famous dream of the ancient Chinese sage Chuang Tsu, who in the dream believed he was butterfly. Upon waking he did not know whether he was Chuang Tsu dreaming of a butterfly or a

---

8. Daniel Dennett, *Consciousness Explained* (Harmondsworth: Penguin, 1991): 107.

butterfly dreaming he was Chuang Tsu. This imaginative capacity has important ramifications for the view of the self. It means that one can avoid the absurdities involved in either strong materialism (i.e., the view that awareness of self is just awareness of one's body), or the equally implausible view that awareness of the self as an item does not depend upon one's body. The first position does not seem to be able to provide any basis for distinguishing rational persons from beasts or brutes. The second seems to disengage the person from the biological condition of conscious agency. The ability to imaginatively inhabit other minds and other worlds also enables us to consider ourselves as essentially the same through and notwithstanding great physical changes. To remain the same person, one needs to hold on to certain skills. In Bernard Williams' 1970 paper "The Self and the Future," he presents the image of a gruff peasant placed (as it were) in the Emperor's body.[9] That seems plausible in relation to the inter-subjective domain. How could one recognize the peasant in the Emperor or vice versa? Yet diachronically, one can see that a parallel puzzle evaporates. Typically, the adolescent feels at odds with his or her body. Consider an adolescent after a strong growth spurt catching a reflection of his lanky form in the mirror or window and the gawky youth not recognizing himself. This need not be pathological, but shows an awareness of a gap between body and spirit.

The small child and the great statesman have a continuous biological and conscious mental states (memories) history. But the child in short trousers and the politician share a common identity. The statesman can remember vividly images of his childhood; perhaps some of those experiences were not merely formative but inspirational for his adult vocation. In the *Bhagavad Gita* it is written that the *atman*, or soul, is beyond "childhood, youth, and old age."[10]

The person is more than the body in the simple sense that personal identity is shaped by memories, fantasies, and hypotheses. The child becomes aware of him- or herself both as an item in space and time with certain properties, and capable of imaginatively engaging in alien domains through the internal theater of consciousness, often as a process of escape. The identification with heroic or archetypal figures is significant, especially for boys. The young in particular explore certain traits that they see in archetypal or heroic types and integrate to varying degrees this imaginative work into their senses of identity.

9. Bernard Williams, "Personal Identity and Individuation," in *Problems of the Self* (Cambridge: Cambridge University Press, 1973), 11–12.
10. *Bhagavad Gita*, 2, 13.

One manner of conceiving these types is, in the wake of Vico, as imaginative universals or poetic characters; that is, as poetic archetypes that lie somewhere both conceptually and historically between Plato's ideas and Jung's archetypes. Such *universali fantastici* are not abstractions, they are living forms that shape the here and now. Vico's central insight is his awareness that we are self-understanding creatures. But our self-awareness is not a stage in his meditations as in Descartes', but is the defining characteristic of philosophy. Reflective human beings are not the straightforward product of instincts and environment but are constituted by an inherited "imaginary," that is, a set of images, symbols, myths and narrative that form a culture. Thus he can claim that "poetic truth is metaphysical truth." Imaginative universals are integral elements of this metaphysical truth:

> Take Godfrey of Bouillon as Torquato Tasso imagines him. He is the true military commander, and all commanders who do not entirely conform to this Geoffrey are not true ones.[11]

Godfrey is not an invention of a particular mind, one which can be traced to a particular mind and psychology. Rather, the minds of individuals must be traced back to such archetypal figures. The archetype, like the Platonic Form, ontologically precedes any subjective awareness of assimilation to it.

The power of the imagination helps us to avoid two egregious philosophical errors. One is the model of the self as a transparent Cartesian ego, substantially distinct from the body. The other is the Humean conception of the self as a bundle of impressions. Both ideas are not without some insights of truth, but present very inadequate ideas of the self.

Descartes correctly stated that thoughts presuppose a thinker. However, the thinking substance Descartes proposes with such confidence is genuinely elusive. There is a fragmented dimension of the human self as Hume recognizes when he claims ignorance of an impression that could generate an idea of a self. But such a theory means that any idea of genuine agency and accountability of the self must evaporate. Kant seems to provide a *via media* through his "I" that accompanies our perceptions but which is not itself an object of possible experience. Kant's characteristically coy solution to the problem of the ego, however, looks like a sterile, formal principle rather than an authentic bearer of consciousness and a rich domain of interior phenomenological and intentional states.

11. Vico, *New Science*, §205, trans. D. Marsh (Harmondsworth: Penguin, 1999), 92.

Purpose, suffering and imagination

The sense of personal identity presupposes a primordial but inchoate sense of unique identity, a thrownness into the world, an idea that is expressed in myths by the idea of the pre-existence of the soul. However, the attainment of a mature and rational self is closely linked to the awareness of the dictates of conscience and the experience of suffering. This is why, I think, the notion of tragedy is so important in our culture. Consider the following speech from Shakespeare's *Hamlet*, delivered from the young prince to Horatio prior to the play-within-the-play in which the murder of a king is enacted:

> Since my dear soul was mistress of her choice,
> And could of men distinguish, her election
> Hath seal'd thee for herself: for thou hast been
> As one, in suffering all, that suffers nothing;
> A man that Fortune's buffets and rewards
> Hast ta'en with equal thanks; and blest are those
> Whose blood and judgement are so well commingled,
> That they are not a pipe for Fortune's finger
> To sound what stop she please. Give me that man
> That is not passion's slave, and I will wear him
> In my heart's core, ay, in my heart of heart,
> As I do thee.[12]

Shakespeare is expressing the Renaissance view of the Christian gentleman. From this perspective, it is the realization of purpose (i.e., the will) that is the task of imagination. *Purpose* is the index of personality, and the healthy personality is orientated to the future rather than the past, and "is not passion's slave." Imagination is the vinculum or bond between "subjectivity" (i.e., the irreducible "my-ness" of the experience, teleology—in short, those purposes and goals that form a coherent identity of self) and the capacity for freedom as the domain of the forging of a self, notwithstanding and sometimes through adverse and painful experiences: "As one, in suffering all, that suffers nothing." In extreme cases, suffering can eclipse and destroy the sense of self and thereby the will to live. But these extreme cases, such as individuals suffering in concentration camps or with very severe illness, need not be taken as paradigmatic. On the contrary, they may be the exceptions that prove the rule. The self needs to overcome suffering

12. Shakespeare, *Hamlet* Act III, scene 2.

and disappointment to forge a coherent sense of self, but that same personal identity may be destroyed by sore adversity.

The distinction between fantasy and imagination is also connected to the metaphysics of the self. Fear grounded upon superstition is the product of those fantasies that pander to the self. Selfishness is reinforced through fantasies and can become extremely disturbing and destructive. The imagination proper is a challenge to the immediate and comfortable ego, and should inspire the soul to the expansion of its interests and concerns.

Hobbes and Spinoza think that *self-preservation* is the primary and ruling motivation of an agent. But human beings clearly have the ability to jeopardize their security and safety on behalf of ideals of self or society. In fact, the sacrifice of the selfish ego and the emergence of a more substantial self requires an imaginative discipline of desire and concentration upon higher values. Polonius says

> This above all—to thine own self be true,
> And it must follow, as the night the day,
> Thou canst not then be false to any man.[13]

It is typical of Shakespeare's dramatic irony that some of his most deeply felt and serious lines are uttered by whimsical characters or in comic contexts. An *ideal* conception of self—requiring imaginative engagement—is only coherent if the Hobbesian view of the self as a raw given or datum is false. In religion and art we find various ideal conceptions of self.

Nature of the artist

Aristotle, hardly the most poetic of philosophers, thought that poetry and philosophy possess a deep kinship. This is because, according to Aristotle, great poetry deals with great human challenges and dilemmas. Thus within the ancient Greek tradition the plots of comedy—relatively trivial matters, or topics of import ironized—can be created by the invention of the dramatist. However, the subject matter of tragedy is always a topic of deep significance and provided by familiar myths. The poet then gives such familiar universal topics and themes particularity. In a related, though more consciously Neoplatonic mode the great Bard says that the

---

13. Shakespeare, *Hamlet* Act I, scene 3.

> lunatic, the lover and the poet
> Are of imagination all compact.
>
> …
>
> The poet's eye, in fine frenzy rolling,
> Doth glance from heaven to earth, from earth to heaven;
> And as imagination bodies forth
> The forms of things unknown, the poet's pen
> Turns them to shapes, and gives to airy nothing
> A local habitation and a name.[14]

Here is a theory of poetry as providing knowledge.[15] Certainly the power of the greatest poems, such as the *Divine Comedy* and *Paradise Lost* or *The Prelude*, rest upon a substrate of philosophical ideas.

One of the perplexing questions in contemporary culture revolves around the nature of art. As a result of Romanticism in the West, art has gained a rank and status that is remarkable, particularly *beaux arts* or *die schöene Kunste*. But with the increased status of the artist it has become increasingly mysterious what their proper task should be. The artist is a mirror of society. As self-conscious and expressive animals—self-understanding creatures, in Charles Taylor's fine phrase—the great task of art is communication. This is not to claim that the artist is necessarily a great philosopher. But the artist is capable of an attunement and imaginative engagement with the environment. This may be merely descriptive: the artist may, like T.S. Eliot in *The Waste Land*, give expression to a widely held mood of decay or anxiety. The great artist, however, is also capable of a prescriptive element, a vision by which the artist can comment upon the world observed. The great artist perceives the infinite in the finite.

In Plato's *Theatetus*, Socrates is described as like a midwife. In *Symposium*, Socrates describes the claim of Diotima that through producing physical offspring "the mortal nature is seeking as far as possible to be everlasting and immortal." Yet artistic creativity is a pregnancy of the soul that guarantees a far more desirable immortality. According to Diotima, "Who, when he thinks of Homer and Hesiod and other great poets, would not rather have their children than ordinary ones?" Drawing upon this tradition, "conceiving" was ambivalent; both physical and a mental propagation were possible.[16] In this

---

14. Shakespeare, *Midsummer Night's Dream* Act V, scene 1.
15. Douglas Hedley, *Living Forms of the Imagination* (London: T & T Clark, 2008), 162.
16. Plato, *Symposium*, 209D. Plato, *Lysis, Symposium, Gorgias*, trans. W. R. M. Lamb (Cambridge, MA: Harvard University Press, 1996), 200–1.

way the ancient, medieval, or Renaissance thinkers could view finite creativity as resembling, or even participating in, Divine creativity. The medieval/Renaissance Platonist Nicholas of Cusa (1401–1464) explicitly developed the idea of creative participation in the Divine mind. Through his doctrine of the *docta ignorantia*, Nicholas attacks both the essentialism of contemporary Aristotelianism and the skepticism and voluntarism of the nominalists. Finite creativity is the unfolding (*explicare*) of that that is enfolded (*complicare*) within the Divine: the creativity of the artist in particular is a sharing in the Divine creative energy. Marsilio Ficino (1433–1499) develops the imaginative power (*vis imaginativa*) that is viewed as divine presence within the human mind.[17] When Michelangelo speaks of "*l'immagine del cor*" or "*un concetto di bellezza*," he is referring to the inner vision that draws upon spiritual mysteries for inspiration. This thought comes to Shakespeare and the English Renaissance from Giordano Bruno and other émigrés from the Counter-Reformation.

Hermetical and magical sources in the Renaissance enhanced the sense of human creativity and imaginative power, especially the "god-making" dimension, so much so that it led even Cardinal Nicholas Cusa to quote from the Hermetic Asclepius in saying that man is the second god.[18] By the seventeenth century, however, the analogy between finite creativity and the Divine *creatio continua* seemed increasingly remote in a Cartesian mechanistic universe. The Romantic extolling of imagination was often the rearguard action of those who lamented the loss of a vital cosmos reflecting the Divine creative energy, the sigh of those who insisted upon viewing art as the perception of the infinite in the finite or, as Coleridge said so memorably, "a repetition in the finite mind of the eternal act of creation in the infinite I Am."[19]

Imagination as the Shechinah in the heart

Imagination presupposes the mind's capacity for memory and retention. Philosophers have often discussed these problems in relation to the association of ideas from Aristotle to Hobbes and Hume. This is the attempt

17. D. P. Walker, *Spiritual and Demonic Magic: From Ficino to Campanella* (Stroud: Sutton, 2000), 76–80.
18. Cusa, De Beryllo VII, *Nicholas of Cusa, Metaphysical Speculations,* trans. J. Hopkins (Minneapolis: Arthur J. Banning, 1998), 794.
19. S. T. Coleridge, *Biographia Literaria,* ed. J. Engell and W. Jackson Bate (Princeton: Princeton University Press, 1985), 106–15.

to expound a mechanism through which memory functions in terms of resemblance, contiguity, and succession. The model is atomistic and mechanical. In fact, David Hartley's eighteenth-century version of the theory was greeted as doing for the realm of the mental what Newton's theory of gravity had done for the physical world. He parallels the work of consciousness with the nervous system. Coleridge, in his critique of Hartley and the Empiricist tradition in his *Biographia Literaria*, is drawing upon the Kantian thought that the association of discrete experiences is an imperfect and at best limited model of knowledge and it overlooks the vital synthetic role of the human mind. Although Coleridge shares this Kantian intuition, his real goal is Platonic: he wishes to expose the intolerable gap between particular sensory images and universal ideas that Empiricism fails to explain. If ideas are derived from impressions and combinations of the kind Locke calls "complex ideas," then the mind's contents are derived causally. Aristotle and Thomas view the mind as a *tabula rasa* and knowledge as the product of experience. Universal ideas occur through the mind abstracting the essence of specific items. This depends upon the mind's capacity to remove the particular images of things and arrive at universal properties. The doctrine of the active intellect should explain this capacity to understand what transcends the senses.

Platonists propose imagination as grounded in an innate capacity of the soul. One might consider the image of the "storehouse," an image that suggests that St. Augustine's explorations about the nature of memory have an evident affinity with Plato's theory, which was linked to the Platonic doctrine of the pre-existence of the soul, further connected to the Classical theory from the *Meno* that the soul could not derive its knowledge from sensory experience, but is remembering that which is derived from a previous existence. Augustine, in thinking about memory, observes that much of its contents could not have been derived from the senses, but was implanted by God.[20] In this Platonic/Augustinian account the human mind is not a *tabula rasa*. This doctrine about memory as the source of genuine knowledge is the key to the Platonic theory of imagination. If the mind does not derive its contents exclusively from sense experience, but rather from God in its creation or from the intelligible realm, one can expect the mind to possess a proleptic awareness or apprehension of realities that transcends its immediate empirical environment.

---

20. Augustine, *Confessions* 10, 19.

This can be seen in Coleridge's famous definition of imagination:"As the prime agent of all human perception, and a repetition in the finite mind of the eternal act of creation in the infinite I Am." Coleridge is assuming a con-substantiality of God and the human mind. Robert Barth helpfully draws an analogy between this doctrine and the medieval theory of the *concursus divinus.* Barth states that God is immanent in all God's creation. God is, however, immanent in a special manner in free agents. Human creativity is thus linked in a special way to divine creativity.

The employment of imagination can "awaken the mind's attention from the lethargy of custom," it can reveal "the loveliness and the wonders of the world before us."[21] Coleridge further claims that an "idea in the highest sense of that word cannot be conveyed but by a symbol."[22] The symbol is "characterized...above all by a transcendence of the Eternal through and in the Temporal. It always partakes of the reality which it renders intelligible; and while it enunciates the whole, abides itself as a living part in that unity, of which it is the representative."[23] Thus, in the symbolic imagination, the transcendent and the finite overlap. Thus Coleridge, employing the terminology of the Jewish Cabbalah, speaks of the imagination in this exalted sense as the "Shechinah in the heart," as immanent Divine presence.[24]

Imagination and the *concursus divinus*

The Empiricist has a greater need of imagination as an epistemological tool, as a means of constructing a world out of the "buzzing, blooming confusion" of sense data. Platonists, however, see the empirical world as an enigmatic image of an intelligible transcendent reality. Ironically, Plato and many Platonists have been critical of confusing the image with its transcendent archetype (a form of idolatry) and dangerous self-serving fantasies. Plato calls this *eikasia* in the *Republic.*

Within the Empiricist tradition imagination is seen as continuous with perception. Hobbes famously defines imagination as "nothing but decaying sense."[25] For another strand of thought, this unduly limits the nature of imagination. Here imagination is not so much a mode of failed or illusory

---

21. Coleridge, *Biographia Literaria* 1, 80.   22. Coleridge, *Biographia Literaria* 1, 156.
23. Coleridge, *Lay Sermons*, 30.   24. Coleridge, *Notebooks* II, 2999.
25. Hobbes, *Leviathan* I, 2 (Oxford: Clarendon, 1958), 14.

perception but a primordial capacity to shape and organize the materials of sensation. Immanuel Kant is important for the development of the idea of imagination, particularly in his distinction between the reproductive and productive (i.e., transcendental) imagination. The productive imagination is the spontaneous power that unifies sense and thought: a foundational power of the soul which furnishes a priori knowledge."[26]

The idea of the productive imagination in Kant becomes central for Fichte, German Romanticism, and in particular the philosophy of Schelling.[27] The fine correspondence of mind-independent objects to the confines of the human understanding is the result of this process. The productive imagination has imbued nature with its shapes and forms unconsciously. It then "discovers," as it were, an order that it has placed into the phenomena. Schelling writes:

> The splendid German word "imagination" (*Einbildungskraft*) actually means the power (*Kraft*) of mutual-forming into unity (*ineinsbildung*) upon which all creation is really based. It is the power whereby something ideal is simultaneously something real, the soul simultaneously the body, the power of individuation that is the creative power.

In the terminology of imagination as the power of "forming into unity" we find a reference to the theological and Platonic background of Renaissance theories in which the universe is perceived as a Divine artwork. Its beauty is a counter-image (*Gegenbild*) of the beauty of God. Philosophical knowledge, according to Schelling in his seminal work *System of Transcendental Idealism* (1800), is ultimately aesthetic as nature is striving towards consciousness (slumbering spirit) and imagination is "the primordial knowledge of which the visible universe is the image."[28]

In Schelling's work, despite the elusive nature of his protean thought phases and his polemic exchanges, we find an increasing tendency to become more explicit in his theology. He was a theologian by training and certain theological themes recur throughout his *oeuvre*. Through his elective affinities, Coleridge was particularly well placed to transmit some of Schelling's insights to the English speaking peoples. Hence, for example, Emerson writes:

26. Kant, *Critique of Pure Reason,* trans. Norman Kemp Smith (London: Macmillan, 1982), 145ff.
27. J. Engell, *The Creative Imagination: Enlightenment to Romanticism* (Cambridge, MA: Harvard University Press: 1981).
28. Schelling, *On University Studies,* ed. E.S. Morgan and N. Guterman (Athens: Ohio State University Press, 1966), 10.

Nature is the true idealist. When she serves us best, when, on rare days, she speaks to the imagination, we feel that the huger heaven and earth are but a web drawn around us, that the lights, skies and mountains are but the painted vicissitudes of the soul.[29]

To see nature properly is to employ imagination and to see the visible cosmos as the enigmatic reflection of the Divine mind.

Conclusion

Much of the Enlightenment critique of religion is a critique of the misuse of imagination. Religion, in this account, is a dangerous fantasy. I would like to argue for the constructive use of imagination in religion and science. For Pascal imagination is characteristically *"cette maîtresse d'erreur et de fausseté"* ("this mistress of falsehood and error").[30] In *Living Forms of the Imagination* I argued for the iconic dimension of the imagination. Theism's espousal of an invisible transcendent God is compatible with the idea that images can be enigmatic signs of the transcendent. Plato's myths offer an illustration of this. Gibbon noted that a pagan philosopher of Antiquity "who considered the system of polytheism as a composition of human fraud and error, could disguise a smile of contempt under the mask of devotion, without apprehending that either the mockery or the compliance would expose him to the mockery of the invisible, or as he conceived them, imaginary powers."[31] Christian writers, however, saw the pagan deities "in a much more odious and formidable light" as "the authors, the patrons, and the objects of idolatry." Gibbon's words can be misleading, however. Indeed, the oldest and most venerable critique of religious belief, from Xenophanes to Feuerbach, is an argument about fantasy. Religious belief is based upon the human propensity to project its interests and longing on the cosmos. The development of philosophical theology in the strict sense, from the idea of an invisible and intelligible deity as the transcendent and supreme being reinforced the fantasy argument.

Theism is often associated by atheists with ignorance and the prescientific. Plato and Aristotle both saw wonder as the inspiration of philoso-

29. Emerson, *Works*, VIII, 26.
30. Pascal, *Pensées,* ed. P. Sellier (Paris: Mecure de France, 1976), §78.
31. Gibbon, *Decline and Fall of the Roman Empire*, XV (1776-1788).

phy. The love of a beautiful and intelligible universe, and the source or principle (*arche*) "that moves the sun and other stars" has inspired much traditional metaphysics. Indeed, one could argue that philosophy is itself chimerical if the universe is a brute absurdity. If consciousness and freedom, the soul and responsibility are systematic illusions, or perhaps at best the epiphenomena of a deterministic universe, these are metaphysical positions and not the simple inferences from scientific facts. More fundamentally still, is there an uncreated necessary Being, the source of the vast contingent cosmos and the realm of becoming? Is there a transcendent Mind beyond the flux of fleeting thoughts, intentions, and aspirations? Plato and Aristotle claim that the answer is yes! The imagination of this transcendent, uncreated reality has inspired the greatest poetry from the Upanishads to the Sufi mystics, from Dante to Wordsworth to Eliot.

False philosophical extremes continue to trouble Christian theology. One extreme consists of a crude essentialism and the other might be loosely deemed nominalism. According to the former, God can be grasped as an object of intellectual inquiry. Theology is not possible if its supreme object is viewed as an entity that can be captured as an item among others; *si comprehendis non est Deus*. However, equally corrosive is the latter option, the nominalism that insists that our abstract names and predicates are universal expressions for a de facto plurality of discrete concrete items. The denial of abstract universals infects theology with a radical and untenable skepticism. The proper balance must consist between the proper respect for the limits of conceptual definition and sufficient epistemological optimism. Imagination constitutes the inward light of the soul. If faith is the substance of things hoped for, the evidence of things not seen, then these objects cannot be seen by the physical organs or deduced rationally. If God is beyond thought and language, then imagination is necessary for theology. As Wordsworth insists:

> This spiritual love acts not nor can exist
> Without imagination, which, in truth,
> Is but another name for absolute power
> And clearest insight, amplitude of mind,
> And Reason in her most exalted mood.[32]

Imagination is an inward light that can be identified with rationality in its most sublime function. Notwithstanding the power of specific arguments

32. Wordsworth, *The Prelude*, VI, 104.

for the existence of God or the nature of the soul, the key to the knowledge of God is that joy of experience of the Divine presence by a living soul that Wordsworth describes as "spiritual love." In book two of *The Prelude* Wordsworth writes:

> Wonder not
> If high the transport, great the joy I felt
> Communing in this sort through earth and heaven
> With every form of creature, as it looked
> Towards the Uncreated with a countenance
> Of adoration, with an eye of love.[33]

Christian theology in particular should be partial to the claims of the imagination, notwithstanding the dangers of idolatry and superstition. Even in an age of disenchantment the mysterious but central doctrine of the *imago Dei* must mean that there is a special and unique link between human beings and God. This doctrine is reinforced by the doctrine of the incarnation. In the political world we can properly imagine inviolable rights and human dignity, even if we no longer see Pindar's "fire darting steeds," the horses of the sun god, in the movement of the sun from east to west. We know the sunset to be an illusion because it is the earth not the sun that is moving, a fact that any rational and educated mind knows since Copernicus. Thus not only is nature rendered devoid of meaning, but even human agency seems redundant: the product of mechanical processes that we are incapable of understanding. We are thus robots deluded by a belief in freedom. As the sense of a meaningful cosmos has been eroded by the scientific revolution of the seventeenth century, so too the belief in human freedom seems battered. A deterministic and scientific view of human nature, however, leaves out the role of ideas upon the events of history. The etymology of words often sheds light on the history of philosophy. Any philosophy overlooks, at its peril, the importance of history and tradition for

> ...a creature who not prone
> And brute as other creatures, but endued
> With sanctity of reason, might erect
> His stature, and upright with front serene
> Govern the rest, self-knowing, and from thence
> Magnanimous to correspond with heaven.[34]

---

33. Wordsworth, *The Prelude*, II.   34. Milton, *Paradise Lost*, book 7 (1667), lines 506–11.

SEVEN

Aesthetics, Phantasia, and the Theistic

Daniel N. Robinson

Mimesis

> Then the first thing will be to establish a censorship of the writers of fiction, and let the censors receive any tale of fiction which is good, and reject the bad; and we will desire mothers and nurses to tell their children the authorized ones only. Let them fashion the mind with such tales, even more fondly than they mould the body with their hands; but most of those which are now in use must be discarded.
>
> *Republic*, Book II

I begin with a passage from Plato, of course, for it is with the dialogues and then with Aristotle that we are drawn into critical appraisals of art, of theology, and of ourselves. The passage from *Republic* records the recognition of the powerful influence of art on both personal and civic life; art as the shaper of minds and, at least as Socrates would have it, *souls*.

To speak of the aesthetic dimension is presumably to speak of beauty and on this point controversy abounds. Lord Shaftesbury was persuaded that, "The most natural beauty in the world is honesty and moral truth. For all beauty is truth. True features make the beauty of a face; and true proportions the beauty of architecture."[1] This is an attempt to assimilate the idea of

---

1. Shaftesbury, *Characteristics of Men, Manners, Opinions* 2 vols., ed. John M. Robertson (1963), I, 94.

beauty to a moral category that seems reasonable enough (as Plato also believed) but Aristotle would regard the conflation as a mistake. The "good" after all, is manifest in action, whereas "beauty" is a property generally possessed by frozen objects.

In *Modern Painters,* John Ruskin reaches a conclusion diametrically opposed to Shaftesbury's, insisting that among the major errors in works devoted to the concept of beauty there is,

> ...first, that the Beautiful is the True; the second, that the Beautiful is the Useful; the third, that it is dependent on Custom; and the fourth, that it is dependent on the Association of Ideas. (4.66)[2]

Against the ancient argument to the effect that beauty requires what is harmonious and proportionate, Edmund Burke dismissed the idea out of hand, as I shall note later in this chapter. For Burke, "Rather, whatever in an object conduces to feelings of love is what is beautiful in that object." Moreover—and directly contrary to Aristotle's view—Burke associates the beautiful with the small:

> What, then, are the real causes of beauty? In the first place, beautiful objects are small. In most languages, objects of love are spoken of under diminutive epithets. We rarely say 'a great beautiful thing,' but often 'a great ugly thing.' There is a wide difference between admiration and love; and while the sublime has to do with great and terrible objects, the beautiful is found in small and pleasing things.[3]

What of "naturalism," that protean concept that would seem to do more work at a distance than it does when viewed close up? A volume devoted to the tension, real or apparent, between "naturalism" and "theism" and drawing upon the aesthetic dimension of life calls for the sometimes tedious but always necessary attempt to make clear just how key terms are to be understood. This is not an easy task. It is sufficient to make clear that the term itself really is protean.

In recent decades, "naturalism" has been used in different senses. Within the field of aesthetics, it has long referred to artistic forms and genres characterized by attempts to represent nature, including human nature, with

---

2. John Ruskin, *Modern Painters,* Vol. II, chap. 4, sec. 1. http://www.gutenberg.lib.md.us/2/9/9/0/29906/29906-h/29906-h.htm
3. Edmund Burke, *A Philosophical Inquiry Into The Origin Of Our Ideas Of The Sublime And Beautiful With Several Other Additions* (1756), part III, sec. 13. http://burke.classicauthors.net/SublimeandBeautiful/SublimeandBeautiful7.html.

faithfulness and accuracy, even brutal realism. The first to use the term in this sense was probably Bellori (1672) in relation to the school of Caravaggio.[4] It is a counter both to the classical ideal and to the *supernatural*. It would restrict the aims of art to the realities of life wherever it is found and however it manifests itself. In literature, perhaps the major progenitor was Balzac, his literary litter of realists including Flaubert, Zola, and later Hemingway and Mailer.

Philosophical naturalism is somewhat resonant with aesthetic naturalism in that it, too, strenuously eschews the transcendent, the supernatural, the ineffable. Some years ago Michael Friedman identified what he took to be its two defining features: First, the rejection of any form of knowledge that is allegedly independent of (a priori in relation to) experience. What counts as knowledge is drawn from the ample domain comprising the subject matter of the empirical sciences. Second, philosophy itself is drawn from that same domain.[5] On this understanding, philosophical naturalism is opposed in principle to the "supernatural." Hence, theists such as C. S. Lewis and Alvin Plantinga must conclude that philosophical naturalism and theism are simply incompatible. Perhaps.

For there to be naturalism, there must be the idea of nature itself as something sufficiently distinct from one's merely subjective states so that the term can be employed inter-subjectively. So, again, it's back to the Greeks, or at least to that obsessive Greek, Aristotle. He offers an invitingly flexible alternative to the incompatibilist thesis owing to his liberated sense of "natural." For him the "natural" includes whatever is a (nearly) universally appearing, non-accidental property of things. What is natural in human nature is that which is coextensive with actual human lives, for example, rationality. Aristotle assumes that whatever is readily and (nearly) universally expressed by human beings in the absence of coercive and inhibiting forces, is "natural." The properties in question must be "essential" as contrasted with accidental or merely coincidental. Coriscus is essentially a human being, coincidentally a musician. Just in case everyone on earth were a musician, this property would still not be an essential property, for if their musical

4. A clear discussion of the term as used in modern times is Thomas Munro, "Meanings of 'Naturalism' in Philosophy and Aesthetics," *The Journal of Aesthetics and Art Criticism*, Vol. 19, 2 (Winter, 1960): 133–7. For Bellori's discussion of Caravaggio, see Giorgio Mancini, Giovanni Baglione, Giovanni Pietro Bellori and Helen Langdon, *The Lives of Caravaggio* (London: Pallas Athene, 2005).
5. Michael Friedman, "Philosophical naturalism," *Proceedings and Addresses of the American Philosophical Association* (1997).

talents were suddenly lost, they would continue to be human beings insofar as they continued to be rational beings. On this understanding, the aesthetic dimension of human life would be no more oddly included within the naturalistic perspective than would digestion. Clearly, then, if there is some fundamental tension between the aesthetic and the natural, it must arise at least in part from the manner in which each is conceived; the manner in which a foundational science or philosophy sets about to assign properties and entities to categories.

The "naturalism" that now commands greatest attention is the bequest of Charles Darwin. He was not the first, of course. Laplace famously contended that the future could be predicted with undeviating accuracy just in case we knew the position and momentum of all particles in the universe. As Laplace understood "naturalism," it was just matter and the laws governing the behavior of matter. Presumably, if one knew the position and momentum of all atomic entities in the universe, one could predict the appearance of both Laplace and his thesis.

It is not out of place, if only parenthetically, to draw attention to the fallacy of conflating prediction and causal determination. Ask all the members of an audience who happen to have blue eyes to raise their hands. One's predictive success will be on the order of 100%, though each of the persons with blue eyes surely raises his or her hand freely. Similarly, just in case selection pressures, brain function, genetic factors and diet permit one to predict that the music of Schubert will be preferred to that of Mahler, it would not follow that the aesthetic basis on which the reactions were based is itself thus determined. True, to have a position on a musical work one usually must hear it (though Beethoven near the end of life was able to make the judgment without that benefit), but there is a distinction worth noting between the conditions that enable an experience and the phenomenology of the experience itself.

Naturalism and evolutionary theory versus aestheticism and theism? The suggested opposition rests on a more fundamental position regarding nature and beauty, nature and the divine. Alfred Russell Wallace arrived at evolutionary theory at about the same time as did Darwin, their two accounts presented together at the Linnean Society on 1 July 1858. It was Wallace whose *Darwinism* presented the most authoritative defense of the theory.[6] But Wallace and Darwin were very different types. If Darwin were given a

6. Alfred Russell Wallace, *Darwinism* (London: Macmillan, 1889).

Rorschach test, he might well have spent the better part of a month on the upper corner of the inkblot, attempting to determine whether the bat was *Myotis sodalist* or *Cynopterus Brachyotic*. Wallace would be more inclined to wonder if such patterns express something mythic and inherent in the substrates of human emotion and cognition, perhaps reaching a Jungian perspective on the matter. It is not surprising that Wallace, in possession of the same data, would find in the aesthetic and moral expressions of our humanity something unheralded in the animal economy. He makes this clear in chapter 15 of *Darwinism*:

> The special faculties we have been discussing clearly point to the existence in man of something which he has not derived from his animal progenitors—something which we may best refer to as being of a spiritual essence or nature, capable of progressive development under favourable conditions... Thus we may perceive that the love of truth, the delight in beauty, the passion for justice, and the thrill of exultation with which we hear of any act of courageous self-sacrifice, are the workings within us of a higher nature which has not been developed by means of the struggle for material existence.[7]

Not to belabor the point, but it is worth repeating that the story one creates with data and with a set of orienting assumptions is itself something of an artistic and aesthetic achievement. I do not imply here that some sort of "social construction of truth" is the proper description of the scientific mission. Rather, not every use of even the most carefully collected and recorded data from the natural world is reserved exclusively for that scientific mission. At some point, the data will be marshaled on behalf of a theory that goes beyond the data. At times, the distance from the data will be so great as to raise questions about violations of what I would call "the rules of evidence." The connection between data and theory in *Origin of Species* is exemplary; the connection in *Descent of Man* borders on polemic. When the dust had settled by about 1900, it was clear that Darwin's story was different from Wallace's. The ultra-naturalistic story is different from the theistic story. It would be extremely useful if there were some Archimedian point from which such competing perspectives might be subjected to an ultimate and decisive test. If there is such a point, it remains hidden.

As noted at the beginning of this essay, Plato did not reach a settled position on the issue and so offered several alternatives as expressed by Socrates.

---

7. Ibid.

On the Socratic account, poetry, drama and music stir the passions, give flight to the imagination, excite a wide range of actions and have the power to neutralize the directives of reason. But the arts, owing to this very power, can fortify one's resolve and give fuller expression to what is virtuous and worthy in our undertakings. It is not surprising that the most frequently cited figure in the dialogues is that of Homer who gets mixed reviews but is the leading exemplar of the power of the poets. It is Homer who heads the list of those who teach the wrong lessons and provide models of weakness and imperfection where the impressionable should be treated to a steady diet of elevating narratives. In Book III of *Republic*, Socrates finds ready agreement with his condemnation of an account of Zeus, intoxicated by the beauty of Hera and, disregarding his chosen course of action, loses himself in the throes of lust.

These lessons were not lost on Aristotle during his two decades as a student in the *Academy*, but neither did they control his understanding of the creative process and the manner in which it should be understood. Where the subject is aesthetics as a *discipline*, it is Aristotle who serves as a principal guide. Choosing him over Plato is deliberate. The rationale is economically expressed by Daniel Greenspan, "Aristotle's *Poetics*, an incomplete set of lecture notes, is the first literary-philosophical analysis of tragedy, the origin of aesthetics and the tradition of literary criticism to come."[8] Once again, why not Plato? Plato, indeed, takes priority in time in his discussion of beauty, developing his fearful appreciation of the power of art and the ultimately *divine* sources of its inspiration. There is criticism, some very pointed. On the whole, the dialogues are hostile to those "fictions" advanced by poets, not to mention the dytherambic music so corrupting of the soul. Moreover, in Book X of *Republic*, Socrates is found condemning the developed inclination to mere imitation caused by regular exposure to the arts which are, one and all, *mimetic* in nature. The Guardians of the *polis* must be courageous, not simply *acting* as would a courageous person but *being* such a person, replacing the "as if" with a "he is." The emphasis throughout is on what is authentic, whereas the productions of art, by their very imitative nature, lack authenticity. In these respects, Plato would have the arts understood as tools to be used to stabilize and defend the political organization of the State by directing and controlling the various strata of society.

8. Daniel Greenspan, *The Passion of Infinity: Kierkegaard, Aristotle and the Rebirth of Tragedy* (Berlin and New York: Walter de Gruyter, 2008), 70.

There is much more to the Socratic position on the arts, but nothing is settled or definite. In his close examination of Plato's conception of beauty, for example, Drew Hyland is finally persuaded that Plato reached no settled position at all.[9] Considering the views defended in the *Phaedrus, Hippias Major*, and *Symposium,* the Socratic view surfaces as a collection of questions and challenges leading finally to still other questions. Hyland is surely correct in his own conclusion that the effect—if not the very point—of the dialogues is to make clear that "beauty" is not to be neatly understood by way of some sort of rational appraisal.

Further evidence, relevant in this context, is found in Plato's *Ion* where the argument is to the effect that the artist creates not by way of rules but through direct inspiration by the Muse. Here Socrates describes the artist as "...a light and winged and holy thing, and there is no invention in him until he has been inspired and is out of his senses, and the mind is no longer in him: when he has not attained to this state, he is powerless and is unable to utter his oracles."[10]

The process owes practically nothing to rationality. Rather, the magnificent rendering of heroic deeds by Homer arises not from a poet's rational plan or template but from an impulse conferred by the Muse. Only then will one be an artist "...make dithyrambs, another hymns of praise, another choral strains, another epic or iambic verses—and he who is good at one is not good at any other kind of verse: for not by art does the poet sing, but by power divine." Here is an *emergentist* conception of the relationship between (or among) the artist, the Muse and the observer of the work. When in the *Physics,* Aristotle tells us that if the art of shipbuilding were in the wood, there would be ships "by nature," he is getting at the same point. While granting the wonderful imagery in Plato's account—granting further that an examination of how or if beauty itself fits into some larger ideal framework that includes truth, justice and the divine—it is nonetheless clear that such an approach will not provide knowledge of the structure, the origins, the sublunary purposes served by the arts.

Plato never did provide a foundation for the philosophical study of aesthetics as such. His treatment is best considered as a recognition of the moral and practical effects art has on the human condition, not as a systematic treatise on the nature of art in its several manifestations and the ingredients

---

9. Drew Hyland, *Plato and the Question of Beauty* (Bloomington: Indiana University Press, 2008).
10. Plato, *Ion* trans. B. Jowett (Charleston: Forgotten Books, 2008), 9.

that qualify a work as poetry, epic poetry, tragedy, and so on. In choosing lines from *Republic* at the beginning of this essay I did not intend to plead the cause of artistic freedom against Ephors in Plato's time or in our own. Rather, the passage draws attention to the Socratic thesis that would have Aesthetics stand chiefly as the moral criticism of art, not as an intellectual-philosophical theater of judgment and analysis.

For a philosophical approach, one turns to Aristotle whose entire orientation is different. It is systematic, taxonomic and genetic. What is the source of the arts? Just what is it that attracts us to art in the first place? How are the different arts to be distinguished? If Empedocles and Homer both use the same poetic meter, why is one understood to be engaged in a scientific exposition and the other in epic poetry? What are the characteristic effects of artistic productions and how do these effects arise from the nature and needs of the percipient?

A useful point of entry is Aristotle's contention that the arts arise *naturally* and make contact with what is an essential aspect of human nature. On Aristotle's account, activities that are virtually ubiquitous in the known history of a species, as well as in the current and evident lives of the members of that species are *natural* and authentic, and are to be understood in terms of ends or needs characteristic of the species itself. Thus, in his *Politics* Aristotle is led by such considerations to declare the *polis* to be entirely of *natural* growth. It is as natural for human beings to enter into essentially political associations as it is for them to reproduce or take nourishment. Even his otherwise dauntingly complex *Metaphysics* begins with the transparently descriptive claim generally translated as, *All men by nature desire to know.* The Greek text [980a] reads " πάντες ἄνθρωποι τοῦ εἰδέναι ὀρέγονται φύσει" where "ὀρέγονται" refers to a process of expanding, stretching out, broadening. The thesis is that the enlargement of what is known arises from nothing less than a need, a natural desire to expand and stretch the canvas of knowledge. He follows this immediately with "σημεῖον δ' ἡ τῶν αἰσθήσεων ἀγάπησις"—the evidence or mark of this is nothing less than the *love* (ἀγάπησις) we have of the senses.[11] This utterly natural inclination to acquire knowledge then feeds naturally on what aids the process. The realm of aesthetics ties in directly as is clear from this passage from the *Poetics*:

11. Aristotle, *Metaphysics*, trans. W. D. Ross in *The Complete Works of Aristotle*, ed. Jonathan Barnes (Princeton: Princeton University Press, 1984), 980a25.

Poetry in general seems to have sprung from two causes, each of them lying deep in our nature. First, the instinct of imitation is implanted in man from childhood, one difference between him and other animals being that he is the most imitative of living creatures, and through imitation learns his earliest lessons; and no less universal is the pleasure felt in things imitated.[12]

The key word in all of this is one or another variant of the verb *to imitate* (μιμέομαι). Aristotle throughout his treatise refers to imitations or representations (μιμήσεις). It can be misleading to reduce the Greek μιμήσεις to a single English word. There are complex ingredients capable of arousing recollections of past experiences; complex ingredients capable not merely of reviving but enriching the recollection and leading to new and unexpected associations. In modern times, Proust describes how a feint odor or one's climbing a staircase may result in the reliving and reinterpretation of bygone experiences. Aristotle surely has all this in mind in the above passage and intends more than a mere conjecture of the sort so common in the Socratic dialogues. He offers a page of descriptive psychology, now by one of the greatest of naturalistic observers. What is his evidence?

We have evidence of this in the facts of experience. Objects which in themselves we view with pain, we delight to contemplate when reproduced with minute fidelity: such as the forms of the most ignoble animals and of dead bodies. The cause of this again is, that to learn gives the liveliest pleasure, not only to philosophers but to men in general; whose capacity, however, of learning is more limited. Thus the reason why men enjoy seeing a likeness is, that in contemplating it they find themselves learning or inferring, and saying perhaps, 'Ah, that is he.' For if you happen not to have seen the original, the pleasure will be due not to the imitation as such, but to the execution, the coloring, or some such other cause.[13]

This passage—which is repeated in his *Rhetoric*[14]—is especially significant. The word Aristotle uses to describe the effect of seeing and contemplating likenesses is "ἥδιστον," which is perhaps stronger than "pleasant"; is more akin to a "sweet pleasure," something craved and savored. Then, too, art, though imitative, arises from what is a natural instinct, planted deeply in human nature, and operating in the service of the cultivation of cognitive powers. To the extent that all human beings (and not merely philosophers) desire to know, there will be a strong and natural impulse toward activities

12. Aristotle, *Poetics,* 1448b. http://www.perseus.tufts.edu/hopper/text?doc=Perseus%3Atext%3 A1999.01.0056%3Asection%3D1448b
13. Ibid.   14. Aristotle, *Rhetoric*, 1371b, 5-10.

that promote and deepen knowledge and render those possessing it ever more resourceful. The process itself is distinguishable from the content. There are depictions of objects and events which, if confronted in reality, would be revolting, even terrifying, as objects of art, however, they lead the observer to a most careful and even joyful examination for they serve as a vehicle for the enlargement of mental life. There is even the intimation of a "pleasure principle" in that this enlargement—being joyful in itself—inclines one to a love of the senses by which this takes place. The universal desire to know explains the delight we take in our senses. What art conveys is not a copy or rehearsal of the same factual experiences but a challenge of sorts. In its imitation of life, the work of art calls for an emotional investment combined with those cognitive powers by which inferences and implications are drawn.

Phantasia

Does evolutionary theory offer a credible account of "imagination"? If "naturalism" is understood as a veiled form of radical physicalism—brain processes now taking over where mental life once held sway—how is "φαντασια" to fit into that sort of account? Some seem to find a ready answer to such questions. Conrad Montell surely speaks for many in the contemporary naturalist school when he writes,

> Imagination evolved to find that which would make the nascent apprehension of death more bearable, to engage in a search for alternative perceptions of death: a search that was beyond the capability of the external senses. I argue that imagination evolved as flight and fight adaptations in response to debilitating fears that paralleled an emerging foreknowledge of death . . .[15]

I should begin to consider the question by noting first that *phantasia* is a term that one scholar has aptly described as "a translator's nightmare."[16] The word itself invites controversy and indecision. In an important essay, Victor Caston notes that "φαντασια" in Aristotle is related not only to imagination

---

15. Conrad Montell, "On Evolution of God-Seeking Mind: An Inquiry Into Why Natural Selection Would Favor Imagination and Distortion of Sensory Experience," in *Evolution and Cognition*, Vol. 8, 1. (2002).

16. H. von Staden, "The Stoic Theory of Perception," Peter K. Machamer and Robert G. Turnbull ed., *Studies in Perception: Interrelations in the History of Philosophy and Science* (Ohio State University Press, 1978), 11.

but also to "memory, expectation, thought, reasoning, desires, deliberation, passion, speech and action."[17] Caston credits Aristotle with launching the subject of "φαντασια" as a philosophical mainstay. He argues that its central-ity in Aristotle's analysis arises from the problem of *error:* Just why and how the otherwise faithful report of the senses leads to faulty representations, judgments, recollections, and so on. It is by way of (the enlarged sense of) imagination that mental content is *about* something—that it is, in modern parlance, *intentional*—but it is also by way of imagination that the manner in which reality is represented can be distorted and misleading.

It is with some diffidence, then, that one ties the word "φαντασια" to a narrowly specific function or process, evolutionary or otherwise. For present purposes I would have it understood as a power or faculty *by which the prop-erties of events and things otherwise not present enter the field of consciousness.* This definition is neutral as to the actual "reality" of such contents, the degree of similarity between the representation and that which is represented, the temporality of the representation and or even whether what the content is "about" is strictly sensible. One surely can represent the personality or char-acter of another such that the other is, as it were, "seen" in a different light; an action once represented as cowardly is later represented as heroic under a different set of descriptions; a sudden discovery proceeds to render one's subsequent experiences as decidedly more optimistic.

Aristotle traces the etymology of the word to light itself, "As sight is the most highly developed sense, the name *Phantasia* has been formed from Phaos because it is not possible to see without light."[18] Quite literally, "φαντασια" brings to light what is otherwise inaccessible to the senses, or not present to the senses. In this respect it is clearly distinct from perception. Perception is of an actual and present object. This is not the case with remembering, dreaming, hallucinating, imagining. One can imagine what was once perceived, but the process or power by which the former is achieved is different from perception itself. It is also different from belief, opinion and knowledge. An entity devoid of sensation could not possess "φαντασια," but the exercise of the latter is independent of the former.

In the normal case, imagination is the means by which one might frame possibilities and strategies, one might "picture" alternative courses of action; one might revive portions of one's personal history and make use of lessons

17. Victor Caston, "Why Aristotle needs imagination," *Phronesis.*Vol. 41 (1996): 1–36.
18. Aristotle, *On the Soul,* 429a.

learned under different but comparable circumstances. Imagination now is liberating rather than controlling. It is part of the preparation to act, part of the planning of a course of action. One is no longer tied to the limits of the immediately present or to the narrow channels revealed by eye and ear. The domain of possibilities is enlarged and the stuff of deliberation can now be worked into a virtually limitless assortment of potential realities. In a word, "φαντασια" is a mixed blessing. It is fraught with error and rich with possibilities. It stands in kinship with representation. Both "μιμησις" and "φαντασια" enlarge the sphere of possibilities and provide grist for complex deliberative processes in those creatures having the power of deliberation.

Aristotle's use of "φαντασια" surfaces importantly in the *Rhetoric,* where he offers this poignant account:

> It is always the first sign of love, that besides enjoying someone's presence, we remember him when he is gone; and we love when we actually feel pain because he is there no longer... There is grief, indeed, at his loss, but pleasure in remembering him and as it were seeing him before us in his deeds and in his life.[19]

Note here again a parallel or complementarity between the imitative and the representation in maintaining contact with the past. The mental representations that collectively restore the missing loved one to a now living memory are themselves a species of imitation. Here, *mimesis* and *phantasia,* though both prone to error, are comparably rich in creative potential. Together they are modes of instruction, akin perhaps to the sort of map-making Tolman refers to in his cognitive theory of problem-solving.[20] It is in imagination that plots and possibilities can be rearranged at will, strategies considered in light of shifting conditions, alternative outcomes pictured depending on how the various possibilities are handled.

To consider "φαντασια" as imagination and, thus considered, as a mode of representation, is to return to Aristotle's foundationalist position on the process. The basic connection is between *sensation* and *imagination,* for the latter requires a content drawn from the realm of the sensible. Here Aristotle anticipates an important chapter in Kant's metaphysics where the role of imagination (*Einbildungskraft*) is essential to the synthesis of a manifold of sensations into a *this* or a *that.* As Kant says,

19. Aristotle, *Rhetoric* 1370b 20–27.
20. E. C. Tolman, "Cognitive maps in rats and man," *The Psychological Review* 55(4) (1948): 189–208.

Synthesis in general...is the mere result of the power of imagination, a blind but indispensable function of the soul, without which we should have no knowledge whatsoever, but of which we are scarcely ever conscious [A78].[21]

Kant locates in the function he calls "imagination" the power of drawing together certain elements in an otherwise disconnected riot of possible sensations, just those that constitute a knowable *something*. Imagination does not yield knowledge but nonetheless makes it possible. It is only when the synthesis of the manifold is then brought into the pure categories of the understanding that knowledge as such arises. The categories, however, must be applied to *something*, for it is only a *something* that stands as, for example, a unity, a reality, something subsisting, having actual existence. These are drawn from the Table of the Categories. They are drawn from the categorical framework that exhausts the a priori concepts setting boundary conditions on human knowledge. *Imagination* is the necessary preliminary stage, that power or function of the soul that synthesizes the flotsam of sensory possibilities into coherence.

Kant is not indifferent to the wider range over which the function of imagination operates. It is not merely a mode of picturing; it is also part of the process of invention. As he says:

If the imagination is not simply to be *visionary*, but is to be *inventive* under the strict surveillance of reason, there must always previously be something that is completely certain, and not invented...namely, the *possibility* of the object itself.   [A770/B798][22]

Where the necessary discipline is not imposed on reason, any number of utterly empty hypotheses might pass for understanding, for a "deeper" insight. The cautionary note sounded by Kant is that the very inventive power of the imagination—the power of synthesizing inventively—is an asset when tied to the possibility of an object of experience, but dangerous when totally "liberated" from such constraints. The dangerous form of liberation leads to what Kant refers to as errors of *subreption* (German: *Erschleichung*), a term borrowed from Roman and Canon Law. Kant often relies on legal procedure and legal terms in his metaphysical writings. "Subreption" appears at A643/B671 in his *Critique of Pure Reason*. He notes there that, "All errors of subreption are to be ascribed to a defect of judgment, never to understanding or to reason."[23] The term when found in legal contexts refers to the *vitium*

---

21. Immanuel Kant, *Critique of Pure Reason*, trans. Norman Kemp Smith (New York: Palgrave-Macmillan, 2003).
22. Ibid.   23. Kant, *Critique of Pure Reason*.

reptionis, generally translated as "the crime of fraud" or an offense arising from a gross misrepresentation of the facts. As Kant would have the term understood, it is a form of delusion based on the misuse or illicit use of judgment. The proper deployment of the various perceptual and cognitive powers results in the correct subsumption of perceptual content within the framework of the pure categories of the understanding. Reason, properly disciplined, draws permissible inferences from the resulting concepts of the understanding. The outcome is *knowledge*. When rightly employed, the perceptual and cognitive powers match up in the right way with the real world and ground the knowledge-claims of the developed sciences.

However, there is a strong tendency to stretch these processes beyond the normal boundaries and seek what Kant refers to as "transcendental ideas" that go beyond the realm of actual or possible experience. The result is to regard the *transcendent* as if it were real; it is to defraud oneself, to perpetrate a subreption.[24] Therein lies the danger. But therein also lie possibilities of great value. Correctly managed, these transcendental ideas:

> ...have an excellent and, indeed, indispensably necessary regulative employment; namely that of directing the understanding toward a certain goal... (giving) the concepts of the understanding...the greatest unity combined with the greatest extension.[25]

Reason is controlled by the canons of logic. The understanding makes use of concepts the source of whose content is empirical. Here, then, are the means by which knowledge is acquired and also limited. But then think of a mirror, which is the example Kant offers. Looking into it, there is the vivid appearance of what is behind the observer, and at a great distance. Now one is aware not merely of what lies before one, but of an entire volume of things and events. All of this is but reflections from a glassy surface but it leads to an apprehension of a greater unity, a greater connectedness among things. Kant uses this imagery to illustrate what he takes to be a basic presupposition of reason; namely, that what is unified within its own limited field is expressive of a wider and total unity, connected by universal laws. It is this presupposition that we *bring to* our examination of nature, not one *derived from* that examination.[26]

24. Ibid.   25. Kant, *Critique of Pure Reason* A644-645/B672-673.
26. The argument for this is developed in his *Critique of Judgment,* sec. V.: "The Principle of the Formal Purposiveness of Nature Is a Transcendental Principle of Judgement." The edition used here is I. Kant, *Critique of the Power of Judgment,* trans. Paul Guyer and Eric Matthews (Cambridge: Cambridge University Press, 2001).

In the third of his great works, the *Critique of Judgment*, Kant extends his analysis, distinguishing between and among the *determinate, reflective* and *teleological* forms of judgment. It is sufficient here to point to his recognition of the need for some foundational or a priori belief or disposition on which the very project of investigating nature would seem to depend. The pure and disciplined rational faculty, combined with concepts firmly tied to possible experience, is too bounded. The imagination moves beyond this. It is served not merely by determinate judgments but by reflective modes of judgment that transcend the level of experience. It is served further by teleological judgments that presuppose *purpose* behind the orderly and lawful productions of nature. The mental life in which these powers are exercised is one in which (as Kant puts it) there is a *free play* of concepts, "lawlessly lawful," and conducive to real pleasure. Here is where art begins and the strictures of metaphysics are left if not in limbo then in reserve. It is here, too, that *theism* supplies a *terminus ad quem* as human reason and imagination construct an ever more unified and intelligible account of reality and the seeming lawfulness and design found within it.

Aristotle and Kant converge, if only circuitously, on this point. A certain liberty—a "poetic license"—is afforded by way of the imagination. This freedom can be abused. The strictures set down by Aristotle as regards plot, character, temporal span and the rest seek to reduce to a system of sorts just what renders the productions of the dramatist and epic poet successful. Comparable principles are clearly at work in art and architecture. The design of a building and its location within a wider context are similar to a plot, for there are some arrangements that would be obviously defective. Aristotle speaks also of those who overdraw characters, inflating their virtues and exaggerating their limitations. If art is imitative, there must be a reality serving as the standard against which one might assess the success of the artistic rendering.

At the same time, there must be *art* in the art. Life's rapid, complex and unrepeatable flow of events affords little opportunity for reflection, little opportunity for a trial-and-error reconfiguration of the events and the conduct of the participants in those events. Moreover, without the benefit of seeing them by way of another and competing perspective, the witness to reality brings a merely personal and perhaps utterly limited perspective to bear on just these events. In the absence of the fully developed plot—the *teleological framework*—there is little more than a congeries of events with no lesson taught and with a set of inferential bridges to nowhere.

The power of rhetoric is also forged from "μιμησισ" and "φαντασια," from imitation and imagination. Aristotle leaves no doubt about this when he declares, "The whole business of rhetoric being concerned with appearances..."[27] He is impatient with the fact, noting that rhetorical style and flare are really unworthy subjects. After all, the success of an address should depend on the facts and on a reasonable weighing of them. The art of rhetoric, designed to "charm" the listener, is able to distract attention from what really matters. Note, he says, that, "Nobody uses fine language when teaching geometry."[28] But style does matter and I submit it matters as *art*. The rhetorical performance, unlike lessons in Euclid, is designed to create images and feelings, opinions and attitudes, otherwise aroused by the actual affairs of life. The audience is moved now to regard a person or event or prospect in a new light revealing what otherwise has been neglected by those less discerning or less knowledgeable than the speaker; perhaps by those caught in the thrall of mere facts! Note how loose and questionable are rigidly *causal* links here. It is the possibility of the imagination playing freely with the facts, the numerous ways in which various combinations of facts give rise to multiple and even competing representations, that one is able to craft and test imagined plots and purposes. That one virtually universally reached possibility presumes to shed light on the Mind of God is surely not to be dismissed on the simplistic complaint that evolutionary theory doesn't credibly account for it. So what!

Theism and scientism

There is no paucity of attempts to objectify beauty and to absorb art into the all-embracing framework of the "natural," this now (oddly) understood as the "scientific." One of the earliest attempts is attributed to Pythagoras and his "Golden Section." Is it the case that the most aesthetically perfect ratio of the length to the width of a rectangle is given by φ, the symbol for the number 1.6180339887? What is this all about?

27. Aristotle, *Rhetoric* 1404a 1–2.   28. Ibid, 1404a 10–12.

1. Take a line of length "A."

2. Mark a segment of that line separating it into segment "B" and segment "C."

3. The relation [A: B:: B: C] is satisfied only when A is φ-greater than B, and B is φ-greater than C.

Pythagoras is also credited with extending φ to the human body where each major anatomical part stands in this specific proportion to others. Vitruvius in ancient times and Leonardo in the fifteenth century were both wed to such notions, providing that famous Canon of Proportion illustrated by "Vitruvian Man." Phidias is said to have designed the Parthenon in accordance with the Golden Section. And then there are the rings of Saturn: If one measures the rings, one discovers that the breaks in the rings seem to reflect the same Golden Section. Examples abound.

Surely the Pythagorean musical scale of harmonies impressed the ancients not merely owing to the mathematical symmetry of the scale but because that very symmetry was reflected in the *experience* of harmony when the music conformed to the mathematics. The well instructed Pythagorean would reject as implausible the claim that there is a merely coincidental relationship between the mathematics of harmony and the nearly universal experience of it by the normal human percipient. The Pythagoreans extended this understanding to Cosmology and the orbital behavior of celestial bodies. Moved by these very considerations, Kepler defended the concept of a "music of the spheres" in his *Harmonice Mundi* which presents and develops his third law of planetary motion: "The square of the period of a planet's orbit is proportional to the cube of its semi major axis."[29] The work itself is actually a sustained argument to the effect that God has fashioned the creation according to strict mathematical principles and that all of creation, properly considered, will reveal a mathematical foundation. Thus, the creation has, as it were, been scored in a *musica universalis.*

Is there, indeed, some fixed standard with which to grade the degree of aesthetic perfection achieved by works of art and architecture? To be told that a building fails as architecture because the ratio of width and height departs from φ would strike today's architects as bizarre. Just as bizarre by

---

29. His *Harmonice Mundi* is the work in which his Third Law is developed. A fine study of Kepler's thinking is Bruce Stephenson, *The Music of the Heavens* (Princeton: Princeton University Press, 1994).

contemporary standards was the "sinfulness" of the diminished seventh chord in early sacred music, the departure from the accepted laws of harmony betokening a satanic influence. Centuries later the same chord would be featured in Bach's *St Matthew Passion*, the devil now nowhere in sight. Reflecting on the issue in one of the early modern treatises on aesthetics, Edmund Burke concluded:

> On the whole; if such parts in human bodies as are found proportioned, were likewise constantly found beautiful, as they certainly are not; or if they were so situated, as that a pleasure might flow from the comparison, which they seldom are; or if any assignable proportions were found, either in plants or animals, which were always attended with beauty, which never was the case; or if, where parts were well adapted to their purposes, they were constantly beautiful, and when no use appeared, there was no beauty, which is contrary to all experience; we might conclude, that beauty consisted in proportion or utility. But since, in all respects, the case is quite otherwise; we may be satisfied that beauty does not depend on these, let it owe its origin to what else it will.[30]

For better and for worse, art presents itself to the world and it is the world's judgment that, at a given time, is decisive. It is, of course, not the last word, for a later age may find a measure of genius in Schubert that the age of Mozart seemed to have missed. Bach's music, it should be recalled, was largely ignored for decades after his death, only to be later revived and revered.

Alas, the debate is likely to continue on the question of whether the chef's talents or the customer's palate serves as the measure of the cuisine or, as Protagoras insisted, whether man is the measure of all things. On this point, Burke was content with what he himself thought of as a "mechanical" principle at the bottom of the experience of beauty:

> Since it is no creature of our reason, since it strikes us without any reference to use, and even where no use at all can be discerned, since the order and method of nature is generally very different from our measures and proportions, we must conclude that beauty is, for the greater part, some quality in bodies acting mechanically upon the human mind by the intervention of the senses.[31]

Matters are surely more complicated than this. To declare that bodies act mechanically on minds is to "solve" the mind-body problem as only an Enlightenment *savant* would dare to do. A much poorer writer but better philosopher, Hegel, found something essential to be missing in the "imita-

---

30. Burke, *A Philosophical Inquiry* Part III, sec. 8.
31. Burke, *A Philosophical Inquiry* Part III, sec. 12.

tive-representational" theory of art. In a study of Hegel's philosophy on this subject, William Desmond offers this instructive summary:

> We can reconstruct the rationale of (Hegel's) rejection of imitation in the following terms. Art as imitation seems to possess what truth it does, not necessarily in virtue of anything in itself as image, but in virtue of something external to it. Hence its value does not reside in the image as such, but depends on an external relation binding image and original. This dependency of imitation seems to make art derivative and of secondary importance compared to the original it imitates.[32]

In his *Lectures on Aesthetics*, Hegel concludes that art thus understood rises no higher than "a parody of life, instead of a genuine vitality." Then, in Part III of the work, he presents his conception of the *Romantic* as distinct from the classical conception of art.[33] Art is seen as originating in a struggle of the imagination to escape the drudgery of imitating nature and to rise to the level of *spirituality*. If it is to *about* something, it must be about that which is not otherwise given to the senses or readily inferred from the data of experience. As Hegel understands it, art was first liberated in the classical age from mere service in providing "external forms for mere natural significations..." The classical age went beyond this, though still unable to separate its object from those natural phenomena yielded by the corporeal and sensuous. Still, the classical achievement of Hellenic art was the ability to present the outer appearances in such an idealized way as to convey at least an intimation of the spiritual. "It is thus that Classic Art constituted the absolutely perfect representation of the ideal, the final completion of the realm of Beauty."[34]

In this, however, the Absolute Idea remains elusive, for beauty is still tied to the sensuous, to an object, to what is finally conditioned by the vagaries of perception. It is only when Beauty itself abandons these attachments, turns in on itself in an act of self-consciousness, that art rises fully to that plane of spirituality otherwise accessible only by way of philosophy and religion. This is the *via reggia* that carries one up toward the Absolute and away from the mundane. The movement is toward the divine: In its classical form, art's mission is, "to bring before perception the spiritual in sensuous form."[35] Art

---

32. William Desmond, *Art and the Absolute: A Study of Hegel's Aesthetics* (Albany: State University of New York Press, 1986), 6.
33. G. W. F. Hegel, *Introductory Lectures on Aesthetics,* trans. Bernard Bosanquet, ed. Michael Lockwood, (London: Penguin Books, 2004). The passage referring to a parody of life is in Part II, sec. LXI at 66.
34. Ibid.   35. Hegel, *Lectures on Aesthetics* chap. 5, part 2.

in this form, constrained by considerations of proportion, symmetry, and abstract mathematical precepts, reconciles the spiritual and the sensuous, anchoring both to the demands and expectations of the rational mind.

"As an escape from such a condition, the romantic form of art in its turn dissolves the inseparable unity of the classical phase," replacing the Greek faith in gods with, "what Christianity declares to be true of God as Spirit."[36]

After testing various theories of art and beauty, Hegel considered the general thesis that nature, as a work of God, must always take aesthetic preference over art, as a merely and ever imperfect human undertaking. Hegel reached the very opposite conclusion, insisting:

> ...that God is more honoured by what mind does or makes than by the pro-
> ductions or formations of nature. For not only is there a divinity in man, but
> in him it is operative under the form that is appropriate to the essence of God,
> in a mode quite other and higher than in nature. God is a Spirit, and it is only
> in man that the medium through which the divine element passes has the
> form of conscious spirit, that actively realizes itself.[37]

God's externalized existence is neither natural nor sensuous. It is elevated to a supersensuous personality, real in a way that the products of mere imagination can never be. In that characteristically "Hegelian" way, Hegel reminds his audience that once man recognized himself as an animal he ceased to be an animal; that through self-consciousness a new reality arises, impelling activity that is differently grounded and designed to achieve still higher degrees of self-consciousness. Art, conscious of its authentic mission, no longer squanders energy on imitations, no longer seeks to represent the sensuously accessible features of nature and physical reality. Rather, it comprehends what is universal and abiding—what is *true*—and manifests it through that which is particular. The singular logical argument illustrates what is universally valid. The individuated and particular life that was Jesus exemplifies the universal and deathless Christ. The work of art, when expressing the true nature and mission of art, particularizes a universal truth by absorbing its mere particularity into the realm of Spirit, the realm of the Absolute. By different paths, philosophy, religion, and art permit humanity to enter into an intimate relationship with the Absolute and direct contact, if only fleetingly, with the true nature of humanity itself. Thus does art nur-

---

36. Hegel, *Lectures on Aesthetics* CVII–Y.
37. Hegel, *Lectures on Aesthetics* XLVIII–C.

ture self-consciousness and in that way does it ground those truths to which merely empirical modes of inquiry and discovery must always be blind.

Science and culture

In the nineteenth century, a debate in print featured two of the most cele-brated essayists of the Victorian era: Thomas Henry Huxley and Matthew Arnold. Huxley had been invited to give the Founder's address at the newly established Mason College, supported by a substantial gift from Josiah Mason. The terms of Mr. Mason's gift included the stipulation that "the humanities not be taught." This was to be a school featuring practical subjects. Huxley's address, published as "Science and Culture"[38] begins with a broadside against those "... classical scholars, in their capacity of Levites in charge of the ark of culture and monopolists of liberal education" who would excommunicate from the House of Intellect those unschooled in Latin and Greek. His target is soon identified: Matthew Arnold, England's "chief apostle of culture;" the Arnold for whom culture just is "the best that has been thought and said in the world."[39]

Arnold replied to Huxley's criticism in his 1882 essay, "Literature and Science."[40] After repeating the humanizing influences of classical study (which, alas, includes far more than the grammar and vocabulary of a pair of dead languages!), Arnold turns to humanity as understood scientifically in the pages of Darwin's *Descent of Man*. Taking one of the very sober con-clusions of that work, Arnold writes:

> And so we at last find, it seems, we find flowing in favour of the humanities the natural and necessary stream of things, which seemed against them when we started. The 'hairy quadruped furnished with a tail and pointed ears, prob-ably arboreal in his habits,' this good fellow carried hidden in his nature, appar-ently, something destined to develop into a necessity for humane letters. Nay, more; we seem finally to be even led to the further conclusion that our hairy ancestor carried in his nature, also, a necessity for Greek.

This "necessity for Greek" is, of course, code for "necessity for culture," and Arnold's pitting this inclination against the creature arising from evolution

---

38. Huxley, "Science and Culture," (1880) http://www.chass.utoronto.ca/~ian/huxley1.htm.
39. This is the definition given and developed in Arnold's *Culture and Anarchy* (Cambridge: Cambridge University Press, 1993).
40. This, too, is available on the internet at http://www.chass.utoronto.ca/~ian/arnold.htm.

is intended to highlight the limitations of naturalistic explanation. What comes to mind is the overworked example of the extraterrestrial being called upon to visit earth briefly, ascertain the real nature of human nature, thereupon returning with an accurate and informing account. The entirely naturalistic account that features hairy quadrupeds with their arboreal habitats is not just an incomplete account, but a flagrantly misleading account. Nothing in the original potions of DNA and the later clumps of protein tells any part of the story worth knowing, just in case one wishes to know what has impelled human progress, surfaced as an enduring human value, summoned the energies and loyalties and passions of the millions.

"Culture" is the useful word for the repository of the things possessing such powers; the word that stands, in Arnold's words, for the best that humanity has thought and done. Arnold is ready and eager to include the extraordinary record of science within this gallery of defining aspirations and achievements. Even failed attempts to unearth the laws and principles of the natural world stand as cultural achievements and thus as part of the overall record that identifies the distinctly human in human nature. Art, needless to say, is even more widely spread, more deeply cherished in human communities. In the concluding pages of Alfred Russell Wallace's incisive and authoritative defense of evolutionary theory, he drew attention to the moral, mathematical, and aesthetic achievements of the human race.[41] In the matter of art, he concluded that,

> ...developments of the artistic faculty, whether manifested in sculpture, paint-ing, or architecture, are evidently outgrowths of the human intellect which have no immediate influence on the survival of individuals or of tribes, or on the success of nations in their struggles for supremacy or for existence.

To be sure, it is always possible to cut and paste the assumptions of any general theory in such a way as to make some contact with the phenomena we seek to explain. Actually, one of the worrisome features of so-called "evolutionary" accounts is that there seems to be no identifiable set of observations that would stand as convincing refutations. Thus, the selfless actions of saints and heroes are "shown" to be consistent with the overall adaptive potential of the species; the arts enhance cooperative behavior and bonding; religious faith fills otherwise dangerous gaps in our powers of prediction and explanation; imagination allows us to come to terms with death. Much of this is at least interesting; some of it is patent rubbish. But the saint and the hero offer a

41. Alfred Russell Wallace, *Darwinism* (1889). http://www.gutenberg.org/etext/14558.

different account in which the adaptive potential of a species is never considered. And just what is it about paintings and music and poetry that actually does draw persons together and strengthen the sense of kinship?

It is a deep and searching metaphysical question as to whether something "unnatural" somehow *emerges* from what is a purely natural substrate, or whether, in fact, anything real is also significantly "unnatural." I have given stress to the differences between the current age of highly developed science and the classical age of Plato and Aristotle in the matter of "nature." For Plato, the realm of the "natural"—at least as it would be understood in scientific terms—is but a collection of shifting and uncertain relations, ephemeral and largely distracting. The value of the "natural" is that the prepared mind (soul) might find in it useful clues to the eternal, the absolute, the true. As noted, the worry about art is that in its imitative function it both distorts reality and draws attention away from what is true.

For Aristotle, though in this I would hesitate to presume to be a spokesman, nature is *what there is essentially*. Humanity is understood to be enlarged by culture and tutored by the *polis*. It is a set of potentialities needing conditions of actualization. There is genuine *emergence* in the process, but not in the sense of the unnatural arising from the natural. There is nothing unnatural about an oak tree, given its origin in an acorn. There is nothing unnatural about greatness appearing on the field of battle where it may have remained dormant and unknown in times of peace.

Book *Lamda* of the *Metaphysics* features Aristotle's "Unmoved mover" in whose absence there could be neither the heavens nor the natural world. This is the god of the *Metaphysics* whose life is one of joyful and creative contemplation. The eternal life of the divine is of a nature that man might approximate for a very brief time as the mind occupies itself with what is best and highest. Thought becomes the same as its object in the sense of its very momentary life being that very object of thought. The essence of cognitive life is receptivity—the power of receiving what are the objects of thought. But the completion of the act is not merely a receptivity but the possession of the object itself.

> Therefore the possession rather than the receptivity is the divine element which thought seems to contain, and the act of contemplation is what is most pleasant and best. If, then, God is always in that good state in which we sometimes are, this compels our wonder; and if in a better state, this compels it yet more. And God is in a better state.[42]

42. Aristotle, *Metaphysics*, 1072b 20–30.

EIGHT

Naturalism Lost: Nature Regained

Conor Cunningham

To us, men of the West, a very strange thing happened at the turn of this century; without noticing it, we lost science, or at least the thing that had been called by that name for the last four centuries. What we now have in place of it is something different, radically different, and we don't know what it is.

Simone Weil[1]

In this chapter we introduce, examine, and critique the philosophical idea of naturalism and materialism, doing so with special reference as to how they relate to the operation of science, and what consequences it has for our understanding of nature and of life. One of the conclusions reached is that ontological naturalism is a contrived stance that rests on an impoverished understanding of science, one that is underwritten by an atrophied imagination, which leaves us bereft of nature.[2]

Naturalism at first blush

Generally speaking, there are two main types of naturalism: methodological and ontological. The former is the approach that science must take when it engages with the universe insofar as it will fail to make any progress unless

---

1. Simone Weil, *On Science, Necessity and the Love of God*, trans. Richard Rees (Oxford: Oxford University Press, 1968), 3.
2. For an exhaustive treatment of many of the issues raised here, see Conor Cunningham, *Darwin's Pious Idea* (Grand Rapids, MI: Wm. B. Eerdmans, 2010), esp. chap. 6.

it brackets the divine. The latter holds that bracketing the divine is not merely methodologically necessary but constitutive of reality as such. A certain methodological naturalism is commonsensical. It would not be very helpful when making a cup of tea if, when the kettle boiled, we became overly entranced by the mystical wonder of the emission of steam, thinking it was the communication of the spirits of our ancestors. Science must preclude this, and thus it seeks to explain phenomena in purely natural terms. This is eminently sensible—we may expect the farmer to pray to his maker, asking for a good harvest, but we don't then expect the farmer to put his feet up and leave God to get on with plowing the fields. Ontological naturalism goes further. While methodological naturalism issues no philosophical or metaphysical opinion of what exists, ontological naturalism suffers no such shyness. It tells us not only that science must stick to what we take to be natural but that the natural is all there is, indeed all there ever could be. Moreover, ontological naturalism deposes philosophy's ancient position as the final arbiter of our understanding of existence to which even science is subjected (what is called First Philosophy). Instead, philosophy now becomes the handmaiden of science, at the most, or science's lackey boy, at the least. Thus for Wilfred Sellars, "Science is the measure of all things."[3] This is what is commonly known as *scientism*, the perspective of which Richard Lewontin captures in one pithy sentence: "Science is the only begetter of truth."[4] Leaving aside the fact that this proposition is extra-scientifc—that is, it is a philosophical thesis and not a scientific one at all—we might be inclined to inquire as to why he asserts something so question-begging? Lewontin gives us an answer of sorts: "We take the side of science in spite of the patent absurdity of some of its contructs, in spite of its failures to fulfill many of its extravagant promises...in spite of the tolerance of the scientific community for unsubstantiated just-so stories, because we have a prior committment to materialism...Moreover that materialism is absolute, for we cannot allow a Divine foot in the door."[5]

There is a saying that offers sage advice: the theology that marries the science of today will be the widow of tomorrow. It is good and constructive

---

3. See "Empiricism and the Philosophy of Mind," reprinted in *Wilfred Sellars, Science, Perception and Reality* (London: Routledge, Keegan & Paul, 1963), 173.

4. Richard C. Lewontin, "Billions and Billions of Demons," review of Carl Sagan, *The Demon-Haunted World: Science as a Candle in the Dark*, in *New York Review of Books* 44, no. 1 (1997): 28–32.

5. Lewontin, "Billions and Billions of Demons," 31.

for theology to engage with science but it cannot act as its "foundation." But this also applies to atheism: the atheism that marries the science of today will be the widow of tomorrow. As the philosopher of science Bas van Fraassen notes: "All our factual beliefs are to be given over as hostages to fortune, to the fortune of future empirical evidence."[6]

When it comes to human nature and culture, scientism and ontological naturalism would contend that we are guilty of what John Ruskin called the "pathetic fallacy." We commit this fallacy when we attribute emotions to what quite obviously cannot have emotion—as in "the wind cried" or "the trees wept." We keep insisting that we have such emotions. We keep attributing terms such as life, death, existence, desire, free will, pain, and so on, to ourselves. But for ontological naturalism—or better, restrictive naturalism—this simply cannot be the case because the very entities to which we ascribe such terms do not exist. We are left in a world that consists solely in the physical or the material. Consequently, what we see before our eyes is merely the agitation of matter; now thus, now so.[7] That remains the case whether such agitation is that of murder, rape, cancer, war, famine, love or joy, birth or death. Moreover, we have to ask if "matter" is all there is. How do we even discern real difference if all events and objects—all change—seem to be wholly arbitrary? To account for real difference, surely we must appeal to something other than matter—yet any such appeal is prohibited in what amounts to a monistic philosophy (the notion that existence is composed of only one type of substance, which we call "matter").[8] As John Peterson puts it, "If matter is the ultimate substrate and is identified with some actual thing, then all differences within matter must come from something besides matter."[9] Consequently, the materialist must admit that his description is metaphysical; it tacitly invokes something that transcends what is basic at the level of immanence or the merely physical. The only other option is to deny all change, just as they must, it seems, deny objects themselves. As Peter van Inwagen writes, "One of the tasks that confronts the materialist is this: they have to find a home for the referents of the terms

6. Bas C. van Fraassen, *The Empirical Stance* (New Haven, CT: Yale University Press, 2002), 63.
7. On the idea of restrictive naturalism, see Barry Stroud, "The Charm of Naturalism," in *Naturalism in Question*, ed. Mario De Caro and David Macarthur (Cambridge, MA: Harvard University Press, 2004), 21–35.
8. Materialism is monistic, yes, but it is a progeny of dualism; see below.
9. John Peterson, "The Dilemma of Materialism," in *International Philosophical Quarterly* 39, no. 156 (December 1999): 429–37.

of ordinary speech within a world that is entirely material—or else deny the existence of those referents altogether."[10] Again: "there is no such thing as a thing."[11] And this includes persons, for as David Chalmers says, "you can't have your materialist cake and eat your consciousness too."[12] But of course, Hegel had already pointed to the vacuous nature of materialism, arguing that the word "matter" remains an ideal unless you pick out something material and that something cannot be just mere matter. But materialism would appear to preclude identity. This becomes clearer when we realize that ontological naturalism cannot, on its own terms, identify what are called persistence conditions for an object—that which an object requires to be what it is (see below).[13] It is little wonder, then, that Michel Henry tells us "there is no person in science."[14] And Henry appears to be correct, for as Thomas Metzinger informs us, "no such things as selves exist in the world: Nobody ever was or had a self."[15] We are inclined to say, "speak for yourself!" But of course, that's the very problem—we can't. Not only is there no such thing as a person, there is no such thing as life.[16]

Those that celebrate scientism and ontological (restrictive) naturalism do so because what they have set out to achieve is the banishment of the divine, no matter what the cost. These fundamentalist atheists will bring the whole house down so as to leave no room for God. They are, in short, willing to cut off their faces to spite their noses—willing to leave us all faceless. Prisons become a cultural artifact, and an eccentric, unjustified one at that. We are now beyond good and evil, as Nietzsche foresaw. If this is true, then naturalism, rather than occupying the high ground of the enlightened, is in truth more damaging than all the wars, diseases, famines, disasters and crimes put together because it is the liquidation of existence itself. It is not heaven that is under threat but earth, the common sense world, the world of nature and of the natural. This is the abolition of the human—not

10. Peter van Inwagen, *Ontology, Identity, and Modality: Essays in Metaphysics* (Cambridge: Cambridge University Press, 2001), 160.

11. G. K. Chesterton, *Orthodoxy* (London: Fontana, 1961), 59.

12. David J. Chalmers, *The Conscious Mind* (Oxford: Oxford University Press, 1996), 168.

13. See Michael C. Rea, *World Without Design: The Ontological Consequences of Naturalism* (Oxford: Clarendon Press, 2002).

14. Michel Henry, *I am The Truth: Toward a Philosophy of Christianity*, trans. Susan Emanuel (Stanford, CA: Stanford University Press, 2003), 262.

15. Thomas Metzinger, *Being No One: The Self-Model Theory of Subjectivity* (Cambridge, MA: MIT Press, 2003), 1.

16. See François Jacob, *The Logic of Life: A History of Heredity*, trans. Betty Spillman (New York: Pantheon, 1973), 299.

of God.[17] On this point Simone Weil makes a crucial observation, quoting first from Adolph Hitler's *Mein Kampf*, which contends that in the natural world "force reigns everywhere and supreme over weakness which it either compels to serve it docilely or else crushes out of existence." According to Weil, "these lines [from *Mein Kampf*] express in faultless fashion the only conclusion that can reasonably be drawn from the conception of the world contained in our science.... Who can reproach [Hitler] for having put into practice what he thought he recognized to be the truth? Those who, having in themselves the foundations of the same belief, haven't embraced it consciously and haven't translated it into acts, have only escaped being criminals thanks to want of a certain sort of courage which he possesses."[18] We must, of course, remember that naturalism recognizes science only. The point is that science should not seek to operate on its own, for if it does then Hitler's position and approach does indeed become a live option. However, such egregious acts or thoughts do not define science; in other words, science does not belong to naturalism, metaphysically speaking. Indeed, in a certain sense it belongs to religion.

Science no more: science once again

Mythologized science is today the opium for the metaphysical enervation of the masses.

Christoph Yannaras[19]

Much as religious fundamentalism presents only an idealized caricature of the history of its own beliefs, so does scientism present the history of science as an unswerving march toward Truth.

B. Allan Wallace[20]

Scientism, and indeed restrictive naturalism, is a massive intellectual pathology being peddled in the West. Van Fraassen calls it the genuflection toward science.[21] It is very evident in the work of the new atheists wherein they

17. See C. S. Lewis, *The Abolition of Man* (New York: Harper and Collins, 1974).
18. Simone Weil, *The Need for Roots*, trans. Arthur Wills (London: Routledge & Keegan Paul, 1952), 129–30.
19. Christos Yannaras, *Elements of Faith: An Introduction to Orthodox Theology* (Edinburgh: T & T Clark, 1988), 38.
20. Wallace, *The Taboo of Subjectivity*, (New York: Oxford University Press, 2000), 38.
21. Van Fraassen, *The Empirical Stance*, 11.

introduce to the public a ridiculous interpretation of science, elevating it to the status of First Philosophy. Scientism seeks to assert a division between hard scientific facts and woolly folk tales most apparent in religions. The reading public are asked to "grow up" and leave childish things (the folk tales of religion) behind, to instead embrace the adult world revealed by the natural sciences with their strong principle of verification—if you can't spray it, it don't exist.[22] The gravity of this pathology can be brought to our attention by borrowing some words from Richard Dawkins, but replacing one of them. "It is fashionable to wax apocalyptic about the threat to humanity posed by the AIDS virus, 'mad cow' disease, and many others, but I think the case can be made that scientism is one of the world's greatest evils, comparable to the smallpox virus but harder to eradicate. Scientism, being a belief that isn't based on evidence, is the principle vice of any militant atheism."[23] We substituted the word "scientism" for "religion." Such scientism appears to have been accommodated by an alteration in our intellectual consciousness. This change is duly noted by Cardinal Joseph Ratzinger: "The separation of physics from metaphysics achieved by Christian thinking is being steadily cancelled. Everything is to become 'physics' again."[24] This unfortunate turn, to say the least, can be seen in the words attributed to Ernest Rutherford: "There is only physics, all else is stamp collecting." One major consequence of this is that science as a discipline becomes less rational, more reductive, and so more nihilistic, undermining itself in the process. For as Gergorios argues, "Divorced from love and wisdom, science/technology becomes an enemy of humanity."[25] More than that, it becomes the root of all evil, for what greater evil can there be than the denial of evil, just as it becomes the denial of people. When society gives people or institutions special privilege, there is generally a proportionate increase in the level of responsibility. This needs to be the case with science, for when it is left to its own devices—or becomes devoid of any constitutive relation to other disciplines and other modes of discourse—then science becomes contorted. It is then transformed into an ideology that we have referred to as scientism. Indeed, there is something

---

22. This we believe is to paraphrase Ian Hacking.
23. Quoted in Alister McGrath, *Dawkins' God: Genes, Memes, and the Meaning of Life* (Oxford: Blackwell Publishing, 2005), 84.
24. Joseph Cardinal Ratzinger, *Truth and Tolerance: Christian Belief and World Religions* (San Francisco, CA: Ignatius Press, 2004), 178.
25. Paulos Mar Gergorios, *Science for Sane Societies* (New York: Paragon House, 1987), 75.

very particular, even special, about science's methodology. Because of that uniqueness, and the unique dangers that go with it, precautions must be appropriate. What is that special status? Quite simply, science is allocated a mandate to explore, examine and analyze the world in a wholly objective fashion. It is allowed to look at the world as if it were dead. As Bulgakov says, "Science deliberately commits a murder of the world and of nature, it studies nature's corpse."[26] This may sound frightening, but it is not necessarily so. Take the surgeon who renders a patient unconscious as if they were dead or bereft of mind, but does so only to perform a life-saving procedure. One would be more than perturbed if, when the patient regained consciousness, the surgeon then only treated them as if they were alive, something which the restrictive naturalist does. Put another way, science becomes dangerous when the unreality (that is, the abstractness) of its methods is mistaken for reality. If the as-if-dead methodology becomes an ontology, in other words, the as if is forgotten. When this happens, science has forgotten itself. It has forgotten that it is scientists as humans who make science, and not the other way around. To quote van Fraassen, "A theory can at best replace real life by a phantasm, even if it is of a particularly useful and survival-adaptive sort."[27] So even if a theory appears to be as real as soil, so to speak—an impression arising from its utility and applicability—we must not forget that its reality is borrowed and that, as with all things borrowed, it will at some point have to be given back. This stands for all scientific theories.

Take the example of matter: surely physics can tell us what it is. But no, for as McGinn—among many others—points out, "physics does not tell us the intrinsic nature of matter, only its operationally definable aspects."[28] (See below). Any such methodological forgetting of life is fine and very necessary. But science must not abuse the very generosity of its own possibility by mistaking itself for ontology. In other words, it must not be removed from its home, which is the subject. Yes, it may look out its front door and analyze what lies before it, but it must also always remember the home that lies behind it, its own soil. After all, do not all scientists return home at the end of the day? Science is practiced at the cost of ignoring its very possibility, and it is only when the human situation interrupts the

26. Sergei Bulgakov, *Philosophy of Economy: The World as Household*, trans. Catherine Evtuhov (New Haven, CT: Yale University Press, 2000), 183.
27. Van Fraassen, *The Empirical Stance*, 178.
28. Colin McGinn, "Hard Questions," in Galen Strawson, et. al., *Consciousness and Its Place in Nature: Does Physicalism Entail Panpsychism?*, Anthony Freeman, ed. (Exeter: Imprint Academic, 2006), 90.

well-greased rails of all such movement that what is actually occurring is brought back into focus. One thinks of certain Germans during the reign of the Nazis—the mechanic, say, who mended vans, concentrating (as if looking down a microscope) at the task in hand, never thinking to look up and see the wider picture. His labors were in collaboration with the Nazi project, enabling the continued transportation of the Jews to their death. It is little wonder that the death camps were named concentration camps. According to van Fraassen, if we appeal only to the scientific worldview, as if it were the final account of reality, then there is no place for ourselves, not to mention those who practice science itself.[29] Moreover, as Charles Taylor writes, "To hold that there are no assumptions in a scientist's work which aren't already based on evidence is surely a reflection of a blind faith, one that can't even feel the occasional tremor of doubt."[30] All science is grounded in forms of faith, some good, and some bad. Good faith is faith in the very possibility of science, one that is based on a belief in the efficacy of reason and the pre-scientific life (Lieb) of the scientist (the hand that wields Ockham's razor, so to speak). Bad faith involves what Eagleton refers to as science's "high priests, sacred cows, revered scriptures, ideological exclusions, and rituals for suppressing dissent," ontological naturalism, presumed atheism, reductive materialism, scientism, universal Darwinism, and instrumentalism are all manifestations of these.

To take a further example, someone like Dennett will argue that religion is natural and, for that reason, cannot be thought of as true, or veridical. But as Hart points out, "Dennett's amazing discovery that the 'natural desire for God' is in fact a desire for God that is natural, it amounts to a revolution not of thought, but only of syntax."[31] This is a fideism of incredible proportions. As Polanyi points out, "Men go on talking the language of positivism, pragmatism, and naturalism for many years, yet continue to respect the principles of truth and morality which their vocabulary anxiously ignores."[32] We can achieve this double bookkeeping only by a sort of schizophrenic suspension of logic. Against this, as Polanyi argues that "the coherence of

29. See van Fraassen, *The Empirical Stance*, 189.
30. Charles Taylor, *A Secular Age* (Cambridge, MA: Belknap Press of Harvard University Press, 2007), 835.
31. David Bentley Hart, *Atheist Delusions: The Christian Revolution and Its Fashionable Enemies* (New Haven, CT: Yale University Press, 2009), 8.
32. Michael Polanyi, *Personal Knowledge: Towards a Post-critical Philosophy* (Chicago: University of Chicago Press, 1974), 233.

science must be regarded as an expression of the common rootedness of scientists in the same spiritual reality."[33] If the fashionable, deluded secular aficionados would dismiss any such corporate rootedness, then they need only take note (as they always do in their everyday lives) of the phenomenon of their own subjectivity, for there lies the common source of all intelligence and rationality, not to mention faith. There is, therefore, a connection between science, faith, and society.[34] Polanyi gives the example of a type of watch, recently invented by some man. If the inventor submits his application for a patent but his application contains only a physical-chemical description of the watch, then any patent issued will only prohibit the production of an exact physical replica—this precise watch, in other words, and not the type of watch it is. To prevent that, the inventor would need to appeal to the form of which this watch is an instance.[35] But though science depends on form, it must receive such insight as it lies outside the competence of its discourse. We cannot, therefore, approach science or the empirical as if we could do so outside tradition, outside selected values, criteria, and so on. This is not to advocate relativism. To deem this a form of relativism would be to share the same default position as the creationists regarding what constitutes truth. It would bespeak a vulgar form of literalism, one that is, in the end, devoid of people.

Like van Fraassen, Edmund Husserl rails against the substructions of science which are approached as if they were reality itself:

> The contrast between the subjectivity of the life-world and the "objective," the "true" world, lies in the fact that the latter is a theoretical-logical substruction of something that is not in principle perceivable, in principle not experienceable in its own proper being, whereas the subjective, the life-world, is distinguished in all respects precisely by its being actually experienceable. The life-world is the realm of original self-evidences.[36]

33. M. Polanyi, *The Logic of Liberty* (Indianapolis: Liberty Fund, 1998), 48.
34. See Michael Polanyi, *Science, Faith and Society* (Chicago: University of Chicago Press, 1964), 73.
35. See Michael Polanyi, *Society, Economics, and Philosophy: Selected Papers*, ed. Richard T. Allen (New Brunswick, NJ: Transaction Publications, 1997), 287.
36. Edmund Husserl, *The Crisis of European Sciences and Transcendental Phenomenology*, trans. David Carr (Evanston, IL: Northwestern University Press, 1970), 127. For a comparison of van Fraassen and Husserl on this point, see Michel Bitbol, "Materialism, Stances and Open-Mindedness," in *Images of Empiricism: Essays on Science and Stances with a Reply from Bas van Fraassen*, ed. Bradley Monton (Oxford: Oxford University Press, 2007), 234.

This is why "objective" knowledge is bankrupt.[37] For it is a lie, denying its own animality, its own life, indeed its own evolution, and lastly its very possibility. Now, such bankruptcy is not inherent but rather contingent. As van Fraassen rightly says, science is an objectifying discourse, one that has brought us untold riches, but he asks, "what does it profit us to gain the whole world and lose our own soul? Riches come with a temptation, a tempting fallacy, namely, to have us view them as all there is to be had, when they are so much. This is true of all riches, and it is true of the riches of objective knowledge. Poor are the rich who succumb to this fallacy."[38] Scientism is just such poverty, as Bulgakov tells us, "Scientism is but a pose assumed by life, a moment in life. Therefore it cannot and should not legislate over life, for it is really its handmaiden. *Scientia est ancilla vitae.* Scientific creativity is immeasurably narrower than life, for the latter is living."[39] All moments, if they are to be true to themselves, must pass. Science must forever return to the source of its possibility and not deny its origins or its future. For all science has arrived from an ena-bling past and will develop and evolve into an unknown future; only the tension between these two poles allows science to be true to itself. Therefore we must realize, as Husserl tells us, that "The concrete life-world, then, is the grounding soil [*der gründende Boden*] of the 'scientific-ally true' world and at the same time encompasses it in its own universal concreteness."[40] Or as Bulgakov puts it, "Science is a function of life; it is born in the process of labour, and the nature of all life is economic, that is, has the aim of defending or expanding life. Life never rests; it is in a state of ceaseless tension, actuality, and struggle."[41] Life is the very possi-bility of the physical, of the physical to appear to itself, to the point that it can speak, to the point that it can write *The Origin of Species*.[42] Consequently, scientism, or reductionism in all its forms, must be "hunted down as persistently as dogmatism."[43] The primal validity of the Lifeworld

37. See Husserl, *The Crisis of European Sciences and Transcendental Phenomenology*, 88.
38. Van Fraassen, *The Empirical Stance*, 195.
39. Bulgakov, *Philosophy of Economy*, 182.
40. Husserl, *The Crisis of European Sciences and Transcendental Phenomenology*, 131.
41. Bulgakov, *Philosophy of Economy*, 181.
42. See Maria Villela-Petit, "Cognitive Psychology and the Transcendental Theory of Knowledge," in *Naturalizing Phenomenology: Issues in Contemporary Phenomenology and Cognitive Science*, ed. Jean Petitot, Francisco J. Varela, Bernard Pachoud, and Jean-Michel Roy (Stanford, CA: Stanford University Press, 1999), 513.
43. Natalie Depraz, "When Transcendental Genesis Encounters the Naturalization Project," in *Naturalizing Phenomenology*, ed. Jean Petitot et al., 474.

(*Lebenswelt*), of the subjective given-ness of experience, both grounds and makes possible the objective world of science, without which science is quite simply impossible. When such impossibility is ignored, destructive ideology is all that is forthcoming.

The problem science presents only arises when its methodology is assigned ontological significance, that is to say, when it is kidnapped by naturalism. As Bulgakov says, "the false assumption that a scientific relation to reality is in fact the deepest and most authentic takes root and flourishes, and the intentional limits of science are forgotten."[44] Moreover, despite the infinite riches that science provides, along with its impressive complexity, it remains "extraordinarily simple, elementary and impoverished in its task."[45] Such simplicity or impoverishment is the secret of science's success, which is more than fine if and when its task is both situated and delineated in proper fashion. Otherwise the temptation to misunderstand science— to make of it a philosophy—will in the end undermine, or at least threaten to undermine, the practice of science itself. We must remember there are no scientists in science. But properly understood, science is itself the opposite of that which it produces. For it may well be the great vivisectionist—it may well turn nature into a corpse, and it does indeed commit a form of murder—but it does so from a position that is otherwise than dead. For science, as we said, is itself a moment of life. If this is forgotten, then science is betrayed by its own brand of fundamentalism, just as religion can also be similarly corrupted by those who misapply it or misunderstand it. As we know, however, this constant temptation is ever-present due to the very methods of science. As Jonas points out, "For its part, the science of biology—being limited by its methods to external physical facts—must ignore the dimension of inwardness that is part of life. In so doing, it leaves material life, which it claims to have totally explained, more mysterious than when it was unexplained."[46] What the scientific worldview desperately needs is systematic inquiry into first-person experience, for then, as Bitbol says, "our soul is regained, even within science."[47] We should point out, however, that the unity of science is a myth—there is no "science" as one

44. Bulgakov, *Philosophy of Economy*, 184.
45. Ibid. 186.
46. Hans Jonas, *Mortality and Morality: A Search for the Good after Auschwitz*, Lawrence Vogel, ed. (Evanston, IL: Northwestern University Press, 1996), 59.
47. See Bitbol, "Materialism, Stances and Open-Mindedness," 259.

thing, so to speak.[48] Nor is there any such thing as a scientific worldview in any monolithic sense. As Bulgakov says, "We mustn't forget that sciences create their own objects, set up their own problems, and determine their own methods. There can thus be no single scientific picture of the world, nor can there be a synthetic scientific worldview."[49]

Materialism's ghosts

> Slowly we are learning,
> We at least know this much,
> That we have to unlearn
> Much that we were taught,
> And are growing chary
> Of emphatic dogmas;
> Love like Matter is much
> Odder than we thought.
> *W. H. Auden*

Materialism fails on every count.[50] It is vacuous and question-begging, unscientific, and indeed self-hating. In other words, materialists hate matter. Moreover, they misrepresent matter, but in so doing they are, like some latter-day Macbeth, forever haunted by the ghost of the very thing they have sought to kill, namely, the material.

In precise terms, materialism is dead. It is dead because it is incoherent at every level of analysis; what we find in its place today is a combination of ideology and wishful thinking. Indeed to invoke matter today as the most basic term of our philosophical worldview is equivalent to saying "God did it." The irony is that in its present guise materialism represents, not a realistic, salt-of-the-earth, away-with-the-nonsense philosophy, but rather an extreme form of idealism that has nothing whatsoever to do with the natural world. Nor has it anything to do with science. Why has this fate befallen

---

48. See John Dupré, "The Miracle of Monism," in *Naturalism in Question*, 39. Also see Nancy Cartwright, *How the Laws of Physics Lie* (Oxford, Oxford University Press, 1983); and, lastly, Nancy Cartwright, *The Dappled World: A Study of the Boundaries of Science* (Cambridge: Cambridge University Press, 1999).

49. Bulgakov, *Philosophy of Economy*, 161.

50. For a recent and comprehensive critique of materialism, see *The Waning of Materialism*, ed. Robert C. Koons and George Bealer (Oxford: Oxford University Press, 2010).

materialism? Because matter has been found out, its pretense rumbled—
because matter, quite simply, does not exist, at least not in the manner that
materialism requires. In short, matter is inscrutable. Likewise, bodies are no
longer available in any simplistic sense. As Noam Chomsky says, "Newton
exorcised the machine, not the ghost," by which he means that the Cartesian
understanding of mechanics was found to be wrong; and in its place it was

> necessary to invoke what Newton called an "occult quality" to account for the
> simplest phenomena of nature, a fact that he and other scientists found dis-
> turbing and paradoxical. These moves also deprive us of any determinate
> notion of body or matter…With the collapse of the traditional theory of
> "matter" or "body," metaphysical dualism becomes unstateable; similarly, such
> notions as "physicalism" or "eliminative materialism" lose any clear sense.[51]

Chomsky continues: "The supposed concepts 'physical' or 'material' have no
clear sense… There seems to be no coherent doctrine of materialism
and metaphysical naturalism, no issue of eliminativism, no mind-body
problem."[52] Bitbol echoes this view: "Material bodies are no longer the
basic objects of physics… Ironically, the notion of material body motivated
the very research that eventually dissolved it."[53]

A major problem facing materialism, already intimated above, stems from
something referred to as "Hempel's Dilemma."[54] In general terms, naturalism
is usually thought to assert that all that exists can be explained naturally, using
the laws of nature and so on; but of course what "nature" is and what quali-
fies as "natural" seem to be rather open. The next move is to appeal to physics, arguing that philosophy should invoke whatever physics says is the basic
and therefore true description of the natural or physical world. But the problem then becomes one of adequacy, for in terms of the mind, for example,
there is no worked-out physical theory. We must, therefore, appeal to some
future physics. But because we have no idea what that future, supposedly

51. Noam Chomsky, unpublished manuscript, quoted in William G. Lycan, "Chomsky on the Mind-Body Problem," in *Chomsky and His Critics*, ed. Louise M. Antony and Norbert Hornstein (Oxford: Blackwell, 2003), 12.
52. Noam Chomsky, "Naturalism and Dualism in the study of Language and mind," *International Journal of Philosophical Studies* 2, no. 2 (1994): 181–209 here 195–6.
53. Bitbol, "Materialism, Stances and Open-Mindedness," 243. Also see Michel Bitbol, "Le corps matériel et l'objet de la physique quantique," in *Qu'est-ce que la matière?: égards scientifiques et philosophiques*, ed. Françoise Monnoyeur (Paris: Le Livre de Poche, 2000).
54. See C. G. Hempel, "Reduction: Ontological and Linguistic Facets," in *Philosophy, Science, and Method: Essays in Honor of Ernest Nagel*, ed. Sidney Morgenbesser, Patrick Suppes, and Morton White (New York: St. Martin's Press, 1969), 179–99.

complete physics will say (what its terms, concepts, or content will be), the whole procedure appears to be wholly vacuous and question-begging. As Crane and Mellor point out, "The 'matter' of modern physics is not at all solid, or inert, or impenetrable, or conserved, and it interacts indeterministically and arguably some times at a distance. Faced with these discoveries, materialism's modern descendants have—understandably—lost their metaphysical nerve."[55] By this Crane and Mellor mean that materialism has just rolled over, remaining now only as a slave to a theoretically complete physics which now defines the empirical world. In other words, materialism is a misnomer. Moreover, it is so weak and paltry that it cannot even hold onto its one, primitive term, namely, matter. Crane and Mellor continue:

> For those whom reduction to physics is the touchstone of the physical do not propose to do it in practice. They simply insist that it can be done "in principle." But what is the principle? It cannot be physicalism. These sciences cannot be reducible in principle because they are physical, if reducibility in principle (RIP) is supposed to tell us which sciences could "in principle" be reduced to physics.[56]

It seems there is no principle involved; rather there is only the dogma of ideology, in this case, "no theology."[57] Indeed, the whole appeal to the physical is one purely of emotion and not of argument.[58] There is something else rather strange going on in this hopeful appeal to the physical, for why should the "physical" permit reduction? In other words, why are subatomic particles, or whatever, so destructive that their very existence would suddenly rid us of the natural world, of the human mind, and so on?[59] Surely this is just Gnosticism.

Van Fraassen refers to the "contrastive nature of explanations."[60] In other words, explanations that say X=B do so in a manner that inform us of why this is the case—why, that is, X is not C. But materialism and physicalism appear to fail this test miserably. Rather, all they offer is the desperate sweat of the compulsion to destroy. It is the Freudian death drive made manifest, for they would rather deny the world and have nothing, than have something there for which they just might have to give thanks, or at least for

55. Tim Crane and D. H. Mellor, "There is No Question of Physicalism," in *Contemporary Materialism: A Reader*, ed. Paul K. Moser and J. D. Trout (London: Routledge, 1995), 66.
56. Crane and Mellor, "There is No Question of Physicalism," 67.
57. Ibid. 70.
58. Ibid. 85.
59. Ibid. 69.
60. See van Fraassen, *The Scientific Image*, chap. 5.

which they should be thankful. So it seems all we are left with is what amounts to a promissory materialism, a presumptive materialism, or indeed a materialism of the gap.[61] Like ghosts of philosophy past, we are haunted by the spirit of materialism.[62] This is somewhat analogous to the idea of fashion, for it keeps changing precisely because nothing is truly fashionable. Likewise, the shifting sands of materialism and its strained efforts belie hollowness, one that Nietzsche would recommend we expose with a hammer, gently tapping the sides of this modern idol, being greeted by a telling sound. This is the intractable *je ne sais quoi* of materialism.[63] Due to the fluid nature of all characterizations of matter in science and beyond, materialism suffers a demarcation problem. In other words, how does it articulate its own stance in a well-principled manner, a manner that would allow it to stand out from other, different stances or philosophical positions? Put another way, if our conception of matter is ever-changing, how does materialism prevent itself from being washed away in a sea of vacuity?[64] Isn't the problem, as already mentioned, that matter is an ideal, a wishful, hopeful thought? Here is van Fraassen's diagnosis of materialism: It is not a theory but merely a cluster of attitudes, including a strong deference to science, which encourages materialism to "accept (approximative) completeness claims for science as actually constituted at any given time."[65] But where, we must ask, is the science in that? Here we are told to fool ourselves into pretending that the provisional is definitive; and then when it does change, which is inevitable, we are told to try and look as casual as possible. Consequently, materialism is, it seems, a prime example of false consciousness, for it presents itself as a cogent theory, when in reality it is more of a stance, an expression of attitudes, even an ideology. This is true because the assertion that "matter is all there is" merely wanders around the lip of nothingness as it is totally lacking in substance. This is why we can speak of materialism's ghosts. As Bertrand Russell said, "Matter has become as ghostly as anything in a spiritualist séance."[66] In short, as Chomsky makes clear,

---

61. Promissory materialism is Popper's phrase; see Karl Popper and John C. Eccles, *The Self and Its Brain: An Argument for Interactionism* (Berlin: Springer, 1977), 96–8. For presumptive materialism, see van Fraassen, *The Empirical Stance*, 49, and lastly for a materialism of the gaps, see Wallace, *The Taboo of Subjectivity*, 128.

62. See van Fraassen, *The Empirical Stance*, 58.

63. Ibid. 59.

64. See Bitbol, "Materialism, Stances and Open-Mindedness," 235.

65. See van Fraassen, *The Empirical Stance*, 59.

66. Bertrand Russell, *An Outline of Philosophy* (London: Routledge, 1927), 78.

"The notion of "physical world" is open and evolving."[67] This is no doubt a veritable crisis for materialism.

Ironically, materialism is a progeny of Cartesianism.[68] It is said that dualism became a rejected philosophical position, and in its Cartesian form that is certainly the case. The point here, however, is that the failure of materialism is the last death throes of that dualism. That is something to be welcomed because, as Jaki makes clear, from a theological point of view,

> Nothing could so badly discredit the glory of the one God than cutting the universe into parts of which some were rational and some irrational. While this procedure is compatible with certain philosophies, it is wholly alien to the philosophical framework of creative science as found in the thinking of all great creators of science.[69]

Along with many others, Siewert draws a parallel between Cartesianism and eliminative materialism.

Descartes granted a certain privileged epistemic status to our judgments about what is "in our minds" relative to judgments about what is "outside of them," in the realm of matter. And the eliminativist recognizes a similar asymmetrical epistemic relation between the "mental" and the "physical"—only the assignments of privilege and subordinate status are reversed. Our right to claims made in a mind-including idiom is made to depend entirely on their providing the best theory of what is conceived of in a mind-excluding one, while our right to apply this latter conception does not in turn depend on our warrant for claims about attitudes and experience.[70]

Importantly, from this reversal or inversion of Cartesian epistemology there came an ontological reversal as well. With Cartesianism there was a temptation to ignore matter or to deny its reality. With eliminativism there is a similar temptation because there is a great deal of difficulty in understanding the mind, so maybe it is just best to give up on the beast and thus deny its existence. As Stapp points out,

67. Noam Chomsky, *Rules and Representations* (New York: Columbia University Press, 1980), 5.
68. See Edmund Husserl, *The Crisis of European Sciences and Transcendental Phenomenology*, 60; Hans Jonas, *The Phenomenon of Life: Toward a Philosophical Biology* (Evanston, IL: Northwestern University Press, 2001), 54, n. 7; John Haldane, "Common Sense, Metaphysics, and the Existence of God," *American Catholic Philosophical Quarterly* 77, no. 3 (2003): 383; and David Braine, *The Human Person: Animal and Spirit* (London: Gerald Duckworth, 1993), 23.
69. Stanley L. Jaki, *Chance and Reality and other Essays* (Lanham, MD: University Press of America, 1986), 176.
70. Charles P. Siewert, *The Significance of Consciousness* (Princeton, NJ: Princeton University Press, 1998), 53.

The conflating of Nature with the impoverished mechanical conception of it invented by scientists during the seventeenth century has derailed the philosophies of science and of mind for more than three centuries, by effectively eliminating the causal link between the psychological and physical aspects of nature that contemporary physics restores.[71]

Naturalizing naturalism

The reason for the failure of rational culture...lies not in the essence of rationalism itself but solely in its being rendered superficial, in its entanglement in naturalism and objectivism.

Edmund Husserl[72]

Materialism is dead. Long live materialism! That is to say, the ever-determined atheist abandons materialism—but only in name. For he then proceeds to establish a successor theory and this is baptized naturalism.[73] As Eddington points out, "Materialism in its literal sense is long since dead. Its place has been taken by other philosophies which represent a virtually equivalent outlook."[74] Naturalism is, according to Quine, the "abandonment of the goal of a First Philosophy prior to natural science."[75] But naturalists do not leave it there—they also claim that "philosophy is continuous with the natural sciences."[76] Things are not so neat and tidy, however, for this progeny of materialism suffers many of the same problems of its forbear, including the lack of any really clear sense of definition, despite what Quine tells us. For even the "science" of which Quine speaks is somewhat misleading, being "simply Philosophy in dark glasses with a phony passport."[77] This philosophy

71. Henry P. Stapp, *Mindful Universe: Quantum Mechanics and the Participating Observer* (Berlin: Springer-Verlag, 2007), 2.
72. Husserl, *The Crisis of European Sciences and Transcendental Phenomenology*, 299.
73. For three very impressive critiques of naturalism, see Rea, *World Without Design*; Charles Taliaferro and Stewart Goetz, *Naturalism (Interventions)* (Grand Rapids, MI: Wm. B Eerdmans, 2007); and lastly, J. P. Moreland, *The Recalcitrant Imago Dei: Human Persons and the Failure of Naturalism* (London: SCM Press, 2009).
74. A. S. Eddington, *Science and the Unseen World* (New York: Macmillan, 1929).
75. W. V. Quine, *Theories and Things* (Cambridge, MA: Harvard University Press, 1981), 67.
76. Paul K. Moser and J. D. Trout, "General Introduction: Contemporary Materialism," in *Contemporary Materialism: A Reader* (London and New York: Routledge, 1995), 9.
77. Mark Wilson, "Honorable Intensions," in *Naturalism: A Critical Appraisal*, ed. Steven J. Wagner and Richard Warner (Notre Dame, IN: University of Notre Dame Press, 1993), 62.

is more of a reactive stance than a creative or positive one. Again, it can be thought of as another version of the "no theology" mantra; naturalism is, therefore, an argument from incredulity. It is what Putnam calls the horror of the normative.[78] The point must be made, however, that physical sciences have nothing to say about the realm of reason and rational explanation, which is precisely that of the normative and not of the factual.[79] In other words, the horror stems from the fact that the presence of the normative—a presence which is necessary for the operation of the sciences but that does not belong to them, since they are subalternate sciences, dependant on logics that reside outside their competence, just as architecture depends on geometry—indicates that this shotgun wedding (for it surely arises out of panic) of philosophy and science is simply not working. And this seemingly work-shy philosophy has a great deal to be getting on with. Yet, at the same time, its adherence to naturalism makes such work nigh impossible. Put another way, the normative announces, in the starkest possible terms, that scientism is a fiction, as is its philosophical lodger, scientific naturalism.

The elusive nature of naturalism is revealed when we realize just how hard it is to give it a substantive definition, and this inability surely belies its ideological nature, as was the case with materialism. Ernst Nagel, in his 1955 presidential address to the American Philosophical Association, noted that the number of distinguishable doctrines for the word "naturalism" is notorious.[80] In fact, naturalism is more of a contemporary shibboleth or a pervasive ideology than a robust philosophical theory.[81] As Stroud points out, naturalism is a bit like world peace: everyone advocates it, but no one has a clue what it means.[82] But apparently, "Naturalism is supposed to be a Good thing. So good, in fact, that everybody wants to be a naturalist, no matter what their views might be."[83] If not world peace, naturalism is certainly like

78. Hilary Putnam, "The Content and Appeal of 'Naturalism'," in *Naturalism in Question* (Cambridge MA: Harvard University Press, 2004), 70.

79. See E. J. Lowe, *Personal Agency: The Metaphysics of Mind and Action* (Oxford: Oxford University Press, 2008), 11.

80. Ernest Nagel, "Naturalism Reconsidered," *Proceedings and Addresses of the American Philosophical Association* 28 (1954–1955): 5–17.

81. See Horst, *Beyond Reduction: Philosophy of Mind and Post-reductionist Philosophy of Science* (New York: Oxford University Press, 2007), 12.

82. Stroud, "The Charm of Naturalism," 22.

83. William Seager, "Real Patterns and Surface Metaphysics," in Dennett's *Philosophy: A Comprehensive Assessment*, ed. Don Ross, Andrew Brook, and David Thompson (Cambridge, MA: MIT Press, 2000), 95.

a religion, one with a very broad church, indeed inclusive to the point of vacuity. As Seager says,

> Naturalism expresses more than a faith in, but also the desire to enter into, orderly community of the real sciences. This religious feeling comes in familiar varieties: At one extreme, the fundamentalist Unitarian is remembered for the doctrine of the unity of the science, which espoused the outright reduction of every field of knowledge to physics, reserving for all that resisted reduction the ontological hell of nonexistence. At the other extreme we find the New Age liberal theology of mere supervenience, unaccompanied by any attempt at reductive analysis, whose hell is the hell of vacuity and quietism.[84]

Indeed, the most accurate definition of naturalism is probably that of hopeful naturalism. We really just hope there's no God—and such hope is willing to sacrifice the natural world entire, especially the person.[85] We should, therefore, maybe follow Stroud, who recommends a much more open form of naturalism but points out that we might just as well call it open-mindedness and therefore drop the otiose, maybe even distracting, tag of "naturalism."

Cognitive suicide

> You can't always get what you want, but…you might just find you get what you need.
>
> *The Rolling Stones*

It is important to bear in mind that nothing in science requires philosophical naturalism. Moreover, the analytic method of philosophy is likewise extrinsic to any attachment we may feel toward naturalism. In short, we can quite happily be scientists or analytical philosophers and reject ontological or restrictive naturalism.[86] There is nothing regressive or reactionary about rejecting naturalism. Indeed the reverse is true, for such naturalism appears to be damaging to both science and philosophy for many reasons. For our purposes, however, the main reason is that naturalism undermines the veracity of reason, that is, it leads to global irrationalism and skepticism. Below we

84. Seager, "Real Patterns and Surface Metaphysics," 96.
85. Ibid. 96.
86. Denis Alexander and Robert White, *Beyond Belief: Science, Faith and Ethical Challenges* (Oxford: Lion Hudson Press, 2004), 29; also see, Antonella Corradini, Sergio Galvan, and E. J. Lowe, "Introduction," in *Analytic Philosophy Without Naturalism* (London: Routledge, 2006), 12.

outline some of the ways in which naturalism leads us into such an intellectual and cultural crisis. When naturalism is ontologized, when it becomes
a metaphysical thesis about what can and cannot exist in the world, one of
the major consequences is cognitive suicide (a phrase used by Lynne Rudder
Baker, Thomas Nagel, and G. K. Chesterton).[87] Why would this be the case?
It is because, as Husserl pointed out, we are then forced into a situation
wherein reason is subjected to species relativism (*ein spezifischer Relativismus*),
which in reality means relativism tout court. There is, in other words, no
universal reason by which our thoughts should be judged. Instead reason
becomes a wholly local affair at best, and is itself subordinated to the utilitarian principle of mere survival. But the problem is that there is now a
disconnect between survival and truth, for they only ever coincide contingently (more on this below).[88] Ironically, this leaves us in a much more
mysterious world than that of the theist, for in an almost Humean sense
everything is now "miraculous," as it is beyond explanation. Not only is
there a disconnect between survival and truth, if we take truth to be objective and normative, but also in the end truth becomes devoid of content as
it is subservient to function: truth is the performance of a function, namely,
survival. In light of naturalism or physicalism, Baker argues that lived life has
become mysterious, almost miraculous; this is what she refers to as the
bizarre spiritualism of the everyday. For example, in the absence of intentional agents—which, given ontological naturalism, must be the case—
social practices that depend upon ordinary explanation and prediction of
behavior become unintelligible.[89] As Stroud points out, "A natural world
conceived of only as a totality of all the physical facts obviously does not
contain any psychological facts. There are not truths to the effect that someone believes, knows, feels, wants, prefers, or values anything."[90] Stuart
Kauffman echoes Stroud when he tells us that "In Physics, there are only
happenings, no doings. Agency has emerged in evolution and cannot be
deduced by physics."[91] This statement of course includes doing science.

---

87. Cf. Lynne Rudder Baker, *Saving Belief: A Critique of Physicalism* (Princeton, NJ: Princeton
    University Press, 1987), chap. 7; Thomas Nagel, *The View From Nowhere* (Oxford: Oxford
    University Press, 1986), 52; also see G. K. Chesterton, *Orthodoxy*, chap. 3.
88. Joseph Catalano, *Thinking Matter: Consciousness from Aristotle to Putnam and Sartre* (London and
    New York: Routledge, 2000), 77.
89. See Baker, *Saving Belief*, 130.
90. Stroud, "The Charm of Naturalism," 27.
91. Stuart A. Kauffman, *Reinventing the Sacred: A New View of Science, Reason, and Religion* (New
    York: Basic Books, 2008), 4.

Thus to deny agency by assuming the perspective of ontological naturalism is in fact to deny evolution. It is to be antievolutionary, for agency is evolution's most impressive fruit. After all, what is the *On the Origin of Species*? It does not exist for reductionism. However, both Stroud and Kauffman are here denying that it is inadequate to only appeal to the physical or to the language established by the natural sciences if we are to retain the common sense world in which we take ourselves to be living. So much the worse for us, says the ontological naturalist; but of course there is no "us," for this seems to be the ultimate victimless crime. Again, this logic is similar to that employed by the Nazis in relation to the Jews, because by the lights of National Socialism, it too was victimless. Moreover, we cannot even find the Nazis culpable—if, that is, we adhere to naturalism. For as Chomsky says, "general issues of intentionality, including those of language use, cannot reasonably be assumed to fall within naturalistic inquiry."[92] Take, for example the statement, *Je suis Napoleon*. If someone believes this claim, then we can decide its veracity only by appeal to logic and not to brain states. But logic is not part of the language of neuroscience.[93]

Alvin Plantinga wisely asks us where the content of belief comes from if it is reduced to the status of a neuronal event. Leaving our friend Napoleon aside for the moment, take the proposition "naturalism is all the rage these days." From where does the naturalist ground the supposed truth of this proposition? Put another way, how does the naturalist discriminate between neuronal events as they may or may not relate to different propositions. Indeed, how do we (naturalistically) individuate neuronal events? To do so suggests that we may in fact have to abandon naturalism; but, then again, naturalism is self-defeating.[94] If this is not to be the case, naturalism must be able to locate a meta–neuronal event, so to speak, which they would call the "naturalism event." But of course that's just plain daft. We must remember, as Uwe Meixner points out, that "no brain event intrinsically signifies anything to anyone."[95] An analogous problem arises when causality of action is dragged through the streets of antecedent neural events, for such an analysis, or pretend analysis, "seems to lose sight of any unifying factor why those apparently independent causal chains of neural events should converge upon

92. Noam Chomsky, "Language and Nature," *Mind* 104, no. 413 (January 1995): 1–61 at 27.
93. See Eric Matthews, *Mind* (London: Continuum, 2005), 45.
94. See Alvin Plantinga, "How Naturalism implies Scepticism," in *Analytic Philosophy Without Naturalism* (London and New York: Routledge, 2006), 33.
95. Uwe Meixner, "Consciousness and Freedom," in *Analytic Philosophy Without Naturalism*, 186.

the bodily movements in question."[96] In other words, this analysis suffers its own version of the binding problem. How do they come together in a manner that allows for the identification of a discrete chain, or indeed action? Put another way, here again we cannot individuate such events or actions by appealing only to a naturalist worldview, as it just doesn't have the conceptual apparatus to cope with this. That is why it tends to deny free will, or eliminate the mind altogether, for that way its profound lack of competence is masked. But if every room into which naturalism walks smells, then you must ask if in fact it is the rooms that smell.

Nietzsche says that "it is unfair to Descartes to call his appeal to God's credibility frivolous. Indeed, only if we assume a God who is morally our like can 'truth' and the search for truth be at all something meaningful and promising of success. This God left aside, the question is permitted whether being deceived is not one of the conditions of life."[97] Nietzsche's question seems to be eminently sensible. In light of adaptationism—the view held by some that natural selection is responsible for all, or at least most, of the features we see in the world[98]—Jerry Fodor appears to agree:

> When applied to the evolution of cognition, the theory of natural selection somehow entails or at a minimum strongly suggests, that most of our empirical beliefs aren't true; a fortiori, that most of our empirical scientific theories aren't true either. So the rumor is that Darwinism—which, after all, is widely advertised as a paradigm of scientific success (I've heard it said that Darwinian adaptationism is the best idea that anybody's ever had, and that natural selection is the best confirmed theory in science)—Darwinism, of all things, undermines the scientific enterprise. Talk about biting the hand that feeds you![99]

The point is simply that Darwin is not in the epistemology business. His theory is not about knowledge but about survival. Therefore, "Evolution is neutral as to whether most of our beliefs are true. Like Rhett Butler in the movies, it just doesn't give a damn."[100] This may well be the case when it

96. Lowe, *Personal Agency*, 53.
97. Friedrich Nietzsche, *Writings from the Late Notebooks* (Cambridge: Cambridge University Press, 2003), notebook 36, June–July 1885, 26; quoted in Plantinga and Tooley, *Knowledge of God (Great Debates in Philosophy)* (Chichester: Wiley-Blackwell, 2008), 30.
98. For a critique of adaptationism, see Cunningham, *Evolution: Darwin's Pious Idea*, chap. 3.
99. Jerry Fodor, "Is Science Biologically Possible?" in *Naturalism Defeated? Essays on Plantinga's Evolutionary Argument Against Naturalism*, ed. J. Beilby (Ithaca, NY: Cornell University Press, 2002), 31. It is no surprise then, that Fodor has been developing a very significant and sophisticated critique of adaptationism.
100. Fodor, "Is Science Biologically Possible?", 42.

comes to extending the reach of Darwinism beyond biology and into our minds. What about naturalism itself, we might ask? The problem is that naturalism is wedded to adaptationism, for otherwise it simply does not have an explanation for the human mind. This uncomfortable situation—uncomfortable for the advocate of naturalism—leads it to indulge in all manner of exotic, desperate explanations of the mind, the best one being that there is no such thing, which seems to be an eminent example of Bill Livant's cure for baldness: you just shrink the head until the remaining hair covers what is left.[101]

Plantinga brings the absurdity of naturalism to our attention:

> If naturalism were true, there would be no such thing as proper function, and therefore also no such thing as malfunctions or dysfunction. Hence, there would be no such thing as health or sickness, sanity or madness, further, and in this epistemological context crucial, there would be no such thing as knowledge.[102]

To this we would add people, life, death, violence, ethics, beauty, and so on.[103] This is not an argument from incredulity. Just because we find it shocking and hard to accept, in other words, does not mean it is not true. The problem is not one of credulity or incredulity in relation to the truth of some view; rather, the problem is whether there is even such a thing as truth. Plantinga's point is that, given naturalism and the emergence of our cognitive faculties through natural selection, it would be nothing short of a miracle if our beliefs turned out to be true.[104] As Plantinga puts it,

> Most human beings think that at least one function or purpose of our cognitive faculties is to provide true belief; although we make mistakes, for the most part we are successful. However, naturalistic evolution, which is the conjunction of naturalism with the view that we and our cognitive faculties have arisen by way of mechanisms proposed by contemporary evolutionary theory, gives us reasons to doubt two things: (1) that a purpose of our cognitive systems is that of serving us with true beliefs, and (2) that they do, in fact, furnish us with mostly true beliefs.[105]

101. William Livant, "Livant's Cure for Baldness," *Science and Society* 62, no. 3 (1998): 471–3; Dawkins' notion of the gene is a similar cure, see chap. 2 above.
102. Alvin Plantinga, *Knowledge of God*, 1.
103. See Cunningham, *Evolution: Darwin's Pious Idea*, chap. 6.
104. Plantinga, *Knowledge of God*, 40.
105. Alvin Plantinga, "An Evolutionary Argument Against Naturalism," in *Faith in Theory and Practice: Essays on Justifying Religious Belief*, ed. Elizabeth Schmidt Radcliffe and Carol J. White (Chicago and La Salle, IL: Open Court, 1993), 35–8.

The point is that survival has the ascendancy over truth, and while truth and survival may at times coincide, such coincidence is contingent. This means that many of our most cherished beliefs have, according to those such as Dawkins, turned out to be patently false—what are memes, after all? Moreover, many scientific views have themselves turned out to be erroneous, yet we have undoubtedly benefited from them. Falsehoods can be beneficial. Indeed does not society benefit from us accepting erroneous ideas like mind, existence, free will, ethics, and even objects? But we are told that none of these ideas are true. At the same time, however, we wouldn't fancy our chances crossing the road to pay a visit to our Darwinian lover without them. In short, truth is not about fitness enhancement.[106] Any fiction that is useful is fair game for natural selection.[107] As the Rolling Stones once sang, "you can't always get what you want, but... you might just find you get what you need." As the saying goes, "In the kingdom of the blind, the one-eyed man is king." In our case it would be, "In the land of the dead, that which mistakenly thinks it is alive, has sex and so breeds." Fitness does not track truth. John Searle famously offered an argument against computers as mindful. While the content and reason of the argument bear no relevance here, the principle at work does. The argument is usually referred to as Searle's Chinese Room. Imagine someone locked in a room, and this person does not understand any Chinese. In the room there are boxes in which there are Chinese symbols. In addition, there is a rule book that instructs this individual how to respond to certain sets of symbols. He or she follows the rules and gives correct responses: "If I [the person in the Chinese room] do not understand Chinese on the basis of implementing a computer program for understanding Chinese, then neither does any other digital computer solely on that basis, because no digital computer has anything which I do not have."[108] The point is that the man in the room has only a grasp of syntax and not of semantics, for the latter requires an understanding of meaning and not just the application of rules. We agree because we believe in the existence of mind, but that is irrelevant here. Transferring Searle's argument to the question of what relation truth has with fitness, we can see that a syntactical grasp of Chinese is sufficient to get the job done. Moreover, a

106. See William F. Harms, "Adaptation and Moral Realism," *Biology and Philosophy* 15, no. 5 (November 2000): 699–712 here at 707.
107. See R. Joyce, "Moral Realism and Teleosemantics," *Biology and Philosophy* 16, no. 5 (November 2001): 723–31 here at 730; and Cunningham, *Evolution: Darwin's Pious Idea*, chap. 5.
108. John Searle, *The Mystery of Consciousness* (London: Granta Books, 1997), 11.

merely syntactical argument can go all the way down; in other words, there is no such thing as a semantical understanding of Chinese. We don't need it, or rather, natural selection does not need it. This being the case, Chinese is not about truth. There is no truth of Chinese but simply the occurrence of tasks, so to speak. Call this major task—SEX. Put differently, any road that leads to Rome does, by definition, get us there, even if we thought we were going to Belfast, and even if we in fact believe that Belfast is Rome (though that's pretty hard to do). After all, Columbus never thought that he had discovered America. He had, but that was beside the point. His belief was irrelevant. In this way, naturalism is the most syncretic, inclusive, and pluralistic of religions. It is not the case that any belief will do the job, however, but that any belief can do the job. This is the case because, again, the intrinsic content of belief is irrelevant. Only its extrinsic relation to the major task—SEX—matters, as it were.

Advocates of naturalism such as Somers and Rosenberg argue that Darwinism is an example of metaphysical nihilism. In addition, however, the authors say it is also ethical nihilism. This means that morality is a complete fiction. But which Darwinian would argue that ethics, morality, and so on, have not been useful—that is, that they are adaptive fictions or lies? Yet that gives support to Plantinga's argument regarding skepticism and naturalism.[109] Stroud too supports his argument: "A restrictive naturalist who holds that what mathematical statements assert is not part of the natural he believes in would have to explain our knowledge of logic and mathematics without himself appealing to any mathematics or logical facts at all."[110] But any such ambition is foolish, to say the least, because we quite simply cannot think without logic or indeed mathematics.[111] The problem does not stop there, however, because as many have noted, naturalism is self-defeating. Stroud continues, "There is an embarrassing absurdity in [ontological naturalism] that is revealed as soon as the naturalist reflects and acknowledges that he believes his naturalistic theory of the world...I mean he cannot say it and consistently regard what he says as true."[112] This statement also applies to universalized Darwinism. Thus ultra-Darwinism and naturalism are like the

109. See Tamler Sommers and Alex Rosenberg, "Darwin's Nihilistic Idea: Evolution and the Meaninglessness of Life," *Biology and Philosophy* 18, no. 5 (November 2003): 653–68 here at 653.
110. Stroud, "The Charm of Naturalism," 32.
111. See Stroud, "The Charm of Naturalism," 33.
112. Stroud, "The Charm of Naturalism," 28. Also see, Steven J. Wagner, "Why Realism Can't Be Naturalized," in *Naturalism: A Critical Appraisal*, p. 218; and John Haught, *Is Nature Enough?: Meaning and Truth in the Age of Science* (Cambridge: Cambridge University Press, 2006), 18.

proverbial drunk man on a moving train who appears to walk straighter than his fellow passengers. Thus as Plantinga says, "the argument isn't against the falsehood of naturalism, but for the irrationality of accepting it. The traditional theist, on the other hand, isn't forced into this appalling loop."[113] Moreover, materialism, physicalism, evolutionary psychology, and so on, consist entirely in revealing the many fictions we live by, including consciousness and a sense of self; after all, according to Dawkins we are disposable vehicles for the transportation of selfish genes.[114] Such fictions are surely adaptive. In this way, it is impossible to be a physicalist and stand opposed to Plantinga's argument. But then, if you are a consistent physicalist, unopposed to Plantinga's argument, you would be in a rather self-defeating position as you could not rationally trust or believe your belief in physicalism. As Stroud says, "If Plantinga and his friends convince others, there will be a general turn away from naturalism. That shows that it is naturalism that is now old hat."[115] We certainly believe it is. For example, it is simply the case that we "cannot understand the world we live in without presupposing normativity."[116] But normativity does not exist in the ontology presupposed by naturalism—when it is taken to be an ontological, as opposed to a methodological, theory. Nor, or course, does normativity exist in the world of ultra-Darwinism—how could it? Another notable contradiction that resides in the philosophy of naturalism is noted by Klapwijk, who points out that the naturalistic thesis "that the living world can be completely reduced to the physical world; the difference between both worlds is the hidden point of departure, its denial a theoretical amendment after the fact!"[117] In other words, naturalism trades on the very thing it denies. Moreover, it seems this lust for reduction is an almost fanatical desire for certainty, in this case the certainty of the grave. But the grave now lies above the ground. Those such as Baker try to remedy the situation by deflating naturalism's content to what she calls "quasi-naturalism." The main difference is that quasi-naturalism honors the achievements of science, without making the claim that science is the only true source of knowledge, but instead there are many such sources (personal experience, for

113. Plantinga, "An Evolutionary Argument Against Naturalism," 60.
114. For a critique of Dawkins' interpretation of genes, see Cunningham, *Darwin's Pious Idea*, chap. 2.
115. Stroud, "The Charm of Naturalism," 24.
116. Lynne Rudder Baker, *The Metaphysics of Everyday Life: An Essay in Practical Realism* (Cambridge: Cambridge University Press, 2007), 51.
117. Jacob Klapwijk, *Purpose in the Living World?: Creation and Emergent Evolution* (Cambridge: Cambridge University Press, 2008), 158.

example). In conjunction with that openness is the way quasi-naturalism refrains from making a metaphysical claim about what there is, or rather, it does not say the natural world is all there is.[118] This seems eminently sensible, because ontological naturalism cannot on its own terms identify, for example, what are called the persistence conditions for an object—that which an object requires to be what it is.[119] Naturalism, then, remains forever barred from such discernment because such conditions are necessary truths and so normative in a manner that resides outside naturalism's remit. Its ontology, not to mention its methodology, cannot cope with such non-empirical concepts. As Baker points out, "the rationality of our attitudes and practices requires that we identify objects over time, and the only objects that we can identify are manifest objects, not collections of particles."[120] But unfortunately for the materialist, everyday objects seem to be an exotic wine beyond the purse of their ontology. Rather tellingly, Quine once compared the simple belief in objects to belief in the gods of Homer.[121] Take the example of the Twin Towers. We of course think an atrocity was committed when they collapsed, but such tragedies come at an ontological price. If we believe that tragedies such as this one actually occur, our philosophies cannot be miserly. The problem with restrictive naturalism is that baby, water, and bath disappear over the fence. If "we" advocate eliminativism, then it is, quite frankly, impossible for the Twin Towers tragedy to have occurred because the ontological inventory attached to this philosophy does not include objects such as towers, not to mention people. To use another example, imagine two cars driving at great speeds, crashing into each other head on. All we are entitled to say is that two carwise-shaped combinations of particles now form another combination, one that we might call accidentwise; but of course, any such combinations we pick out are, in then end, arbitrary.[122] In short, nothing real actually happened, just as now the idea of a wound is impossible—arrangements do not really exist, they are not true objects.[123] Terms such as "accident," "tower," "person," and so on, are not referring terms. Consequently, all we can speak about legitimately are particles now arranged otherwise. But

---

118. See Baker, *The Metaphysics of Everyday Life*, 87.
119. See Rea, *World Without Design*.
120. Baker, *The Metaphysics of Everyday Life*, 6.
121. See W. V. Quine, "Two Dogmas of Empiricism," in *From a Logical Point of View: Nine Logico-Philosophical Essays* (New York: Harper and Row, 1951), 44.
122. See Baker, *The Metaphysics of Everyday Life*, 7.
123. Ibid. 27.

even that will not do, for our speech is, likewise, simply an arrangement of air and not itself a referring term. We might think this is an outrageous philosophy, but to be fair it is the most consistent position that falls under the umbrella term "naturalism." Even if we appeal to a weaker philosophical version of naturalism, such as reductionism, the situation is not much better, for again all we can say is that the term "tower" is just a description we give to the mereological sums of particles. Such descriptions merely reflect our interests—they are parochial colloquialisms, quaint primitive stories we tell each other at the fireplace. They are not, therefore, ontological, for reality does not reflect our interests. We need to move to a non-reductionist position if we are to believe that the Twin Towers tragedy actually happened, but this is not an easy thing for naturalism to do without begging the question. A non-reductionist position will say the towers did in fact exist and that now they no longer do—therefore the Twin Towers collapsed. Yes, they were composed of particles, but they were not identical to those particles.[124] The same stands for the unfortunate people in the car crash: yes, they were made from atoms, but they were not identical to those atoms. This should not surprise us for our bodies are always changing, and we are not therefore identical to any set of materials that at some point in time make up our bodies. Therefore, to believe in people, cancer, violence, or tragic events—not to mention sex, marriage, death, and life—we need to have a more interesting ontology, one that allows for a variety of primitive kinds. That is, the ontology must allow for kinds with different persistence conditions—conditions that are necessary for something to actually be or remain what it is. As Baker puts it: "An object X has K as its primary kind only if: X is of kind K every moment of its existence and could not fail to be of kind K and continue to exist. Something that has K as its primary kind cannot lose the property of being a K without going out of existence altogether."[125] According to Baker, a person is a primary kind, while a "human animal" is one's body's primary kind. In this way such a body is a human animal nonderivatively, and a person derivatively. Our primary kind is to be a person, while our body's is that of being a human animal, and a body only becomes related to a person contingently insofar as it constitutes you.[126] Now what distinguishes a person

---

124. Ibid. 26.   125. Ibid. 35.

126. See Baker, *The Metaphysics of Everyday Life*, 38. "The self is what it is, and not another thing," (Lowe, *Subjects of Experience*, 51). Also, see E. J. Lowe, *An Introduction to the Philosophy of Mind* (Cambridge: Cambridge University Press, 2000), 16–18.

184 TURNING IMAGES IN PHILOSOPHY, SCIENCE, AND RELIGION

as a primary kind is the existence of a first-person perspective, whereas the human animal or the body only has a third-person perspective. The persistence conditions of a person therefore entail a first-person perspective. It is this difference that means that a person cannot be identified with their body.[127] Moreover, "no objectifying inquiry can reveal what persons are or who the persons are among things in the world."[128] The notion of a person is beyond the ken of science and of all objective modes of thinking, for the simple reason that a person is not an object. Just because science cannot identify persons is no reason to deny their existence, as that is just begging the question. Indeed, if a philosophy jettisons a first-person perspective, they are no longer talking about people but maybe about bodies—if, that is, such a philosophy can even accommodate bodies. Crucially, first-person perspectives cannot be duplicated. They are irreducibly singular.[129] Consequently, it does not matter out of what "stuff" a person is made, as that is merely a contingent relation. What is necessary is the existence of the first-person perspective. There is, so to speak, no game to be played until this emerges. Moreover, as Baker points out, "First-person perspectives do not appear to be biologically significant... [but] first-person perspectives are ontological significant."[130] The point is that if we only appeal to Darwinism, as naturalists must in this regard, we will seek in vain to find a person. But that is only a problem for those who seek to make Darwinism a universal philosophy.

Naturalism is also self-defeating in its slavish following of science and its rejection of all things metaphysical. As E. J. Lowe points out, "without a coherent general concept of the whole of reality, we cannot hope to render compatible the theories and observations of the various different sciences: and providing that conception is not the task of one of those sciences, but rather that of metaphysics."[131]Moreover, any arguments given in opposing metaphysics seem to be employing the very thing that they are denying, for they are inevitably making metaphysical claims.[132] For example, it is self-defeating to assert that philosophy must relinquish its claim to formulate a First Philosophy, and that it should instead be subservient to science, as

127. See E. J. Lowe, *The Four-Category Ontology: A Metaphysical Foundation for Natural Science* (Oxford: Oxford University Press, 2006), 7.
128. van Fraassen, *The Empirical Stance*, 191.
129. See Baker, *The Metaphysics of Everyday Life*, 69.
130. Ibid. 70.
131. Lowe, *An Introduction to the Philosophy of Mind*, 4.
132. See Lowe, *An Introduction to the Philosophy of Mind*, 4; Also, see Oliva Blanchette, *Philosophy of Being: A Reconstructive Essay in Metaphysics* (Washington, DC: Catholic University of America Press, 2003).

science allegedly provides the best account of reality. Such an assertion is self-defeating because it is, quite obviously, not a scientific claim but rather a metaphysical one. As Lowe says, "science only aims to establish what does in fact exist, given the empirical evidence available to us. It does not and cannot purport to tell us what could or could not exist, much less what must exist, for these are matters which go beyond the scope of any empirical evidence."[133] In addition, science cannot tell us why something does exist—what makes its existence possible, whether that something is a carrot or mathematics. Even less can it tell us why anything at all exists. Lowe continues, "It would be a complete abdication of philosophical responsibility for a philosopher to adopt the metaphysical outlook of some group of scientists just out of deference to their importance as scientists." This temptation to abdicate arises, it seems, because naturalists believe in the myth of a physicist's paradise.[134] But as we know from above, and as Kanzian makes clear,

> ...while physicalists refer to physics (they believe in physics), there is no serious physicist who is looking for the ultimate world formula, the physical principles of all other sciences, the reducibility of all true sentences to a physical language, etc. Serious physicists are no physicalists. They even deny what physicalism asserts.[135]

Another source of this seductive temptation to abdicate philosophical responsibility stems from a particular embarrassment, namely, the very possibility of philosophy itself: From where does it issue, or where does it reside, as it were? Naturalism finds it very difficult to accommodate philosophy at all, just as it finds it extremely difficult to naturalize itself. In other words, naturalism cannot itself be naturalized. For if naturalism were, in a sense, true, then it would never be spoken of. In short, it would not be a philosophical position at all.[136] Naturalism is in a similar position to ultra-Darwinism: their posture as universal theories causes them to eat their own discourse, so to speak. They therefore become like a racing driver who, to avoid friction, chooses tires that are so smooth they offer no resistance, which in turn causes the driver to remain at a standstill, unable to move.

---

133. Lowe, *An Introduction to the Philosophy of Mind*, 5. Also see Lowe, *Four Category Ontology*.
134. See Christian Kanzian, "Naturalism, Physicalism and some Notes on 'Analytical Philosophy': Comment on van Inwagen's Paper," in *Analytic Philosophy Without Naturalism*, 90.
135. Kanzian, "Naturalism, Physicalism and some Notes on 'Analytical Philosophy,'" 92.
136. "One thing that seems not to have been naturalized is naturalism itself," Stroud, "The Charm of Naturalism," 22.

Likewise, if Darwinism dissolves other discourses it comes to a standstill itself. Naturalism's dissolution of philosophy leaves it in a similar place, for its sycophantic relation to science renders it devoid of rationality. But thankfully, as Lowe points out, 'We cannot rationally believe that we lack freedom of rational action.'[137]

Conclusion: persons, naturally

Robert Spaemann argues that "Persons are not something else the world contains, over and above inanimate objects, plants, animals, and human beings. But human beings are connected to everything else the world contains at a deeper level than other things to each other. This is what it means to say there are persons."[138] This type of connection is reflected in the notion of common ancestry, but arguably only accurately when the Patristic notion of recapitulation (*anakephalaiōsis*) is included. In short, the human is a microcosm, uniting the inanimate, the animate and the intelligent, and opening it up to the divine, that is, the immaterial. It should be noted—before the fashionable despisers of humans tell us that such a view is pompous and self-serving—that what in fact is special about man's place in the world is precisely his relationship with the rest of nature. As St. Gregory Nyssa says, "There is nothing remarkable in Man's being the image and likeness of the universe, for earth passes away, and the heavens change…[I]n thinking we exalt human nature by this grandiose name (microcosm, synthesis of the universe) we forget that we are thus favouring it with the qualities of gnats and mice."[139] Indeed, as St. Maximus the Confessor tells us, "man was introduced last among existent things, as the natural bond mediating between the extremes of the whole through his own parts, and bringing into unity in his own person those things which are by nature distant from each other."[140] In other words, persons naturalize nature, which is to say they actualize nature. They reveal nature to itself, doing so in all its forms, colors,

---

137. E. J. Lowe, "Rational Selves and Freedom of Action," in *Analytic Philosophy Without Naturalism*, 177.

138. Robert Spaemann, *Persons*, trans. Oliver O'Donovan (Oxford: Oxford University Press, 2008), 4.

139. St. Gregory of Nyssa, quoted in Alexei V. Nesteruk, *Universe As Communion: Towards a Neopatristic Synthesis of Theology and Science* (London: T & T Clark, 2008), 174.

140. Maximus the Confessor, *Ambigua*, 41.

and structures, for without them all is dark, or at least shadow. Thus they do not flee nature, as do the philosophical naturalists who destroy all that is natural. Moreover, Lowe is surely correct when he argues that "Selves as persons are not created through biological processes but rather through socio-cultural forces, that is, through the cooperative efforts of other selves or persons. Persons create persons, quite literally."[141] This is correct. But one should not read such creation in a purely cultural manner, for that can lead to a damaging sense of nominalism. In thinking something is a product of culture we tend to presume that this means it is not truly real. But no, culture is itself an emergent phenomenon, with its own modes of causality.[142] More importantly, if persons only come from persons, then it is for this reason that God, according to Christianity, is personal, indeed the arche person. Jacques Maritain echoes this sentiment: "How can it be that I am born? It is the certitude of being born common to all men, which suppresses in us the blossoming—There is only one solution: I have always existed, this I who thinks; but not in myself …nor in some impersonal life. Where, then? It must have been in a being of transcendent personality."[143] Henry makes the same point when he says "More original than the truth of Being is the truth of man."[144] The more we are repulsed by the apparent anthropocentricism of this, the more anthropocentric we are. For, according to Henry, Man's truth, insofar as Man is, is the Incarnation.[145] Inspired by such insight, Henry argues that there is no birth in the world. He says, "In the world, according to Christianity, no birth is possible."[146] Indeed Christ prohibits the "natural attitude" to birth: "Do not call anyone on earth Father, for you have one Father, he in Heaven" (Mat 23:9). This may seem to some to be only metaphorical. But it is here that our preceding analysis of both materialism and naturalism reveal their worth, for if we search the "purely" natural world for an actual birth of a person, we will not find one. Alas, we cannot even find a person, no matter their birth. Thus these ostensibly atheistic philosophical positions are in the end servants of the truth, that is, of theology. They are servants of theology insofar as what they take to be

141. Lowe, *Subjects of Experience*, 48.
142. See Cunningham, *Evolution: Darwin's Pious Idea*, chap. 5.
143. Jacques Maritain, *Approaches de Dieu* (Paris: Alsatia, 1953), 83–6.
144. Michel Henry, *The Essence of Manifestation*, trans. Girard Etzkorn (The Hague: Martinus Nijhoff, 1973), 41.
145. See Cunningham, *Evolution: Darwin's Pious Idea*, chap. 5.
146. Henry, *I am the Truth: Toward a Philosophy of Christianity (Cultural Memory in the Present)* (Palo Alto, CA: Stanford University Press, 2002), 59.

negative findings can be read as iconic revelations of creation ex nihilo, which is to say, the nothingness they strive to find. This is the case only because what is presented in nature declares the dependence of all upon their very source. Like Darwinism—which, as Aubrey More pointed out, came in the guise of a foe but did the work of a friend—the bid to capture nature has returned us to the font of subjectivity, to the sacramentality of each and every day. Little wonder then that Merleau-Ponty appeals to the Eucharist so as to elucidate this idea:

> Just as the sacrament not only symbolizes in sensible species, an operation of Grace, but is also the real presence of God, which it causes to occupy a fragment of space and communicates to those who eat of the consecrated bread...in the same way the sensible...is nothing other than a certain way of being in the world suggested to us from some point in space, and seized and acted upon by our body...so that sensation is literally a form of communion.[147]

Indeed, all talk about emergence is to some degree the recognition of just this situation, no matter how oblique. Strange as it may seem, philosophies that seek to destroy nature, doing so by reducing it, despite their apparent hate of religion, are indeed handmaidens to theology: *Scientia est ancilla vitae.*

> The miracle is the only thing that happens, but to you it will
> not be apparent,
> Until all events have been studied and nothing happens that you
> cannot explain
>
>   W. H. Auden, For the Time Being, Recitative

147. Maurice Merleau-Ponty, *Phenomenology of Perception*, trans. Colin Wilson (London: Routledge and Keegan Paul, 1962), 212.

NINE

The Sacred Beauty of Nature

Gordon Graham

I

The resurgence of religion that occurred in the last decades of the twentieth century has had the effect of unsettling a longstanding and hitherto dominant belief in "secularization." Quite suddenly, Christianity, Judaism, Hinduism and especially Islam, exhibited a dramatic power to attract new generations of adherents, a power wholly incompatible with the "secularization" thesis—the sociological claim that the demise of religion is an inevitable concomitant of economic and technological development. This surprising reverse was made the subject of a collection of essays edited by the sociologist of religion Peter L. Berger, significantly entitled *The Desecularization of the World*. In his opening chapter, Berger notes an import-ant exception to the new cultural trend—the resilient persistence of secu-larization in a key subculture.

> There exists an intellectual subculture composed of people with Western-type higher education, especially in the humanities and social sciences, that is indeed secularized. This subculture is the principal "carrier" of progressive, Enlightened beliefs and values. While its members are relatively thin on the ground, they are very influential, as they control the institutions that pro-vide the "official" definitions of reality, notably the educational system, the media of mass communication, and the higher reaches of the legal system...
> I cannot speculate here as to why people with this type of education should be so prone to secularization. I can only point out that what we have here is a globalized *elite* culture.[1]

1. Peter L. Berger, ed., *The Desecularization of the World* (Grand Rapids and Cambridge UK: Eerdmans, 1999).

The secularized intellectual elite to which Berger refers is the principal bastion of secularism. Secularism is not an explanatory thesis but a normative doctrine, and its "official definition of reality" has been determined by the supposed triumph of naturalism. That is to say, modern secularists infer from the indisputable success of the physical and biological sciences that reality *as a whole* is the outcome of natural processes which those sciences can ultimately be expected to explain. It is this expectation that drives research in the modern academy—a sustained attempt to naturalize mind, language, the emotions, knowledge, aesthetics, morality, and even religion itself.

The potential conflict between a naturalistic "definition" of reality and traditional religion is evident. Since the concepts of the sacred and the holy seem so closely connected to belief in the *supernatural*, a thoroughly naturalistic account of the world can hardly be expected to have any place for them, and so a radical conflict between secularism and religion appears to be inevitable. Yet, interestingly, in recent years a number of writers have striven to prise naturalism and secularism apart, to retain the sacred while abandoning the supernatural, and in this way find a rapprochement between science and religion in what has come to be called "religious naturalism." Karl E Peters is one of these writers, and in his book *Dancing with the Sacred* (subtitled "Evolution, Ecology and God") he sets out the task with commendable clarity:

> How can we portray [the] creative transformation of an evolving universe in a way that someone who thinks within the worldview of modern science might find it religiously meaningful? How can we develop a modern, naturalistic idea of our sacred center, the source, sustainer and transformer of all existence?[2]

Uncovering a path to religious naturalism is also Ursula Goodenough's aspiration, as the title of her book—*The Sacred Depths of Nature*—indicates. Goodenough is a biologist with an enthusiasm for the language, practices and artifacts of all the world religions. For Goodenough, however, these religions are so embedded in distinctive cultural histories, that we must abandon any attempt to affirm one of them as "true."

> I stand in awe of these religions. I am deeply enmeshed in one of them myself. [But] I have no need to take on the contradictions or immiscibilities between

---

2. Karl E. Peters, *Dancing with the Sacred: Evolution, Ecology and God* (Harrison PA: Trinity Press International, 2002).

them, any more than I would quarrel with the fact that Scottish bagpipes coexist with Japanese tea ceremonies.[3]

The analogy with the contrasting cultures of Scotland and Japan, however, turns out to be a little misleading. Unlike these practices, culturally distinct religions (whether because of the less enlightened attitudes they encourage, or because of the more serious understanding of religion they incorporate) have tended to generate conflict. If cultural conflicts are to be avoided, Goodenough thinks, we cannot rest content with this plethora of religions. Humanity needs more than local traditions and loyalties. The antidote to conflict is consensus around a "common religious orientation" or "global tradition." This is what religious naturalism can provide.

> Any global tradition needs to begin with a shared worldview—a culture independent, globally accepted consensus as to how things are. From my perspective, this part is easy. How things are is, well, how things are: our scientific account of nature, an account that can be called The Epic of Evolution. The Big Bang, the formation of the stars and planets, the advent of human consciousness and the resultant evolution of cultures—this is the story, the one story that has the potential to unite us, because it happens to be true....It is therefore the goal of this book to present an accessible account of our scientific understanding of nature and then suggest ways that this account can call forth appealing and abiding religious responses—an approach that can be called religious naturalism. If religious emotions can be elicited by natural reality…then the story of Nature has the potential to serve as the cosmos for the global ethos that we need to articulate. (ibid: xvi–xvii)

The project of religious naturalism as outlined by Peters and Goodenough raises a good many questions, the most crucial of which relate to underlying assumptions about the nature of reality and of religion. In this essay, I shall not be concerned primarily with the specific arguments they make for their versions of religious naturalism. My focus, rather, will be three quite general questions that confront *any* attempt to articulate a religious naturalism. Why does naturalism need a conception of the sacred? What resources does it have to provide one? If naturalism cannot accommodate any cogent conception of the sacred, what does this failure imply?

3. U. Goodenough, *The Sacred Depths of Nature* (New York and Oxford: Oxford University Press, 1998).

II

Peters seeks the source of the sacred in a radically reconstructed concept of God as "universal creative process." He refers to "God or the Sacred" interchangeably, and describes his position as that of "naturalistic theism." It is plausible to regard the expression "naturalistic theism" as a contradiction in terms, but the idea of "rescuing" God from supernaturalism is an intriguing one, and can in fact be elaborated with much greater philosophical sophistication than Peters gives it, as Mark Johnston does in his *Saving God* (2009). At the same time it is important to distinguish between two questions that are related, certainly, but also easily confused. The first asks whether there is any version of belief in God that is consistent with scientific naturalism. Answering this question with a "No," may still leave us with the second question—whether a world that has abandoned God can still have religious meaning. Can a world *without* God retain anything that is properly designated sacred?

It is the second issue that I mean to address, and it obviously requires us to begin with this question. What is it for something to be sacred? A useful opening is to be found in the observation that the concept of the sacred (in its established uses) has both positive and negative dimensions. On its positive side, to say that something is sacred is to say that it warrants attitudes and actions that go beyond respect and admiration, and reach the more intense level of veneration and worship. On the negative side, sacred objects invite awe and dread—fear and trembling, to use a familiar expression—but this is much more than the sort of anxiety about risk that is appropriate when we face, say, the prospect of an epidemic or a famine. We disregard the sacred at our peril, certainly, but what is at risk is something far more important than health or strength—in traditional language, upon our attitude to the sacred hangs our fate for all eternity.

Curiously, it is perhaps the negative aspect of the sacred that is most easily connected with the worldview of the thoroughly secularized mind. The still familiar mantra "Life is sacred" is a warning against taking life, rather than a prompt to celebrate it. The plaintive question "Is nothing sacred?" is not merely an inquiry, but an expression of concern, the anxiety that without some conception of the sacred to hold them in check, human beings are likely to reach new depths of "bestial" behavior (though as has often been observed, human depravity regularly exceeds anything that other animals have proved capable of manifesting). In short, naturalists, who are broadly persuaded by Nietzsche's announcement of the "death of God," still seem to fear acts of desecration, and to fear them more than they long for objects of veneration. It can be inferred from this, I think, that a promising route into a naturalized concept of sacred may lie with the old idea of "taboo"—that is to say, an absolute prohibition on certain kinds of action.

To make any sense of the idea of "absolute prohibitions" in a wholly naturalistic world, we need to specify some classes of action that it is intuitively plausible to regard in this light. What might they be? There are some types of human behavior—traditionally called "abominations"—that continue to be viewed with the deepest loathing, even by those who think there is no God and that scientific naturalism is the truth (and the whole truth) about reality. The most longstanding of these "abominations" are cannibalism, incest, corruption of minors and the mistreatment of the dead. The reaction that such actions consistently elicit among human beings in general would appear to provide a powerful incentive for an enlightened naturalist to retain (or reformulate) some idea of the sacred. Many modern naturalists would add something new to this list—the abusive subjection of other species and/or disregard for the natural environment. This new addition will be returned to at a later stage, since as I hope to show, it has special significance for contemporary ideas about naturalism and the sacred.

For the moment though, it will serve the investigation best if we focus on the traditional examples of abominable behavior. It is true that a few human societies have engaged in reverential practices of eating the dead, and occasionally individuals have been pressed to it by dire necessity. But in general people find the idea of eating other human beings deeply abhorrent. It is worth observing, though, that this is not just a matter of intense disapproval or immediate revulsion. Such acts are also, in a special sense, fascinating. This special sense is reflected in the fact that those whose fascination leads them to commit such ghastly actions do not regard them as any the less deviant. It is key to understanding profanation that it has the capacity to charm as well as repel. The same point can be made about the other "abominations." There is something truly abhorrent about a parent using his or her own offspring as the means of satisfying sexual appetite—though often this abhorrence, strangely, is an important part of incest's allure.

It is a noteworthy feature of very highly secularized societies that the mistreatment of children calls forth unusually intense and widespread condemnation. One way of analyzing this is to say that the innocence of children has a "sacred" character. There are adults who find amusement in teaching children to swear, who happily encourage them to steal, give them intoxicating drink or drugs, or photograph them in sexually provocative poses. These actions are not objectionable because of the harm they cause. This may be slight, and indeed deliberately teaching little children to use foul language may not cause them harm at all. But this is no mitigation of the act. Something much worse than physical or psychological harm is at issue—namely their simple innocence. These actions are more properly described as filthy than harmful. Purity, it seems right to say, has been sullied.

Treatment of the human corpse makes the same point even more forcefully. A dead body can be damaged, but it cannot be harmed. Yet more importantly, since it is no longer a person, it does not possess the rights, or experience the feelings, that generally make actions against persons wrongful. At one level of description, human remains are inanimate physical objects like any other, and viewed in this light, a burial ground becomes merely the place for their hygienic disposal. Yet no culture views the human body simply in this way. Every culture has held that denying human corpses proper respect is hateful, and a form of desecration. This supposition is crucial to Sophocles's *Antigone*, for example, a play that the societies of many times and places have found equally intelligible. It is by extension that the harmless defacing of memorials to the unknown dead amounts to an act of desecration also.

All these instances of violating sacred taboos are guaranteed to provoke horror in the vast majority of human beings. Yet, though cannibalism, incest, pederasty and necrophilia are all universally abhorred, they can also exercise a ghoulish fascination. Any admission of having performed them generates loathing and shame, even if in the secret recesses of many human hearts they have the attractiveness of the forbidden. Within traditional religious ways of thinking these are only extreme cases of a much more general phenomena—impiety—which is to say, crossing a boundary set by God (or the gods). Such boundaries are acknowledged as absolutely wrong for human beings to cross. At the same time it is this very same feature that tempts some human beings to cross them in acts of Promethean defiance—and thus commit the sin of *hubris* or *superbia*.

Assuming (as most secular naturalists do) that there is no God, the following question obviously arises. What should we think about acts like these? One possible response—Nietzsche's in part—is to hail scientific naturalism as a liberator. The growth of knowledge and the advance of science has finally freed humanity from attitudes originally formed by pre-enlightenment ignorance and superstition. There are some people who do indeed take this attitude to incest, believing that just as enlightened attitudes to sex have liberated women from the "bonds" of marriage, and liberated gays from ignominy and suppression, so the self-directed sexual choices of members of the same family group should be accepted and respected. But whatever plausibility this particular example may have, the same approach is unlikely to command much support when applied to the consumption of human flesh, the corruption of minors (sexual and otherwise) or the treatment of dead bodies. Few people, if any, think that we should welcome "liberation" from the "confining" ideas of childhood innocence or respect for the dead. On the contrary, attitudes to the sexual and commercial use of children have tended to harden amongst progressive secularists for whom few other acts are quite so "sinful."

Even if it is true that most people can be expected to refuse "liberation" from inherited ideas of desecration, this fact obviously does not constitute a *refutation* of naturalism, no matter how deep-seated the intuitive conviction on which that refusal rests. Naturalists can coherently contend that if naturalism is true, nothing is sacred. This returns us to the question of this section. Why should it be thought that naturalism *needs* a conception of the sacred? Surely the concept of morality can be called upon to handle "abominable" phenomena like cannibalism, incest and so on. So long as these practices can be classified as immoral, the language of desecration, profanity and so on can be left behind.

The problem, though, is to decide just what immoral means in the context of secular naturalism. Theistic versions of naturalism have the conceptual resources to condemn "unnatural" practices because the "natural" is a norm, established by God in the specific nature that he has given to his creatures, much in the way that an engineer establishes the proper way to use a machine that he or she invents. We are organisms not machines, of course, but the same teleological perspective applies. Incest is wrong for human beings in something like the way gluttony is bad for them. Without God, however, what is "natural" for an organism can only mean the kind of behavior that observation reveals as characteristic or typical in that kind of organism. The fact is, though, that incest, the use of children for sexual purposes, and (at times) cannibalism can all be observed as occurring quite widely among human beings. Overall, perhaps, they are relatively rare, but this does nothing to affect the general point: "on average" is merely a descriptive summary without any evaluative force. Of course, while naturalists are unlikely to attempt to ground immorality on any natural/unnatural distinction, their difficulty lies in the fact that other resources are not obviously available to them. The arguments here are familiar. If morality is a matter of utilitarian calculation—harms against benefits—then, as has been shown many times, no strictly absolute prohibition is possible; some contingent circumstances may justify courses of action that would be abominable in most. The alternative appeal to "rights" does not seem promising either. To say that a young child or dead body has a "right" not to be used for sexual purposes will quickly turn out to be just another way of saying that the act of doing so is "immoral." A deontological morality can of course be construed along more Kantian lines, as neither the calculation of contingent costs and benefits nor an appeal to "rights," but an exercise in pure practical reason. But in this case the naturalist must either find some ground for rejecting Kant's own contention (in the *Critique of Practical Reason* II/II/V) that divine creation and control of the natural world is a necessary postulate of morality, or provide an alternative to God in Kant's theory. Elsewhere I have argued at some length that Kant's contention about God and morality is a cogent one.[4] If that is correct, then the first alternative is ruled out, which leaves only the second—the need for naturalism to find an alternative to God—that is, a naturalistic conception of the sacred.

In summary, while the deep seated responses that most people have to the traditional "acts of abomination" cannot show scientific naturalism to be false, they do provide strong motivation for it to find some conception of the sacred that will serve as a ground for at least some of the absolute prohibitions on human action that the concept of impiety hitherto sustained. Though it is possible for naturalists to embrace these actions as part of "life's rich tapestry," were they to do so, it would almost certainly undermine the credibility of the secular view of the world that scientific naturalism is generally called upon to underwrite. Secularists no less than religionists want to condemn the abominations of human wickedness. We are thus led to my second question. What intrinsic resources does naturalism have to sustain a conception of the sacred?

---

4. Gordon Graham, *Evil and Christian Ethics* (Cambridge: Cambridge University Press, 2001).

III

Goodenough is rather unrestrained in her appropriation of religious language. She finds it easy to use despite its apparently supernatural implications, partly because she is happy to interpret the "words of the traditional texts [in ways] that sound different to us than they did to their authors,"[5] and partly because she thinks that such substance as there is to these implications, can be captured by a wholly naturalistic conception of the sacred. Importantly, though, in her explication of this naturalistic equivalent she lays almost exclusive emphasis on the sacred's positive side.

> Our story tells us of the sacredness of life, of the astonishing complexity of cells and organisms, of the vast lengths of time it took to generate their splendid diversity, of the enormous improbability that any of it happened at all. Reverence is the religious emotion elicited when we perceive the sacred. We are called to revere the whole enterprise of planetary existence, the whole and all of its myriad parts as they catalyze and secrete and replicate and mutate and evolve. (ibid: 170)

Though the scientific "story" to which Goodenough refers may owe much to the immense strides that science made in the course of the twentieth century, this passage expresses a view strikingly similar to nineteenth-century American Transcendentalism, and indeed Goodenough's very next paragraph cites Ralph Waldo Emerson, referring approvingly to his conception of prayer as "the contemplation of the facts of life from the highest point of view." The Transcendentalism of Emerson, Thoreau, Margaret Fuller and so on, is somewhat misnamed, however. Though it sought to transcend the confines of empiricism's appeal to the physical senses, its search for meaning was limited to an exploration of the *human* spirit. It did not seek or invoke anything properly called *super*natural. It is not entirely clear that Goodenough succeeds in observing the same limit. Her assertion that "we are called to revere the whole enterprise of planetary existence" inevitably invites this question: Who or what it is that *calls* us to an attitude of reverence? And whoever or whatever it is, why should we obey the call?

5. U. Goodenough, *The Sacred Depths of Nature* (New York and Oxford: Oxford University Press, 1998).

I shall leave these potentially telling questions aside, however, because there are several other no less important issues that arise even were there no reference to being "called." First, why should we think that the emotional response we experience in the face of the complexity, vastness, and improbability of the world that science has revealed to us (if we do experience such a response) is properly described as "religious?" There is good reason to insist that the attitude of wonder generated in us ought to be thought of as itself scientific, rather than religious. After all, it is precisely a disinterested wonder, or curiosity, about natural phenomena that has driven the whole enterprise of science since the time of the Pre-Socratics. Wonder in the sense of puzzlement lies at the heart of every scientific inquiry, and is no less characteristic of human beings, or common to them, than religious awe. Secondly, there is equally good reason to question Goodenough's underlying assumption that emotion or feeling (rather than theological beliefs and/or ethical principles) is key to religion. Schleiermacher, to whom such a view is often attributed, did indeed hold that religious faith is misunderstood if it is identified with either metaphysics or ethics, but the "intuition" that he thought central to religion is not merely affective but in an important way cognitive. Thirdly, and crucially, even if we were to grant Goodenough's assumption that a feeling of reverence lies at the heart of religion, there is still the matter of what the proper object of this feeling is. It is philosophically naive to think that necessarily emotions are properly directed at the things which engender them. Sometimes they are and sometimes they are not. For example, fear is an appropriate response to tigers, but not (in general) to spiders. Of course, we are quite familiar with human beings who are afraid of spiders. But their fear does not *make* spiders dangerous, any more than the real danger that man-eating tigers constitute can be averted by teaching ourselves not to be afraid of them. Similarly, a racist may have such strong feelings that the sight of a black man and a white woman walking hand in hand leads to genuine and intense revulsion. In this case, while there is no denying the reality of the racist's feeling, its reality does nothing to make her revulsion *warranted*.

Precisely the same point can be applied to religious emotion. It too can have, and lack, proper objects. Setting the first two points aside, let us suppose (though it is not obviously true) that contemplating the complexity of the world that science reveals to us generally induces a sense of reverential "awe," and that this is plausibly described as religious. The third point shows the mistake in inferring from this that the world is therefore "awesome." We need some reason to take this further step. The feeling may be real enough, and yet it may also be nothing more than the residue of religious attitudes that modern science ought to have enabled us to abandon by now.

An initially plausible rejoinder to this point lies in the contention that religious emotions are special precisely because they do not have proper objects in the way that other emotions do. This is because they are directed at the *totality* of things—the world as a whole rather than the various items in it or aspects of it. The spider has a specific nature that is independent of our feelings about it, and with which those feelings may or may not be in accordance. By contrast, the totality of things cannot be conceived independently of the way we apprehend it. "The world of the happy man," Wittgenstein famously remarked, "is a different one from that of the unhappy man."[6] That is to say, the person who is "glad to be alive," finds joy in life's struggles and strains no less than in its successes and satisfactions. Similarly the person to whom life is a "vale of tears" finds evidence of this in the transience of beauty as much as in the experience of pain.

With this contrast between finite experiences, and the infinite context within which they necessarily take place, we both come much closer to Schleiermacher's conception of religious "intuition," and can better appreciate its dual character as affective *and* cognitive. Nevertheless, if talk of "the infinite" in this connection is stripped of all supernatural overtones, then the best that naturalism can do is give a psychological account of the sacred—how people generally feel with respect to the totality of things, or life as a whole. In this case, though, "the sacred" can only have a very precarious foundation, too precarious to sustain either the absolute character of taboo or the inescapable obligation to worship. This is because "the sacred" exists only so long as human beings have feelings of certain kinds, and it can be eliminated completely by training ourselves not to have those feelings. Applied to the acts of desecration discussed in the previous section, this means that any "absolute" prohibition attaching to them is really conditional upon human feeling. Only cease to be horrified by them, and they will cease to be prohibited—which means that they were never "absolutely" prohibited at all.

This unwelcome conclusion must follow from any attempt (like Goodenough's) to derive "sacred depths of nature" from human attitudes of awe and wonder. As if this were not problem enough, however, all such

6. Ludwig Wittgenstein, *Tractatus Logico-Philosophicus* (London: Routledge and Kegan Paul, 1922), §6.43.

attempts encounter a yet more striking difficulty. Ignoring the conclusion of the argument up to this point, let us make the following assumptions— first that the vastness and complexity of evolved natural systems do prompt us to awe and wonder; secondly, that this is properly described as a religious response; thirdly, that in some way we can legitimately infer from this the sacredness of the natural world; and fourthly that without any theistic over- tones we can speak of its thereby "calling" for veneration. If all these propos- itions are true, the "sacred depth of nature" is indeed a proper object of religious contemplation. But how does awe-filled contemplation of this kind relate to human action? Is there anything to be *done*, or is it enough to pause for a moment now and then in an attitude of wonder and reverence? And what would it be, on this account, to commit an act of *desecration*? Does an improper response to the sacredness of nature consist simply in a failure to adopt the right attitude towards it? If this is all there is to desecration, then, though such a failure may be regrettable, it could not intelligibly pro- voke any of the horror and revulsion universally elicited by those "abomi- nable" acts discussed earlier. What is lacking, clearly, is any obvious ground for *opprobrium* rather than mere disapproval.

Indeed, we might reasonably ask whether this deficiency in response is properly described as a failure of action at all. Or, to put the point the other way round: can feeling awe in the contemplation of nature be properly described as an *action*, something that we are "called" to perform? What could such an action be, other than voicing certain sentiments when the occasion seems to make it appropriate? In modern versions of the Psalms, the Biblical injunction "Stand in awe and sin not" is translated "Let awe restrain you from sin" (*Psalm* 4:4). What "sin" could, or should, the contem- plation of nature's complexity and vastness restrain us from?

One possible answer to this question invokes the idea of "respect for nature," a conception that has increasingly been appealed to in the context of formulating an environmental ethic. In what is such a "respect" properly grounded? There is a familiar and protracted debate between "deep" and "shallow" ecology, prompted by Arne Naess's 1973 article in which the dis- tinction was first introduced. At the heart of that distinction is the percep- tion that a concern about environmental degradation based on long-term human interests and inter-generational justice—the kind of concern that underlies almost all political and governmental interest in "the environment"—is not really "respect for nature" properly so called. Its focus is not the value of nature in itself, but the value of nature to human beings, both present and future. This is what makes it "shallow." So what "deep" alternative is there? The topic is a large one,[7] but one interesting line of thought lies in trying to construct a generalized conception of "respect for nature" from (for example) the sort of respect that an experienced sailor has for the sea. Like a sense of the sacred, such respect has a positive and a negative side. An admiring appreciation of the enlarged perspective that comes from harnessing the power and vastness of the oceans must nonetheless be combined with a clear understanding of the dangers that these very same features constitute. In an interesting sense, sailors are doubly dependent on the sea. It makes their mode of life possible, while at the same time being a constant threat to its continuance. To have respect for the sea is to sail in the light of this dual understanding. The successful sailor is one who has achieved a harmonious relationship with the sea by acquiring the wisdom that knows when to use its power for the advancement of human purpose, and when to yield those purposes to its power, all the time accepting that the sea will have the final word.

Can this model be extended to the naturalist's life on earth? Many writers employ concepts in this context that seem to assume it can. They talk of human existence requiring to be in harmony with the natural world of which it is inescapably a part. Peters is one such writer. He speaks of encountering "all forms of life, streams, rocks and stars" in a "state of consciousness called my sacred center." In this state of consciousness he is enabled to "live in peace and love in this wonderful evolving world—in the dance of the sacred."[8] The tone of this may sound optimistically Romantic, but like the experienced sailor, Peters acknowledges Nature's dark side, and for this reason resists any conception of the "sacred center" as a "Mother Earth" that would incline us to ignore it.

The key concept in this ideal is an aesthetic one—harmony, the concordant beauty of sound. Indeed, the whole conception is really an aesthetic one—humanity dancing through life to nature's music. It contrasts interestingly with an alternative aesthetic conception that is often invoked in this context—nature in the beauty of landscape and wilderness. This second conception focuses on the visual, and by inviting comparison with great painting resonates with the appeal to awe and wonder that Goodenough

7. See, Gordon Graham, *Theories of Ethics* (New York and London: Routledge, 2010).
8. Karl E. Peters, *Dancing with the Sacred: Evolution, Ecology and God* (Harrisburg, PA: Trinity Press International, 2002).

and others make. But it encounters the same problem. As an essentially contemplative conception, its connection with human action is obscure. By contrast, the alternative aesthetic ideal of humanity dancing to the rhythms of nature is quintessentially active.

Of course, "dance" is a metaphor here and has to be filled out—and expanded. James C Edwards provides something of a clue to this expansion in his book *The Plain Sense of Things* (1997) where he reflects at length on Heidegger's philosophical investigation of what it means "to dwell poetically on the earth as a mortal."[9] In his reflections Edwards—like Goodenough—has recourse to American Transcendentalism, in this case Henry David Thoreau. In 1845 Thoreau built himself a small house on land owned by Ralph Waldo Emerson around the shores of Walden Pond in Concord, Massachusetts. For the next two years he experimented with the idea of "simple" living, and during this time drafted *A Week on the Concord and Merrimack Rivers*, a long essay describing a trip he had taken with his brother. This essay, which he published privately, formed the basis of a book finally published in 1854—*Walden, or Life in the Woods*—now widely regarded as a notable contribution to American literature in which the ideals of natural simplicity, harmony, and beauty are explored as key to a spiritually adequate mode of life.

Edwards takes *Walden* to be a concrete example of Heidegger's "poetic dwelling" and illustrative of one possible answer to the dilemma that confronts Berger's subculture of Western intellectuals—how to "be religious when we can't really believe any of that glorious stuff…we used to believe" (ibid: 195). Unlike Goodenough, though, Edwards understands the pursuit of the sacred without the supernatural to be a matter of finding something to be limited by, as well as finding something to enlarge our horizons.

> While traditional supernatural religion is no longer possible for us, we still need something: something to bound our temptation to eat up the earth and ourselves in pursuit of ever new, and ever more reckless, forms of self-fashioning; and—simultaneously—something to loosen our captivity to whatever particular form of life is commonsensically dominant here and now. (ibid: 197)

There is no denying the appeal that a vision like *Walden* has to many minds, or its seeming fittedness to a world in which concern with "the environment" has won widespread if less than universal assent. Yet insofar

---

9. James C. Edwards, *The Plain Sense of Things: the Fate of Religion in an Age of Normal Nihilism* (University Park, PA: Pennsylvania State University Press, 1997).

as it is called upon to supply us with a naturalistic concept of the sacred, it confronts two crucial problems. First, it seems highly individualistic in the way that Romanticism in general tends to be. What could *Walden* possibly tell us about the possibilities for "poetic dwelling" in the teeming tower blocks of Chicago or Beijing? The very aptness of the sailing analogy reveals this, in fact. Harmonious "respect for the sea" conjures up an image of the lone yachtsman, not the crew of a super tanker. Secondly, however admirable the ideal of "poetic dwelling on the earth" as a mode of human life, it is just one more "form of self-fashioning." No will but mine imposes it. How then can human temptation be "bound" by it? Whether or not we can any longer believe "the glorious stuff" of monotheism, we can see easily enough that the very idea of Divine Law stands over against *all* human choice and contrivance. And since this Law emanates from a God who is both omnipotent Creator and just Judge of human kind, a God who will not be mocked forever, conceptually it provides a kind of "bound" that no individual or collective act of human will can ever do.

Besides, the concept that lies at the heart of this vision—natural harmony—will not bear much close scrutiny. How does one live harmoniously with the sacred depth of nature that shows itself in earthquakes, volcanic eruptions, tornados and tsunamis? How are we to dance to the natural rhythms of bone cancer, Lou Gehrig's disease or bubonic plague? These last examples point us in quite a different direction, and a radically different vision—that of human life as a *battle* with nature, one in which we call upon human intelligence, integrity, ingenuity and fellow feeling, to defeat the onslaught of nature, and thereby wrest a meaningful and satisfactory existence from the powerful, but blind and mindless Earth on which we find ourselves. This may be the vision that leads to industrial pollution as well as technological captivity within a world of airplanes, freeways, computers and cell phones. But it is also the vision that has drastically reduced infant mortality, put an end to smallpox, and built the Parthenon.

This Promethean alternative is not one I mean to commend. I articulate it only in order to show that *both* of these visions are essentially humanistic, resting as they do on the remarkable degree to which science has enabled us to understand the processes of nature, and on our desire that human life should be more than a mere passage of time from cradle to grave. The former is currently fashionable, and the latter formerly so. Both can point to limits on human conduct that it is wise to observe; neither can show us that it is sacrilege to cross them.

IV

We thus arrive at the last of my three questions. If naturalism cannot accommodate any cogent conception of the sacred, what does this failure imply? To a degree it has already answered itself, since the argument to this point has shown that there is indeed some basis for the thought that "religious naturalism" is a contradiction in terms. For all that the ideal of natural harmony which surfaces so clearly in Peters and Goodenough receives classic expression in Thoreau, and is given philosophical sophistication by Edwards, its proscriptions enjoy no greater authority than human beings individually or collectively can lend them—and what is self-legislated can always be repealed. Moreover, the fact that it can be (and often is) articulated in quasi-religious language does nothing to alter its essentially human character. After all, it is not hard to construe the contrasting Promethean vision as finding expression in language similar to that of the Christian hymn "Fight the good fight with all thy might." Imagining nature as foe need be no less emotionally stirring than imagining it as friend.

But there is perhaps a little more to be said about the implications of naturalism's failure to supply us with anything properly called "sacred." As was observed earlier, such failure is more significant with respect to limits than aspirations. We need not be much troubled by the claim that simple wonder at "the starry heavens above" is not properly called religious. The heavens are still there to be wondered at. Much more troubling is the thought that our revulsion at the "abominable" act of making pornographic pictures of children or feeding human remains to pack animals, though it may be stronger, is no more normative than our revulsion at the smell of rotting vegetables. Now as was also observed earlier, we cannot use our psychological reluctance to accept this equivalence as a logical ground against naturalism. This is because the logical form *modus tollens* is simply *modus ponens* in reverse. We might reason thus: Acts of desecration imply the existence of the sacred, and if the sacred exists, then naturalism is false. Such a line of reasoning, however, enjoys no logical advantage over its converse: if naturalism is true, nothing is sacred, and therefore acts of desecration are impossible. Still, while our psychological reluctance to accept this second line of reasoning is no proof against it, it is a legitimate ground for re-examining some of the naturalist's assumptions.

Peters aims to address the person "who thinks within the worldview of modern science." Goodenough identifies this view—in her terms, "our scientific account of nature"—with an explanation of "how things are," an explanatory "story" that "has the potential to unite us, because it happens to be true." It is to be noted that scientific accounts of "how things are" do not consist in lists of observational "facts" or empirical statistics about the natural world around us. They are rather general formulations of the natural laws that govern empirical facts about that world. The spectacular advances of scientific understanding consist in its successfully devising ever more abstract and encompassing laws of this kind, laws that at the highest levels must be given mathematical expression. Science's continuing success raises an interesting question. What is it that makes it possible for a human invention—mathematics—to render intelligible the fundamental workings of a world that is not of human making?

This is a familiar philosophical question, and a variety of responses have been made to it, including the response that doubts the intelligibility of the question itself. Though it is obviously far too large an issue to engage properly with here, it nonetheless provides a context for the following thought. Does "the worldview of modern science" not presuppose an idea of harmony quite different to that which religious naturalism aims to capture? Consider once more the "natural harmony" between the experienced sailor and the sea. If we examine this a little more carefully we will find, I think, that whatever the relation between the two, it is not rightly described as "harmony." In the literal case harmony consists of two or more musical notes played simultaneously. Their differing pitches are such that *together* they have a musical outcome that neither on its own could produce—a chord rather than a discord. Now the sailing case does not seem properly analogical to this. The yachtsman tacking into the wind and riding the waves moves *against* these natural elements. The skill of the sailor lies in using the elements' force to counteract their immediate effect, that is, resist a natural inclination to be blown in the direction the wind is going. Consequently, in one sense the yacht makes progress *despite* the wind and waves. Of course it is true that the sails are harnessing the latent energy of the wind, and that if the wind dies down no progress can be made. Nevertheless, though the yacht's journey is dependent on the wind, the distance it travels is not a joint accomplishment of yachtsman and elements, but of the sailor alone.

Compare this with the case of science. A scientific theory is successful only insofar as it is "in harmony" with the aspect of nature that it seeks to explain, and nature is intelligible only insofar as its operations are "in harmony" with the concepts science employs. A common account of this "harmonic" relation is the correspondence theory of truth. The problems encountered by such a theory have led to coherentist alternatives, but we need not enter into this difficult territory to see that, on either approach, science must track the natural world in a way that seamanship does not track the sea. Likewise, while the ocean is wholly indifferent to the human purposes of those who sail on it, the natural world must in some sense be accessible to the scientific minds that study it. In short, sea and sailor are in opposition, but world and science must agree.

At its simplest, agreement between human beings takes the form of a convergence of mind and will. Theistic conceptions of nature can invoke something similar in explaining the success of science and technology—a convergence between the divine mind of the creator as embodied in the physical world on the one hand, and the mind of human beings as they seek to understand and manipulate that world. The sense of mystery that this endeavor frequently generates is not to be interpreted as a feeling of awe-filled wonder, so much as a perception of the inevitable limits of human understanding. Just where such limits fall may be uncertain, but their existence is necessary nonetheless. The boundaries of our understanding constitute an intellectual counterpart to the practical absolutes that a sense of the sacred imposes and that a proper piety bids us observe.

These brief remarks point towards a version of theistic supernaturalism that I am strongly inclined to defend. They are not offered here as a defense, however, since they amount to little more than a gesture. Even so, they may provide a reasonable indicator of how a rapprochement between science and supernaturalism might be affected such that any aspiration to a religious naturalism is rendered unnecessary. We need not strive to find the sacred within nature if we can more plausibly continue to look beyond it. And, to return to my starting point, the secularization thesis no longer has the power to make this seem impossible.

TEN

Imaging Religious Thoughts in the Appearance of Sensory Things

Mark Wynn

In this essay, I shall be concerned with the idea that religious thoughts can shape our experience of the sensory world. Specifically, I shall be interested in the possibility that religious thoughts can infuse the appearances of sensory things, and that their content can then be imaged by those appearances, and can contribute thereby to our aesthetic appreciation of the world. Drawing on this general picture, I shall explore some of the ways in which the religious imagination can help to shape the rational, behavioral and phenomenological structure of the life of faith. In concluding, I shall consider one further, more radical way in which the appearances of sensory things may mediate a religious meaning.

Religious thoughts and sensory appearances

I am going to begin by considering a little more closely the idea that religious thoughts can enter into the appearances of sensory things. In his book, *The Aesthetics of Architecture*, Roger Scruton comments that the appearance of a Gothic church can be structured by the thought of the heavenly city depicted in the Book of Revelation. The thought of the heavenly city need not just sit alongside the experience of the building, as a kind of commentary upon it, Scruton suggests, but can instead inhabit the appearance of the building. Accordingly, the thought can be rendered in experience, rather than simply being illustrated by or evidenced by experience. Scruton develops the point in these terms:

> ...it is clear from Abbot Suger's account of the building of St Denis...that the architects of the Gothic churches were motivated by a perceived relationship between the finished church and the Heavenly City of Christian speculation. Sir John Summerson has further suggested that the Gothic style aims at a certain effect of accumulation. Each great church can be considered as a concatenation of smaller structures, of aedicules, fitted together as arches, chapels, windows and spires, and so can be seen as an assembled city, rather than as a single entity minutely subdivided...But the "interpretation" here is not a "thought" that is separable from the experience—it is there *in* the experience, as when I see the dots of a puzzle picture as a face, or the man in the moon.[1]

So the distinction between thinking of a building as "a single entity minutely subdivided" and thinking of it as "a concatenation of smaller structures" has, Scruton is saying, a phenomenological counterpart: these conceptions of the building can be inscribed in its appearance. And for our purposes, it is noteworthy that once the building's appearance has been infused by the thought of the heavenly city, or by the thought of a "concatenation of smaller structures" which together comprise some overarching structure, then the church will present an image of the heavenly city. As Scruton says, it will then be possible to "see" the heavenly city in the structure of the building.

In Scruton's example, a person approaches a material object with a religious thought already in mind, and uses that thought to guide their construal of the object. It is also possible, surely, for a religious thought to arise out of the appearances, rather than being imported into them. However, for ease of exposition, let's keep the focus of our discussion on the case which Scruton has described. Of course, it is a familiar truth of human experience that we are able to arrange the lines of a shape or drawing, in our experience of them, so that they present a variety of perceptual gestalts. What is of particular interest in Scruton's remarks is the suggestion that religious thoughts can contribute to the formation of such a gestalt. If he is right about this, then the religious imagination can play a role in structuring our experience of the sensory world, and religious thoughts can be articulated—and contemplated

1. Roger Scruton, *The Aesthetics of Architecture* (Princeton, NJ: Princeton University Press, 1979), 74–5.

and reckoned with—not only in verbal form, but as inscribed in the appearances of sensory things.

In general, there is no great difficulty in the idea that the appearance of a spatial entity should be capable of being informed by the thought of another such entity. For example, I can use my knowledge of a racing car to guide my construal of a cloud (providing that the cloud is of the right general proportions!) so that the cloud's appearance comes to be patterned on the shape of the car. The thought of the heavenly city is, like the thought of a car, the thought of a spatially extended entity; and here too, there is no cause for surprise if the thought should be capable of structuring the appearance of sensory things. We might contrast this sort of case with the case where an abstract thought, rather than the thought of a spatial entity, enters into the appearances of things. This further case is of particular interest for an account of the relationship between religious thought and the appearances of the sensory world, because it points to the possibility that relatively abstract claims, including creedal claims, may be able to enter into the appearances. Some of Scruton's examples concern this further kind of case. Take for instance the following passage, where he suggests that the thought of a religious order's ideal of life can infuse the appearance of a building that has been constructed by the order:

> ...one might think of a Romanesque cloister in terms of the industrious piety of its former inhabitants: in terms of an historical identity, a way of life, with which this habit of building was associated. But were a man to present this as his reason for looking favourably on some particular cloister, say that of S. Paolo Fuori le Mura in Rome...then the onus lies on him to show exactly how such an idea finds confirmation in an experience of the building. Perhaps he could go on to refer to the variety of forms employed in the columns, to their fine industrious detailing, and to the way in which none of this abundance of observation disturbs the restful harmony of the design. He might trace the rhythm of the arcade, and describe the Cosmatesque mosaic, with its bright and childlike inventiveness that never transgresses the bounds of sensible ornamentation. In all this, he might say, we see how energetic observation and monastic piety may be successfully combined. A certain idea of monasticism becomes a visible reality: the idea is not merely a personal association occasioned by some anecdotal or historical reminiscence: we *see* it in the details of the building.[2]

2. Ibid. 109.

Here it is an abstract idea—the idea of a certain mode of life or a certain ideal of monastic piety—which enters into the sensory appearances of things. The thought of the order's charism is, therefore, like the thought of the heavenly city in having a phenomenological correlate. In this case, the relevant gestalt turns on the perceived relationship between the cloister's ornamentation, which suggests "energetic observation" of the world, and the "restful harmony" of the building's overall design. The perceptual field of a person who experiences the building in these terms will, presumably, afford the detail of the ornamentation a degree of salience, but in such a way that this detail remains integrated within the graceful, harmonious structure of the building as a whole. In this way, the order's charism can be imaged by the appearance of the building. As Scruton says, we will then be able to "see [this ideal of the monastic life] in the details of the building."

So the example of the cloister extends the example of the Gothic church by raising the possibility that abstract thoughts can enter into the appearances of sensory things. It also introduces the idea that the interpretation of an object can be assessed according to its ability to enhance the "look" of the object, once it enters into the object's appearance. Whether or not this was, as a matter of historical fact, the way of life which was professed by the builders of the cloister, this interpretation succeeds in aesthetic terms, Scruton is suggesting, insofar as it enriches the appearance of the cloister. It is easy to multiply examples of our willingness to rank thoughts on the basis of their capacity to enter unifyingly or enrichingly into the appearances of things. There is for example a famous line drawing which can be interpreted either as an old woman in a shawl looking down her nose or as a young woman turning her head away. No doubt other readings of this picture are also possible—there are, after all, other interpretations that will enable the lines of the drawing to hang together in some degree in our experience. But we prefer these two because they introduce a particularly satisfying unity into our perception of the picture. So one possible outcome of thought-infused perception is, as Scruton says, that "ambiguities are resolved and harmonies established."[3]

So far, we have been considering two ideas: religious thoughts, including abstract religious thoughts, are capable of entering into the appearances of sensory things; and, secondly, we can rank thoughts, including religious thoughts, on aesthetic grounds, according to their capacity to enter enrich-

3. Ibid. 119.

ingly into the sensory appearances. Let's consider now some implications of these two ideas for an account of the rational and phenomenological structure of the life of faith.

The pragmatic case from the appearances of sensory things

I am going to begin by considering how the aesthetic potency of a religious thought, or its capacity to enter enrichingly into the appearances of sensory things, may yield a reason for subscribing to the thought, at least to the extent of holding it in mind in some relatively focused and disciplined way.

Many of our contemporaries entertain religious thoughts, and engage in associated religious practices, without affirming the truth of those thoughts. Religious affiliation of this kind can be a religiously serious act. It may involve, for example, a determination to rehearse certain religious ideas in a regular and disciplined way—and in a spirit of reverence, or as a kind of spiritual exercise. The position of the moral philosopher Raimond Gaita suggests a perspective of broadly this kind. Gaita is well-known for his defense of the idea that "afflicted" human beings—such as the person who suffers from a serious psychiatric condition—belong fully within the moral community. Given his atheism or agnosticism, it is perhaps surprising to learn that Gaita also maintains that this insight is preserved most securely in the language of theistic faith, and above all in the prayerful language which represents God as a loving parent.[4] Although Gaita does not say as much, an atheist who shares his stance on these moral questions, and who shares his sense of the special resonance of the language of prayer, might well commit themselves, for good reasons, to rehearsing certain religious thoughts—and to thinking of other human beings as objects of divine love—as a kind of spiritual exercise, or as a way of refreshing their commitment to the full humanity of all human beings regardless of capacity or predicament. Gaita's case for the importance of religious thought in these matters is made in a broadly Wittgensteinian mode, but the same sort of perspective could also be developed in phenomenological terms, by supposing that certain

---

4. Gaita's case is set out in *A Common Humanity: Thinking about Love & Truth & Justice* (Melbourne: Text Publishing, 1999), 17–27.

religious thoughts, especially when they are entertained habitually or as a matter of spiritual discipline, can enable a person to enjoy a livelier perception of other human beings and in turn, therefore, a deepened appreciation of their significance.

So far, our discussion has been more concerned with the aesthetic than with the moral dimensions of our experience; and the same sort of case can be made here. As we have seen, a person might choose to adopt a religious thought because of its capacity to enter enrichingly into their experience of a church or cloister. And there is no reason to doubt that our experience of many other objects can also be enhanced, in aesthetic terms, once their appearance is informed by relevant religious thoughts. Indeed, we might plausibly speculate that by adopting relevant religious ideas, a person may be able to enjoy not simply an aesthetically enhanced experience of a certain type of object, or a restricted set of objects, but an aesthetically enhanced life world, where such a world encompasses a broad swathe of experience. If that is so, then a person may have good reason to rehearse a set of religious thoughts, in a regular and disciplined way, in order to share in the life world of the correlative faith tradition. Here we have the rudiments of a non-doxastic case for a certain kind of religious commitment.

It might be objected that this sort of commitment is bound to be rather "thin" religiously. There is, surely, a world of difference between entertaining a set of religious ideas purely on aesthetic grounds, because of their capacity to enhance the appearances of things, and holding them in the spirit of religious faith as traditionally conceived. This objection raises at least two issues. First, there is a question about the difference of epistemic standpoint between the person of religious faith and the person who adopts a set of religious thoughts simply for the sake of their appearance-enhancing powers. Someone who adopts a set of religious thoughts simply for aesthetic reasons could, after all, take those thoughts to be overwhelmingly improbable, and it is hard to see how the person of faith could take this view. Secondly, there is potentially a distinction of motivation. Someone who adopts a set of religious thoughts simply for the sake of their appearance-enhancing power would be acting, it might be alleged, in a spirit of self-interest, whereas a genuine commitment of faith surely implies a transcending of narrowly self-interested concerns.

The pragmatic justification of religious commitment which I gestured at just now will need to be extended in these two respects if it is to be relevant not only to the aesthetically motivated and, potentially, religiously serious contemplation of a set of religious thoughts, but also to religious faith as conventionally defined. This is not too difficult to do. For instance, we might simply stipulate that someone who acts on the basis of this pragmatic case will only count as a person of faith providing that they satisfy certain epistemic conditions—such as the condition of not taking the relevant thoughts to be overwhelmingly improbable. That leaves the objection from self-interest. Objections to pragmatic justifications of religious faith commonly hold that these justifications fail because they rest upon an appeal to self-interest. An objection of this kind may have some force if the relevant pragmatic benefits can be specified independently of any reference to religious concerns. (Suppose, for example, that benefit is understood as the enjoyment, whether in this life or the next, of a peace of mind which is devoid of any specifically religious content.) The account which we have been considering is relatively immune from this sort of objection, I suggest, because in this case the benefit has inherently a religious content: it consists, after all, in the enjoyment of various religious thoughts, or in the contemplation of these thoughts as rendered in sensory form.

It is noteworthy that many traditions require their adherents to appreciate the aesthetic dimension of the tradition's picture of reality. The person who fails to do this will to that extent have an impoverished apprehension of the significance of that picture.[5] So a person who derives aesthetic enjoyment from the contemplation of religious thoughts as rendered in sensory form, and who holds these thoughts in mind because they take pleasure in their aesthetic excellence, is not evidently moved by considerations which are contrary to the spirit of genuine faith—for the contemplation of such thoughts for the sake of their aesthetic excellence is surely, in the view of many traditions, a religiously worthy ambition. Of course, this is not to say that the motivations of the person of faith are exhausted by such aesthetic considerations. I am suggesting only that these considerations can have a part to play within a broader account of the motivational structure of the life of faith.

The recent literature on non-doxastic faith has been much concerned with the conditions which need to be satisfied if a commitment to a set of religious thoughts is to count as a case of faith. The account that we have been developing can be extended a little further by considering how it

---

5. For further discussion of these themes in relation to the Christian tradition, see for example David Bentley Hart, *The Beauty of the Infinite: The Aesthetics of Christian Truth* (Grand Rapids, MI: Eerdmans, 2003).

might relate to these accounts. For example, in his discussion of non doxastic propositional faith, William Alston notes that the person of faith should consider the truth of relevant religious thoughts to be a "good thing," and he adds that the person of faith should also take these thoughts as a basis for action.[6] Our aesthetic account provides one way of understanding why the person of faith may consider the truth of relevant religious thoughts to be a "good thing." Folk psychology (not to mention the practice of advertising agencies!) suggests that "a picture is worth a thousand words"; and the long-standing concern of the religions to regulate images is a further testament to their motivational power in religious contexts. If all of this is so, then we might suppose that religious thoughts are especially capable of engaging the affections when inscribed in the appearances of things. And in that case, we might respond to the question of why a particular person should hold that the truth of certain religious thoughts would be a good (or bad) thing by noting that this person has encountered these thoughts in sensory form.

The phenomenological perspective that we have been exploring is also relevant to Alston's requirement that the person of faith should take their religious thoughts as a basis for action. Here again, we could appeal to the capacity of religious thoughts to engage the affections and the will once they are inscribed in the appearances. But another account is also possible. Suppose I am visiting the site of an ancient settlement, and have little experience of such sites. Under these conditions, the site may strike me initially as little more than a heap of rubble; but with the help of my guidebook, I may be able to piece together an account of how these remains constitute a humanly meaningful whole. Suppose now that my experience of the site comes to be inhabited by this account of its significance. It is plausible to suppose that I will then be able to orient myself practically at the site with new assurance—for my sense of how its parts fit together, in humanly meaningful terms, will now be available to me directly, in perception. In the same sort of way, we might suppose that the thoughts of the person of faith can serve as a basis for action when those thoughts inhabit the sensory appearances. In such cases, a thought enables a new set of perceptual discriminations when it enters into the appearances, and thereby it also enables a new set of practical discriminations.

6. William Alston, "Audi on Nondoxastic Faith" in *Rationality and the Good: Critical Essays on the Ethics and Epistemology of Robert Audi*, ed. M. Timmons, J. Greco, and A. Mele (Oxford: Oxford University Press, 2007), chap. 11. For another instructive account of these matters, see John Schellenberg, *Prolegomena to Philosophy of Religion* (Ithaca NY: Cornell University Press, 2005).

In his account of religious faith, John Henry Newman famously distinguished between "real" and "notional" assent, where the first sort of assent depends upon having a "real image" of relevant objects. The details of this distinction are of no great consequence here, but it is noteworthy that Newman uses this distinction to develop the idea that the deeper kind of religious faith rests upon first hand experience. For instance, it is only when I have encountered God as my judge, in the experience of conscience, that I will be able to acquire a "real image" of God as judge; and it is only then, Newman says, that I will be able to give a "real assent" to the thought that God is my judge. The account of faith that we have been developing is like Newman's in seeking to ground faith in first hand experience, and to show how faith therefore requires more than a purely verbal assent to a set of creedal claims. Specifically, we have been interested in the idea that the content of a religious thought can be encountered in experience, not so much because we have direct experience of, for example, the heavenly city, but rather because the heavenly city can be imaged in the appearances of sensory things. This is not exactly Newman's position, but it shares with his an emphasis upon the role of "images," and of relevant first hand experience, in the life of faith.

To summarize, the phenomenological perspective that we have been considering generates at least a partial answer to a number of important questions. How could a person be moved, for sound, non-doxastic reasons, to adopt the perspective of faith? Why might someone take the truth of a religious thought to be a good thing? How might the perspective of faith inform our everyday relationship to the sensory world—perceptually and practically? And how might faith involve more than merely intellectual assent? Using this same phenomenological framework, I am going to turn to a further question now: what reasons might a person have for affirming the truth of a religious thought?

The epistemic case from the appearances of sensory things

Let's begin by returning to Scruton's example of the Gothic church. Suppose someone tells me that the designers of the Gothic church intended these structures to provide an image of the heavenly city. And suppose that I view a Gothic church with this thought in mind, and discover that the thought is capable of entering enrichingly into the appearance of the building. In that case, will I not have acquired a reason for thinking that these buildings were in fact constructed for the purpose of imaging the heavenly city?

Why think this? Well, if this was the purpose for which these churches were made, then it should be possible to grasp intellectually how the lines of a Gothic church can be fitted together so as to constitute an image of an assembled entity. If we cannot do this, then the church can hardly function as a representation of a city. And if the church is to "image" a city, rather than just lending itself to the thought that it shares certain structural features with a city, then it should be possible for this intellectual grasp to be rendered in experience, so that we acquire a perceptual grasp of the building's likeness to a city. And if the design is a good one, then the gestalt which is produced in this way should constitute a clearly defined unity, which encompasses the various elements of the building without undue strain. So the truth of the hypothesis that this building was made, as a matter of historical fact, for the purpose of imaging the heavenly city should generate a reasonably strong expectation that the thought of the heavenly city will be able (assuming the skill of the designers) to enter unifyingly into the appearance of the building. It follows that if the thought of the city can enter unifyingly into the appearance, then this hypothesis concerning the designers' intentions is to that extent confirmed, and if it cannot, then the hypothesis is to that extent disconfirmed.

Here we have an aesthetically grounded argument in support of a design hypothesis: it seems that, in cases of this kind, we can test the hypothesis that an object was made for a certain purpose by considering whether the thought of that purpose (in some relevant respect) is able to enter unifyingly into the appearance of the object. Admittedly, the example of the Gothic church is a rather special kind of case, because here the purpose concerns specifically the provision of an image. But even this rather specialized sort of case seems to lend itself pretty readily to theological application. There is, for instance, a long tradition of supposing that the world was designed by God so as to constitute an image—on the received view, an image of eternity or of the divine nature. (Aquinas, for example, develops this theme in the *Summa Theologiae*: 1a.47.1.) And if we understand God's purpose in creation in these terms, then why should we not reason in relation to the world in rather the way that we just reasoned in relation to the Gothic church? And would we not then be entitled to conclude that if the thought of the world as an image of God is able to enter enrichingly into the appearance of the world, then the hypothesis that this was indeed God's purpose in creation is to that extent confirmed; and if the thought is unable to do this, then it is to that extent disconfirmed?

As we have seen, it is not too difficult to understand how the thought *this church images the heavenly city* might be inscribed in the appearance of a Gothic church, so that it is rendered in phenomenological terms. But what phenomenology are we to associate with the thought *the world images God?* Indeed, how might *the world* function as an image of any kind? It is hardly possible, after all, for the world as a whole to be presented as a perceptual object.

The tradition of "extrovertive" mystical experience suggests one possible answer to this question. Experiences of this kind seem to involve a perceptual or quasi-perceptual grasp of a unity which is taken to underlie or infuse the objects of everyday experience.[7] And since the being of God is on all hands supposed to be supremely integrated or simple, should we not conclude that, to this extent, the world's likeness to God, or its imaging of God, can be apprehended in perceptual terms? In fact, extrovertive mystics of a theistic persuasion have presumably been interested in this sort of experience precisely because it allows us to understand how the world might become transparent to the being of God.

Of course, the world's unity can also be understood more in scientific than in religious terms, as when its unity is characterized in terms of its conformity to natural law. It seems that unity of this kind can also be apprehended in perceptual terms. Fridjof Capra's well-known remarks in *The Tao of Physics* appear to provide an illustration of such an experience:

> I was sitting by the ocean one late summer afternoon, watching the waves rolling in and feeling the rhythm of my breathing, when I suddenly became aware of my whole environment as being engaged in a gigantic cosmic dance. Being a physicist, I knew that the sand, rocks, water, and air around me were made of vibrating molecules and atoms, and that these consisted of particles which interacted with one another by creating and destroying other particles. I knew also that the earth's atmosphere was continually bombarded by showers of "cosmic rays," particles of high energy undergoing multiple collisions as they penetrated the air. All this was familiar to me from my research in high-energy physics, but until that moment I had only experienced it through graphs, diagrams, and mathematical theories. As I sat on that beach my former

---

7. See Caroline Franks Davis, *The Evidential Force of Religious Experience* (Oxford: Clarendon, 1989), 58–60.

experiences came to life; I 'saw' cascades of energy coming down from outer space, in which particles were created and destroyed in rhythmic pulses; I 'saw' the atoms of the elements and those of my body participating in this cosmic dance of energy; I felt its rhythm and I 'heard' its sound...[8]

Of course, Capra is interested in the possibility that experiences of this kind might confirm an Eastern, mystical conception of the world. But however that may be, his account also suggests that it is possible to apprehend the unity of the world, conceived scientifically, in perceptual terms. And if this possibility is granted, then we can make some sense of the idea that the world images the divine nature.

Capra's experience and the experiences of extrovertive mystics are evidently of a somewhat exceptional character. But there are other, more everyday kinds of experience which could also be taken to confirm the thought that the world was made in order to image God. To name an obvious example, there are artistic and other traditions, across cultures, which rest on the idea that it is possible to experience not just individual natural objects but whole landscapes and seascapes, and skyscapes, as beautiful. Insofar as beauty in this context is conceived in terms of a harmonious bringing together of disparate elements, experiences of this kind provide a further reason for supposing that the unity of the world can be registered in perceptual terms. And again, if that is so, then we have some reason for admitting the possibility that the world can function as an image of God.

Of course, there is a long-established tradition of natural theological speculation which has appealed to the experience of beauty in nature. F. R. Tennant is perhaps the most notable recent exponent of this tradition. He argues that the pervasiveness of the sensory world's beauty constitutes a weighty reason for thinking of that world as a designed object.[9] For Tennant, the world's beauty points to the truth that God's purpose for the world is, among other things, that it should be beautiful. But for the reasons we have been considering, the same range of phenomena might also be taken to support the claim that God intends the world to image the divine nature. Perhaps we could say, more simply, that God intends the world's beauty to image the divine beauty? But this claim will need to reckon with the objection that the beauty of material things can hardly present a likeness to the

8. Fridjof Capra, *The Tao of Physics* 3rd edn. (London: Flamingo, 1992), 11.
9. F. R. Tennant, *Philosophical Theology*, Vol. 2: *The World, The Soul and God* (Cambridge: Cambridge University Press, 1930), 89–93.

beauty of the immaterial God;[10] and in responding to this objection, we may need to invoke, after all, the idea that it is the unity of the material order that enables it to image a non-material realm.

Granted all of this, it makes sense to suppose that someone might allow their construal of sensory things to be guided by the thought that the world is an image of God, and might discover thereby that this thought can inhabit the appearances of sensory things. Such a person would have a reason (not necessarily an all-things-considered reason) for concluding that the world was in fact made so that it would image God. This case presents a relatively straightforward counterpart to Scruton's example of the Gothic cathedral. Equally, a person might begin from their experience of unity in nature, and then come to construe such experience as an experience of the divine unity or the divine beauty. In this case too, the experience of unity in the material order could be taken as confirmation of the thought that God intended the world to serve as an image of the divine nature. Of course, a person might experience the sensory world as beautiful or unitary with no thought of God. This sort of experience could also be taken to confirm the thought that the world was made in order to image God, because it shows that the world is in principle capable of imaging a unitary God, albeit that some individuals do not read their experience in these terms.

So far we have been concerned with imaging as a form of design. But in the human domain at least, we might suppose that a similar train of reflection will hold for other kinds of design. Suppose for example that an object is made for the sake of purpose P, where P has nothing to do with imaging anything. And suppose that this design is a good one: suppose, that is, that the object fittingly serves P. In that case, it should be possible to grasp intellectually how the various parts of the object constitute a unity—in so far as these parts are all fittingly ordered to P. I do not see that there is, in general, any presumption that an intellectual grasp of this kind should be capable of entering unifyingly into the appearance of the object. So I do not think that the failure of the thought of P, in some relevant respect, to enter unifyingly into an object's appearance has, in general, any tendency to disconfirm the hypothesis that the object was in fact made for this purpose. However, if the thought of P, in some relevant respect, can enter unifyingly into the appearance of an object, then the hypothesis that the object was made for purpose

<hr>

10. As Patrick Sherry asks, "how can a corporeal being be like God, who has no body or matter?" in *Spirit and Beauty: An Introduction to Theological Aesthetics* (Oxford: Clarendon Press, 1992), 141.

P is, presumably, to that extent confirmed. For in this case, we will enjoy a kind of perceptual verification of the claim that the parts of the object do indeed mesh together, fittingly, for the sake of serving P. We might appeal to this sort of consideration in some kinds of empirical enquiry. For example, an archaeologist might propose that a newly discovered artifact was made for such and such a purpose. And this hypothesis will be found more compelling, and rightly so, in so far as we can "see" (in Scruton's sense of seeing), rather than simply apprehending intellectually, how the parts of the thing fall together so as to serve this purpose.

If an argument of this kind can apply to human artifacts, then we might wonder, once again, whether a similar train of reflection might hold for the non-artifactual world or, as we might put it, for the world considered as a divine artifact. I take it that this is possible in principle. The hypothesis that the world was made for some divinely ordained purpose will be confirmed to the extent that the thought of that purpose, in some relevant respect, is capable of entering unifyingly into the appearances of sensory things. However, once again, we may doubt whether the failure of the thought of that purpose to enter into the appearances of things will, in general, count against the hypothesis.

Arguments from design in the tradition of William Paley invite us to think of the world as made from various parts which work together for the service of a purpose. Typically this Paleyan sort of argument rests upon the identification of a finely tuned relationship between the parts of a thing and its purpose. Thus Paley argues, famously, that we can show that a watch is in the strict sense a mechanism because we can establish the truth of relevant counter-factuals. We can show, for example, that if the watch's springs had been made from some metal other than steel, then they would have lacked the elasticity that is a prerequisite of accurate time-keeping.[11] The case we have been considering amounts to a perceptual and aesthetic rendering of the same sort of idea. If an object fittingly serves a given purpose then, relative to that purpose, its parts should constitute a satisfying unity; and if we can apprehend that unity in our perception of the object, then the thought that this is indeed the object's purpose will be to that extent confirmed.

Of course, this is not a wholly novel idea. It has, after all, long been supposed that design in nature can be registered perceptually, and not simply by

---

11. William Paley, *Natural Theology; or Evidences of the Existence and Attributes of the Deity, Collected from the Appearances of Nature*, Vol. I, (London: R. Faulder, 1803), 1–4.

way of inference.[12] These two approaches can of course work together; as we have seen, the perceptual case can corroborate the discursive. However, for the reasons we have been considering, the perceptual case may have a particular role to play in virtue of its motivational efficacy. If the sensory appearances can be inscribed with the thought that the world exists for the sake of a certain purpose, then this purpose will come to seem, in perceptual terms, part of the fabric of the world; and our affections and our will can be engaged accordingly. It is also worth noting that the aesthetic approach need not be wedded to a mechanistic conception of design. What matters is the perceptual recognition of a relation of fittingness, and this relation will obtain whenever several parts, or a number of independent variables, are elegantly adjusted to one another so as to serve an overarching purpose.

I have been arguing that the data supplied by the religious imagination can be applied to the question of how likely it is that the world was made for a certain end. So far, I have been talking in very general terms. A more persuasive presentation of this case would need to descend to the detail of particular religious traditions, and to ask whether the worldview of a given tradition gives us much reason to think that its doctrines will be able to inhabit the appearances of sensory things. Some traditions will generate a relatively strong expectation that certain of their doctrinal claims will, if true, be capable of informing the sensory appearances. For example, Christians have sometimes supposed that genuine conversion is distinguishable from its simulacra because of its phenomenology.[13] And on some accounts, this new phenomenology will consist, at least in part, in a re-ordered perception of the sensory world. As William James notes, "a not infrequent consequence of the change operated in the subject [following conversion] is a transfiguration of the face of nature in his eyes. A new heaven seems to shine upon a new earth."[14]

Of course, when its content is specified in these rather generic terms, a re-ordered experience of this kind is open to a number of interpretations. But one account would proceed along the lines that we have been sketching. Perhaps the convert was unable to give even verbal assent to various

12. See for example Del Ratzsch, "Perceiving Design," in *God and Design: The Teleological Argument and Modern Science*, ed. N. A. Manson (London: Routledge, 2003), chap. 6.
13. See Jonathan Edwards, "Religious Affections," in *Jonathan Edwards: Representative Selections* ed. C. H. Faust and T. H. Johnson (New York: Hill & Wang, 1962), 239.
14. William James, *The Varieties of Religious Experience: A Study in Human Nature* (London: Longmans, Green, 1910), 151.

creedal claims prior to conversion. And perhaps they find that, all of a sudden, these claims come to life, and come to seem compellingly persuasive. We might speculate that in some cases at least, this story will obtain when these creedal claims enter into the sensory appearances of things. Perhaps this is what conversion consists in, in some cases, from a phenomenological point of view. Jonathan Edwards testifies to the possibility of an experience of broadly this kind when he writes of his own conversion that "God's excellency, his wisdom, his purity and love, seemed to appear in everything: in the sun, moon, and stars; in the clouds and blue sky; in the grass, flowers, and trees; in the water and all nature..."[15] To the extent that Christians read conversion in these terms, and to the extent that they treat conversion as a prerequisite of authentic Christian commitment, then their tradition will be open to a significant degree of confirmation or disconfirmation depending upon whether certain of its doctrinal claims are able to enter into the appearances of sensory things. Alternatively, we could tell a somewhat similar story in which the initial, pre-conversion state is one of merely notional assent, and where the transition to real assent is equally an achievement of the religious imagination to the extent that it requires various thoughts to be imaged in the appearances of sensory things.

It is not difficult to see why the subject of such an experience might take this "transfiguration" of the appearances to show that the relevant doctrinal claims are true—for from their perceptual vantage point, the content of these claims will now be inscribed in the fabric of the world. Our earlier discussion suggests that this shift from a transformed phenomenology to a new assessment of the epistemic status of certain claims may well be in order; for a thought's capacity to enter into the appearances of things can, under the right conditions, serve as index of its likely truth.

So some traditions will generate a relatively strong expectation that at least some of their creedal claims will, if true, be able to enter into the appearances of sensory things. Other traditions may be much less likely to generate phenomenologically testable consequences. For instance, a tradition might maintain that human experience is so corrupt that it is only rarely, if at all, capable of being penetrated by a true conception of things. For a tradition of this kind, human experience will remain relatively opaque to religious truth. The epistemic case which we have been considering

15. Cited in *The Varieties*, 249.

might still apply prima facie to such a tradition; but this case will lack ultima facie force, once we take into account the particular understanding of human experience that is favored by the tradition. Here, the failure of certain doctrines to enter into the appearances of things will not yield an ultima facie case against the truth of those doctrines.

I have been concentrating on the case of theistic traditions, not least because these traditions take an interest in design, and their approach can be related with particular ease, therefore, to Scruton's examples of design in architecture. But the truth of the doctrines of non-theistic traditions may also generate phenomenologically testable expectations, and the religious imagination may have an epistemic role to play in this context too. Indeed, a striking feature of many such traditions is precisely their interest in effecting some transformation in the subjective quality of the believer's experience, under the impact of relevant teaching. The sage's experience of the world is often supposed to be infused by the thought of certain fundamental metaphysical ideas—such as the idea that sensory things are all transitory, or all in some important respect unsatisfactory. So we might say that the sage is precisely the person who has grasped these truths perceptually and who is, therefore, liberated from illusion, because for him the appearances are now truth-bearing—because inhabited by a true conception of things. A tradition which speaks in these terms will of course be open to a significant degree of testing on phenomenological grounds.

A concluding thought: encountering God in the appearances

We have been exploring some of the implications of the idea that religious thoughts can be inscribed in the appearances of sensory things. I would like to close by alluding very briefly to one further way of developing this idea within a rather specific doctrinal context.

Christians have long supposed that, in some sense, God identifies with afflicted people. This tradition derives in part from the passage in Matthew, chapter 25, where Jesus says to those who have fed the hungry, clothed the naked, and visited prisoners: "as often as you have done this to one of these my lowliest brothers, you have done it to me" (v. 40).[16] Interestingly, there is

16. I have based this translation on the English rendering of the text given in Ulrich Luz, *Matthew 21–28: A Commentary*, trans. J. E. Crouch (Minneapolis, MN: Fortress Press, 2005), 264.

a long tradition of taking this passage at its word, and supposing that Jesus is not just proposing that when we treat marginal people with decency, we treat people *like him* with decency, but that in so doing, we treat *him* with decency. When commenting on this passage, and the case of those who have refused to extend help to the sick, and other marginal people, Gregory of Nyssa comments: "In condemning the sickness that preys upon the body of this man, you fail to consider whether you might be, in the process condemning yourself and all nature. For you yourself belong to the common nature of all. Treat all therefore as one common reality."[17] Here it is not only Jesus whom we treat decently when we treat the marginal person decently, but in a sense all human beings, and ourselves, because of the "common nature of all." Whatever we make of the ontology of natures that is implied here, it is clear that Gregory intends to endorse a reading of our passage which licenses a closer identification between the marginal person and the figure of Jesus than is implied in the "like him" reading. And it is easy to generate other examples of this stronger reading of the text.[18] Let's consider now how we might relate this particular doctrinal complex to our earlier reflections.

In our experience of other human beings, we can distinguish broadly speaking between three cases. First, there is the case where their personhood is denied or in some way bracketed out. On some accounts, pornography provides an example of this sort of experience. We might say that here we experience the body of the person, rather than the person as embodied.[19] In this sense, it is the body of the person and not the person themselves who is presented in the appearances. Then there is the case where the personhood of the other is acknowledged, but where this recognition does not infuse the appearances. When we are tired, for example, or when our sensitivities are blunted for some other reason, we may find that our experience of others fails to be infused by the thought of their personhood, even though we do not set aside this thought or cease to think of them as persons. In this case too, we may say that while the person is the object of our experience,

17. Gregory of Nyssa, in Susan R. Holman, *The Hungry are Dying: Beggars and Bishops in Roman Cappadocia* (Oxford: Oxford University Press, 2001), 201. The text is taken from Gregory's sermon "On the Saying, 'Whoever Has Done It to One of These Has Done It to Me'." I am grateful to Morwenna Ludlow for this reference.
18. A particularly well-known medieval example is the story of Martin of Tours, who gave half his tunic to an impoverished person, and who then had a dream in which Christ said that it was he himself who had received the tunic. See Luz, *Matthew 21–28*, 272.
19. The distinction is noted by Scruton in *Beauty* (Oxford: Oxford University Press, 2009), 47.

the person themselves fails to be presented in the appearances. Then finally there is the case where the appearance of another human being is infused by the thought of their personhood. This sort of experience is, I take it, quite different morally and phenomenologically from experience of another person which is vacant of any such thought. Here the person themselves is presented in the appearances.

The "strong" interpretation of Matthew 25 suggests that we can distinguish somewhat similarly between three cases of experience of God. Even if it is in fact God whom we encounter in our relationship to another human being, as Gregory supposes, God may fail to be presented to us in the appearance of this person. This may be because we do not acknowledge the reality of God, or because while we do acknowledge that reality, the thought of God fails even so to enter into the appearances. But there is also a further possibility. Suppose that a person subscribes to Gregory's account, and suppose that this account is in fact the truth of the matter; and suppose that this person allows the thought of God to infuse the appearance of another human being. (How exactly this might be done is, I am afraid, beyond the compass of this paper, but I trust that the earlier discussion provides some clues! For an example of such an experience, the reader is referred to Jonathan Edwards' account of his conversion, cited just now.) Should we not say of this case not simply that God is the object of the experience, but that God is presented in the appearances of the other person?

In this way, the idea that the thought of God can inhabit the appearances of sensory things can be used, within a specific doctrinal context, to support a particularly radical assessment of the significance of the sensory world. Not only can various religious thoughts be inscribed in the appearances of the world, and not only can God be recognized in the sensory world as its sustaining cause, and not only can God be encountered in the sensory world insofar as Gregory's ontology of natures holds true, but God can also be presented in the appearances of sensory things.[20]

20. I have benefited from the opportunity to present this paper on a number of occasions, in particular at the research seminar of the Department of Theology and Religion, Exeter University; at the D Society, Cambridge University; at the Natural Theology Group, London; at the symposium "*Renouveaux Analytiques en Philosophie de Religion*," hosted by the *Institut Romand de Systématique et d'Ethique*, University of Geneva, 2010, and at the Glasgow University Philosophy of Religion conference, 2010. I am very grateful for the helpful comment I received on all of these occasions. I have addressed some related issues in a paper which is forthcoming in *Religious Studies*, and I am also indebted to the editor and to a reader for the journal for their comments on a draft of that paper.

Figure 11.1 Espagnola Tourists. © Jonathan Wells 2011

ELEVEN

Re-Imaging the Galapagos

Jil Evans

"Philosophical analysis at its best is an aesthetic undertaking."[1]

Hovering over the equator with a bird's eye view and his tongue firmly planted in his cheek, well-known naturalist Richard Dawkins imagines in his mind a Tinker Bell of biology, performing an act of metamorphosis. What emerges is the archipelago of nineteen islands that has come to symbolize for many a first garden of ultimate metamorphosis: evolution.

> The good science fairy flew right round the world, looking for a favored spot to touch with her magic wand and turn it into a scientific paradise, a geological and biological Eden, the evolutionary scientist's Arcadia. You may question her motives or her existence, but of the place she lit upon there is no doubt.[2]

Later on, he describes why this location is so special for the study of evolution:

> But this volcanic hell-mouth placed—as it is—at just the right distance from the mainland, and with the islands themselves neatly spaced out, all evolutionary hell breaks loose. But it breaks loose with that controlled moderation that marks the well-designed experiment: just enough richness to be interesting and revealing, not enough to confuse and smother the take-home message.[3]

1. Daniel N. Robinson, in his introduction to *Neuroscience and Philosophy: Brain, Mind, and Language*, by M. Bennett, D. Dennett, P. Hacker, and J. Searle (New York: Columbia University Press, 2007), ix.
2. Richard Dawkins, in his forward to *Galapagos: The Islands That Changed The World* by Paul D. Stewart (New Haven: Yale University Press, 2006), 6.
3. Ibid. 7.

Animal life cycles through birth and death in the Galapagos Islands, regardless of our observations. But there are all kinds of human observations of non-human life that have been carried out before and after Darwin's visit to that archipelago of volcanic islands in 1835–from the scientific data gathering of evolutionary biologists, to conservationists who work to rid or control the effects of non-endemic species on the eco-system of the islands, to eco-tourists who march in single lines along narrow paths, guided by trained naturalists, in order to experience *Las Encantadas*.

Reactions to the Galapagos range from the ecstatic to the contemptuous. Ecstatic reports come from scientists like Dawkins who find the Galapagos an ideal location for observing and studying animals in their natural habitat, and tourists who find the intimate proximity to animals to be Eden-like, reviving an old, cherished dream of the peaceable kingdom. There are, however, less than positive responses, including this famous account by Herman Melville:

> Take five-and-twenty heaps of cinders dumped here and there in an outside city lot, imagine some of them magnified into mountains, and the vacant lot the sea, and you will have a fit idea of the general aspect of the Encantadas, or the enchanted Isles. A group rather of extinct volcanoes than of isles, looking much as the world at large might after a penal conflagration. It is to be doubted whether any spot on earth can, in desolateness, furnish a parallel to this group.[4]

Melville's portrait gives us an experience just as human as Dawkin's merited excitement about the islands as a brilliant laboratory. Melville pictures land masses devoid of enchantment, instead the islands loom up quickly, gigantic piles of abandoned scrap hurled into the ocean by indifferent gods. Hanging over and surrounding the islands is a vast emptiness, an infinite oppressive space. Dawkins' vision of the Galapagos is one of a fertile, ceaselessly productive site. Out of the "hell-mouth" magma explodes in contact with the water, forming the islands just where they should be. Dawkins finds them perfectly fitted to a scientist's work and goals. Everything can be found in its right place and in its right portion.

Dawkins and Melville work to persuade us of their experience through the aesthetic properties of language: how words sound alone and in proximity to another, the rhythm of their placement in a forward motion, the

---

4. Herman Melville, "The Encantadas; or Enchanted Isles," (originally published in 1854) in: *Billy Budd and Other Tales* (New York: Signet Classic, 1998), 235–6.

bearing of their stature, the density, shape and direction of motifs and images. Their compositions of experience arrive, not through lifeless abstractions, but through our senses. Such different pictures, and such different conclusions, but both writers are engaged with how we inhabit the world and how we should inhabit the world.

This engagement with habitation "bodies forth"[5] ideas about both the nature of our species and the nature of mind. This chapter addresses the subjective experience of longing, our longing to know the answer to the question "What am I doing here?" Human habitation on the Galapagos Islands has a complicated and fitful history.

The islands came under jurisdiction of Ecuador in 1832, and there were a number of attempts by non-Ecuadorian immigrants to create permanent settlements. In the 1800s a man named Manuel Cobos, who was murdered by a convict wielding a machete, established a penal colony on San Cristobel Island. Norwegians were lured to the islands by an Oslo promoter's talk of diamonds; others were drawn to the Galapagos through the published watercolors and photographs of William Bede and his team of scientists. People on the islands are still talking about the visit and bizarre events involving a possible murder, an attempt to establish a monarch on the islands, and the unanswered disappearance of the infamous Baroness Eloise Wagner-Bousguet and her all-male entourage.

The utilitarian use of the Galapagos that benefits its human population has gradually come into greater balance with the scientists, ecologists, and concerned citizens who work to save the islands from the ever-expanding deleterious effects of human habitation and invasive species. Today, large-scale illegal fishing is pervasive in the archipelago, and many of the inhabitants live in poverty with inadequate education and health care. Still, we have moved on from the eighteenth and nineteenth centuries when whalers demolished the whale population and ate nearly all of the giant tortoises.[6]

The Galapagos have attained mythic status for a variety of reasons. For those of us who value the prolific growth of knowledge in the biological

5. Shakespeare, *Midsummer Night's Dream*, 5.1.14.
6. Among recent books on the Galapagos Islands, I highly recommend: Pierre Constant, *Galapagos Islands* (Hong Kong: Odyssey Books & Guides, 2000); John Hickman, *Galapagos: The Enchanted Islands through writers' eyes* (London: Eland, 2009); Edward J. Larson, *Evolution's Workshop* (New York: Basic Books, 2001); Carol Ann Bassett, *Galapagos at the crossroads* (Washington DC: National Geographic, 2009); K. Thalia Grant and Gregory B Estes, *Darwin in the Galapagos* (Princeton and Oxford: Princeton University Press, 2009).

sciences, the islands live in a story that is bound up with Darwin's journey on HMS Beagle, his development of the theory of evolution by natural selection, and the subsequent image of the natural world as a realm with only the appearance of intention, agency and design. Because of the enduring importance of Darwin's work and the almost continuous philosophical explorations of theories of evolution and emergence, two images of the islands come into view, manifestations of two radically different images of the universe itself and how we understand the relationship of consciousness, purpose, and nature. These images yield very different pictures of habitation.

Two images from the bird's eye

The two images I would like to compare in this final chapter of *Turning Images* involve the image of the natural world according to theism and according to naturalism. The theistic tradition grounds the earth and the cosmos itself and all its content and laws (galaxies, dark matter, consciousness, and so on) in a purposive, intentional Being who creates "fittingness" into the very structure of reality itself. Theism offers one explanation for our ability to apprehend order and disorder, to make sense in gaining new knowledge and the new opportunities to care for the well being of the planet. Our ability to do this is grounded in the existence of an irreducible goodness and an aesthetic quality of fittingness.[7] There is fittingness or goodness in the moral realm as well as in the physical processes and states that constitute what we understand as the realm of nature.[8]

The competing, longstanding image of the world is naturalistic. Naturalism comes in many forms, but in the present context my focus is on the stringent and popular form of naturalism which is physicalistic and understands the whole cosmos, including all experience in terms of physical/material

---

7. I develop a sustained concept of aesthetic fittingness in the co-authored work, *The Image in Mind*. Suffice to note here, I am invoking the notion that we have an affective sense of when acts and events are fitting, proper or good and an affective sense of when such acts and events are unfitting, improper, bad or dysfunctional. This is not to say that we cannot be mistaken in our judgments, but that this sense is an irreducible sense that we consult when making judgments. *The Image in Mind* also includes a defense of the coherence and plausibility of Platonic Theism, a view of God that gives a central role to beauty, truth, and goodness. For a sympathetic treatment of theistic views of the environment see "Christianity" by Robin Attfield in *A Companion to Environmental Philosophy*, ed. D. Jamieson (Oxford: Blackwell, 2001), 96–110.

8. For an elaboration and defense of this position, see by R. M. Adams, *Finite and Infinite Goods: A Framework for Ethics*, (Oxford: Oxford University Press, 1999).

processes. In this schema, consciousness, our curiosity and relentless drive to understand the natural world and its meaning must ultimately be accounted for in physical terms. This is the stance taken up in different but similar ways by David Armstrong, Paul and Patricia Churchland, Daniel Dennett, David Papineau, Willard van Orman Quine, J. J. C. Smart, and others. Richard Dawkins seems to recognize consciousness as a genuine, emergent reality (not reducible or eliminated by the physical sciences), but because he has dedicated himself to the absolute replacement of theism with biology, I will regard him as an honorary strict naturalist. The naturalism I am engaging is one that insists on the causal closure of the physical world; it is a worldview that does not allow for independent (irreducible to physical states) mental causation or teleology (purpose). The philosophy of naturalism only allows the mental and purposiveness to have causal roles if these are fully determined by non-mental, non-purposive causes.[9]

The naturalist therefore seeks to explain our experience using a mechanistic model, consisting of only physical forces, while the theist understands the physical to be only part of reality, made possible and sustained by what Aristotle and Darwin both thought of as a First Cause.[10] If naturalism is true, how do we reconcile all our interests, purposes, and experiences of awe and disappointment with a universe that has no purpose? Can reductive naturalism really answer not only why and how the laws and forces of nature account for the shape and extension of the mockingbird's wing fitted for flight, but also the moment in time when the mockingbird enters a poem? I don't mean a scientific description of that moment, which the natural sciences can certainly provide. I refer to the claim that Richard Rorty made that:

> Every speech, thought, theory, poem, composition, and philosophy will turn out to be completely predictable in purely naturalistic terms. Some atom-and-the-void account of micro-processes within individual beings will permit the prediction of every sound or inscription which will ever be uttered. There are no ghosts.[11]

9. See Stewart Goetz and Charles Taliaferro, *Naturalism* (Grand Rapids: Erdmanns, 2008) for an overview of the different forms of naturalism; in their terminology I am focusing on strict naturalism or forms of broad naturalism according to which the mental has no independent causal role, but is completely determined or as completely supervening on the physical. For a helpful analysis of the problems facing naturalistic-physicalism, see Daniel Stoljar, *Physicalism* (London: Routledge, 2010).
10. Charles Darwin, *The Autobiography of Charles Darwin 1809–1882*, (London: Collins, 1958).
11. R. Rorty, *Philosophy and the Mirror of Nature* (Princeton: Princeton University Press, 1979), 387.

Naturalists Dawkins and Daniel Dennett illustrate naturalism (and critique the theistic alternative) by using the images of a crane and a skyhook. The crane is quite a tangible thing, handy and strong. The crane is pictured as a machine that is operating on simple objects and processes that gradually build greater levels of complexity. The bottom-up order of explanation has a grounding and logic that is, in the judgment of Dawkins and Dennett, utterly lacking in theism, which is pictured as a skyhook. The latter is an imaginary, invisible (impossible to locate) "hook" on which to hang something. Dennett sets up the two images as follows:

> Let us imagine that *a skyhook is a "mind first" force or power or process, an exception to the principle that all design and apparent design is ultimately the result of mindless, motiveless mechanicity.* A *crane*, in contrast, is a subprocess or special feature of a design process that can be demonstrated to permit the local speeding up of the basic, slow process of natural selection, and that can be demonstrated to be itself the predictable (or retrospectively explicable) product of the basic process.[12]

Dawkins offers a similar portrait of naturalism versus theism.

> One of the greatest challenges to the human intellect…has been to explain how the complex, improbable appearance of design in the universe arises. The natural temptation is to attribute the appearance of design to actual design itself…The temptation is a false one, because the designer hypothesis immediately raises the larger problem of who designed the designer. The whole problem we started out with was the problem of explaining statistical improbability. It is obviously no solution to postulate something even more improbable. We need a "crane," not a "skyhook." For only a crane can do the business of working up gradually and plausibly from simplicity to otherwise improbable complexity. The most ingenious and powerful crane so far discovered is Darwinian evolution by natural selection. Darwin and his successors have shown how living creatures, with their spectacular statistical improbability and appearance of design, have evolved by slow, gradual degrees from simple beginnings.[13]

Contemplating the images of the crane and the skyhook, I am struck first with the concreteness and repetitive motion of the crane's moving arm, and in contrast, the no-where-ness (in the clouds? the starry heavens?) of the "mind-first" power. The crane is doing something functional; the skyhook is nowhere to be found. The images employed here to create a

---

12. D. Dennett, *Darwin's Dangerous Idea* (New York: Simon & Schuster, 1995), 76.
13. R. Dawkins, *The God Delusion* (New York: Houghton Mifflin, 2006), 157–8.

comparison are deliberately (and most appropriately) of different kinds. However, in religious thought, when making comparisons between two kinds of things, often it is to posit two realities—one that is contingent and decays, and one that is of a different order all together. The image of the golden calf and a burning bush that speaks, the grass that withers and the enduring word, are presented as real things that are finite or as metaphors for things that open up to the transcendent. Each is presented as a reality that we are asked to acknowledge, but also to know the difference. The crane and skyhook are images of origins; and the crane awakens a kinesthetic response in us to weight, physicality—something that we can quantify. The skyhook isn't just weightless or inadequate; it is an absurdity.

Equating theism with a skyhook ignores the central claim of theism: the very potential for existence in theism is not in a thing, but in a being. The grounding of the cosmos (with all its cranes, suns, cosmic growth and decay, equilibrium and dynamism) in a deeply personal Reality is in a great, omnipresent, intentional being who is anything but (in Dennett's terms) mindless or motiveless. In theism, God is understood as necessarily existing; God is not dependent upon any external causal laws or forces to sustain God in being. Both Dennett and Dawkins write as though if there is a God, God's existence needs to be explained through physical laws. If one imagines God as one of a species, a material thing or a blind force, their view makes sense, but as many have pointed out, including the philosopher and atheist Thomas Nagel, Dennett and Dawkins seem to completely misunderstand the nature of theism. They reason that in order to recognize the existence of God, one must have a causal account of how God came into being, whereas the very concept of God is of a being that cannot have come into being or pass into non-being. If God exists, God's existence is not due to any sort of explanation, or at least not one involving probabilities.[14]

The use of the crane or the whole naturalistic framework of arguing from the ground up does not make any less mysterious the existence of consciousness and the existence of the cosmos itself. Dawkins seeks recourse in natural selection, but the biological account of consciousness itself is deeply

14. See "Dawkins and Atheism" in Thomas Nagel, *Secular Philosophy and the Religious Temperament* (Oxford: Oxford University Press, 2010) 19–26, especially 22.

problematic, as I have argued in *The Image in Mind*, a position that is reinforced in Steve Jones' book, *Darwin's Island*:

> Scientists are often asked to explain what makes men different from chimpanzees or oranges, but in some ways that is scarcely an issue for science. Such questions deal not with the body or the brain but the mind, a topic most biologists consider to be outwith their expertise.[15]

A naturalistic account of the cosmos itself will have to run deeper than Darwin's account of the origin of species, for (ultimately) naturalism will need to address not just the emergence of life and consciousness, but the existence of the laws of nature that make evolution possible at all. Some naturalists (perhaps most) have treated such laws as basic and not requiring explanation (for, arguably, none is possible within naturalism). But if we focus on the desire for a *complete explanation*, one might wonder (to use the Dennett-Dawkins idiom) what the crane is resting on.

To conclude this initial look at the two images of crane and skyhook, a modest point is in order about the shifting nature of both science and images. The conception of biological explanation that Dawkins and Dennett employ (of moving from the simple to the complex) is not a model that most biologists are working with today. Many, if not most contemporary biologists think a better model draws on the sciences of complexity. The field of epigenetics treats the organism as an irreducible entity, existing in self-organizing patterns of networks, involving genes, but also the constraints of the environment and physical laws.

This shift in models does not make all of reality suddenly and obviously explainable in naturalistic terms, but it could serve as an important critique of genetic reductionism by providing a model that pictures complex entities that are irreducible.

Rather than investigate theism and naturalism in formal analytic terms, I would like to consider both in the language of fittingness (our sense or view that some attitudes, emotions, actions are fitting or unfitting) and habitation, or what may be called *a longing or desire to be at home* in the natural world or the cosmos as a whole. This will involve weighing theism and naturalism in our experience of values. To do so, let us return to the Galapagos Islands.

---

15. Steve Jones, *Darwin's Island* (London: Abacus, 2010), 82. For a further defense of this position see Robinson's *Consciousness and Mental Life* (New York: Columbia University Press, 2008).

The naturalist Galapagos

Many of us who have traveled to the Galapagos hold in our minds images that reflect shifts in our perceptions over the course of the voyage. I am concerned with our conscious apprehension of where our status lies on an inner map, an inner map that demarcates the depth and breadth of our desire to feel at home in the world we know in our subjective experience, and beyond that the cosmos. As noted earlier, the majority of the islands are not fit for human habitation, and vast expanses of ocean are traversed to visit various islands. We carry our assumed understanding of our place in the world into terrain that will never be domesticated to provide for our needs. Markers that we often take for granted are nonexistent. Walking across a landscape with no fresh water, no possibility of agriculture, and little protection from the equatorial sun, we experience a place on the planet that does not make a good fit for our species, and so we are not at home. Most of the islands in the archipelago are experienced as being indifferent to our well-being. As day visitors carefully guided over vast beds of aa and pahoehoe lava, and along paths that wind through the Giant opunita cacti, our existence is vulnerable, as it truly is wherever we are. The tourists who witness, probably for the first time, the abandonment of the young sea lion by its mother are reminded that they are not in Eden. It is distressing to watch a baby sea lion wander up and down the beach looking for its mother, or for any female to be adopted by, and watch as it collapses, exhausted and alone. Why are we distressed?

The imagination is engaged in our experience of place, for in experience our perception includes more than what is immediately apparent to us in sensations. As Mark Wynn and Douglas Hedley have argued, our perception can involve extrapolation and filling out.[16] Is our experience of the islands to fit the early naturalistic portrait of conflict and does this seem fitting?

In some respects, the islands do seem to reflect the old picture of the cosmos, going back at least to Empedocles, that the world is shot through with warfare. In his zoogony, the presence of strife and the power of love work in a continuous dialectic to create and then destroy wholeness. Empedocles presents images of dismemberment that startle our necessary and abiding sense of organic unity.

16. See Douglas Hedley, *Living Forms of the Imagination* (London: T&T Clark, 2008), and Mark Wynn's *Emotional Experience and Religious Understanding* (Cambridge: Cambridge University Press, 2006), and *Faith and Place* (Oxford: Oxford University Press, 2009).

Here sprang up many faces without necks, arms wandered without shoulders, unattached, and eyes strayed alone, in need of foreheads.[17]

In Empedocles' world the carnage of the battlefield is our beginning, born of strife. Love then works to combine what is broken and whole creatures are born. Many centuries later, Thomas Hobbes' continued this general portrait, arguing that our natural state, without government, is a "war of all against all."[18] This fits with a naturalist view of the cosmos.

These two portraits of nature by Empedocles and Hobbes, inclusive of brokenness, war and violence, are attempts to bring our experience and our witness of suffering into reconciliation with the good we desire, and even sometimes experience. We need to make sense of it. Taking the imagery of war as a metaphor for our natural origin will be carried onward in the language of Darwinism: "survival of the fittest" and in what Marilynne Robinson deems as Freud's parascientific model of reality, "...one in which the world in itself is an intolerable threat, and only the strict rationing awareness of it, by grace of the selectivity of the senses, makes the organism able to endure it...Freud's model of the origin and nature of consciousness is of a being first of all besieged and beleaguered, not by the threats posed by the vital, amoral energies of Darwinian nature, but by, so to speak, the cosmos, the barrage of undifferentiated stimuli which is everything that is not itself."[19] So bothered was Freud by our persistent desire to abide in the cosmos as friend and not as stranger—for our existence to have meaning that transcends the utilitarian needs of an impersonal universe—he sought to reduce this longing to a pathology.[20]

In proper scientific investigations into life cycles, adaptation, biological function, and so on, there is neutrality over theories of value, whether this involves the Hobbesian warfare model or theism. Scientists are not asking ontological questions when trying to determine functions or probabilities. Change happens; it is not good or bad; it just is what it is. (Though their scientific practice is grounded in what are epistemological and metaphysical claims about the nature of evidence and its relationship to truth.)

There is a strange, and confusing complexity of meaning and non-meaning in the analogies of life as war emerging here in looking at the history of

17. Empedocles, (B57).
18. Hobbes, *Leviathan*, xiii, various editions.
19. Marilynne Robinson, *Absence of Mind* (New Haven & London: Yale University Press, 2010), 102.
20. Ibid. 102–3.

images used in the naturalism-theism debate. The confusion becomes apparent when we look at our subjective experience and compare it to the language used to develop the larger, grander theories of our place in the order of things.

In actual war, the hope for unity or wholeness in our human experience is severed and gives way to deprivation and murderous retaliation. In actual war our image of wholeness dies in language itself, confronted with the spoken and pictured testimony of those who must live through it, and die of it. New vocabularies of death and killing (*casualties, friendly fire*), clichés, and a state-controlled narrative invade to dominate public discourse.[21] Attrition, alienation and closing down are now foregrounded in the language of what is possible or what was potential.

Paul Celan, who lost both parents in the Holocaust, wrote poems heeding the necessity to find a form that would hold in its silences the very nature of what is at stake in the face of humanity's destruction of humanity. After such a rupture, how do you begin to speak again? The poet is constantly aware of the failure of the word to provide wholeness. Poetry makes the gap explicit and then invites us to leap over. Celan took on the terrible task of trying to find a way to use the German language, the language of both Holderlin and the Third Reich, to hold on to what war threatened to erase.

> *Tubingen, January*
> Eyes talked into
> blindness.
> Their—"an enigma is
> the purely
> originated"—their
> memory of
> Hölderlin towers afloat, circled
> by whirring gulls.
>
> Visits of drowned joiners to
> these
> submerging words:
>
> Should,
> should a man,
> should a man come into the world, today, with

---

21. For a sober account of the culture of war and its effect on culture, as well as a historical look at war found in the writings of the Greeks and Romans, see the war correspondent Chris Hedges' book: *War is a force that gives us meaning* (New York: Public Affairs, 2002).

the shining beard of the
patriarchs: he could,
if he spoke of this
time, he
could
only babble and babble
over, over
againagain,

("Pallaksh. Pallaksh.")[22]

One consequence of violence is the erosion of our ability to "make sense." Celan's "riddling poems" conveys a self who is working, not dreaming, to keep sense from drowning in non-sense.[23] And here the longing for sense, what Camus called our "longing for happiness and reason" in the face of our capacity to kill and be killed, to find in the world an answer to injustice, is ultimately, in naturalism, an intellectual mistake on our part.[24]

For as Dawkins notes, in naturalism, there is no problem of evil in the sense that evil is anomalous or a monstrous aberration, a rent in the fabric.

> On the contrary, if the universe were just electrons and selfish genes, meaningless tragedies like the crashing of this bus are exactly what we should expect, along with equally meaningless good fortune. Such a universe would be neither evil nor good in intention. It would manifest no intentions of any kind. In a universe of blind physical forces and genetic replication, some people are going to get hurt, other people are going to get lucky, and you won't find any rhyme or reason in it, nor any justice. The universe we observe has precisely the properties we should expect if there is, at bottom, no design, no purpose, no evil and no good, nothing but blind, pitiless indifference.[25]

By way of an immediate response to the above passage, note that Dawkins at the very least misspeaks when he uses the phrase "meaningless tragedies." Tragedy is marked by destruction and lamentation; to say something is tragic is to recognize the value of a loss. Contrary to Dawkin's dismissal of meaning, to be replaced by mindless forces at work in a universe of chance, it was the presence of evil that accounted for Darwin's own misgivings about Christian theism.

The problem of evil has long been, for some, evidence that God does not exist. When one considers the magnitude of suffering endured by animals

22. *Poems of Paul Celan*, trans. Michael Hamburger (London: Anvil Press Poetry, 1988), 177.
23. G. Steiner, *Grammars of Creation* (New Haven & London: Yale University Press, 2001), 324.
24. Albert Camus, "Absurd Walls," in *The Myth of Sisyphus and Other Essays*, trans. J. O'Brien (New York: Hamish Hamilton, 1955), 21.
25. R. Dawkins, *River out of Eden* (London: Weidenfeld and Nicolson, 1995), 132–3.

and humans alike through the ages, it is clear that the presence of suffering and evil is persistently difficult for theists to reconcile with the classical understanding of a loving God.[26] Now we are moving from a discussion in Dawkins of blind functions and processes, to a discussion about values, and these are two different kinds of things. In the following passage Darwin acknowledges the problem of evil for theists (evil is back on the table), but then finds a "good" in a naturalistic justification for its existence.

> A being so powerful and so full of knowledge as a God who could create a universe, is to our finite minds omnipotent and omniscient, and it revolts our understanding to suppose that his benevolence is not unbounded, for what advantage can there be in the sufferings of millions of lower animals throughout almost endless time? This very old argument from the existence of suffering against the existence of an intelligent first cause seems to me a strong one; whereas, as just remarked, the presence of much suffering agrees well with the view that all organic beings have developed through variation and natural selection.[27]

Darwin acknowledges that ideas about scale, the means we use to attempt to measure the amount of suffering and evil in the cosmos, are important to grasp and express the magnitude of what is at stake for his theory. His theory requires that animals have the motive (or drive) to live, and this would not be feasible if animals were in a state of absolute misery. Darwin needed to acknowledge a general state of animal well-being. "But pain or suffering of any kind, if long continued, causes depression and lessens the power of action; yet is well adapted to make a creature guard itself against any great or sudden evil."[28] In the following passage Darwin finds fittingness in the relationship between good and evil:

> But passing over the endless beautiful adaptations which we everywhere meet with, it may be asked how can the generally beneficent arrangement of the world be accounted for? Some writers indeed are so much impressed with the amount of suffering in the world, that they doubt if we look to all sentient beings, whether there is more misery or of happiness;—whether the world as a whole is a good or a bad one. According to my judgment happiness decidedly prevails, though this would be very difficult to prove. If the truth of this

26. For a recent overview of the case for and against animal suffering, see Michael Murray, *Nature Red in Tooth and Claw: Theism and the Problem of Animal Suffering* (Oxford: Oxford University Press, 2008).
27. Charles Darwin, *Autobiographies* (London: Penguin Books, 2002), 52.
28. Ibid. 51.

conclusion be granted, it harmonies well with the effects which we might expect from natural selection. If all the individuals of any species were habitually to suffer to an extreme degree they would neglect to propagate their kind; but we have no reason to believe that this has ever or at least often occurred. Some other considerations, moreover, lead to the belief that all sentient beings have been formed so as to enjoy, as a general rule, happiness.[29]

Darwin then goes on to naturalize goodness, using the strategy he used to naturalize suffering. Darwin recognizes a utility for goodness or happiness in serving the process of adaptation, turning our traditional images of what is being served and to whom, upside down. Darwin's view of goodness and happiness replaces a classical view of values. While the most and least happiness, and the best and worst health is in an ever-changing dynamic in our personal experience, most of the time the presence of goodness and beauty direct our attention to the value of existence as a good, recognizing goodness and beauty and existence as not *having* a meaning (utilitarian purpose), but *as* meaning.[30]

Darwin reasons that in a necessary struggle for existence, beauty comes along with happiness to cheer us on for the sole purpose of keeping a biological process going. Ever growing is the search for the survival value of all our desires, pleasures, violence and accomplishments. In Denis Dutton's book *The Art Instinct: Beauty, Pleasure and Human Evolution*, people create things in order to attract mates:

> Darwin's *Descent of Man*, by regarding the mind as a sexual ornament, presents us with a first step toward explaining those features of the human personality that we find most charming, captivating, and seductive. Adding sexual selection to natural selection, we begin to see the possibility for a complete theory of the origin of the arts.[31]

Darwin himself extended the implications of natural selection, the implications *as he saw them*, to all of human agency and potential. Darwin believed that there was an obvious difference in the cognitive abilities amongst people, found especially in the comparisons of human racial groups—even referring to "race" as possibly interchangeable with the term "species." "The

29. Charles Darwin, *The Autobiography of Charles Darwin* (Barnes & Noble Publishing, 2005), 67.
30. Iris Murdoch, in her book exploring the Platonic notion of beauty and goodness, calls this re-direction of our attention "un-selfing." See *The Sovereignty of the Good* (London: Routledge & Kegan Paul, 1970).
31. Denis Dutton, *The Art Instinct: Beauty, Pleasure and Human Evolution* (New York: Bloomsbury Press, 2009), 152.

variability or diversity of the mental faculties in men of the same race, not to mention the greater differences between men of distinct races, is so notorious that not a word need here be said."[32] Darwin considers racial extermination: "Do the races or species of men, whichever term may be applied, encroach on and replace one another, so that some finally become extinct?"[33] He drew on his extensive travels on the Beagle to justify a positive relationship between struggle and progress:

> Since we see in many parts of the world enormous areas of the most fertile land capable of supporting numerous happy homes, but peopled only by a few wandering savages, it might be argued that the struggle for existence had not been sufficiently severe to force man upwards to his highest standard. [34]

Darwin is so concerned with the progressive nature of natural selection, he questions why we should devise ways to help the weaker members of our species, and why it is that there is value placed on the individual.

> We civilized men, on the other hand, do our utmost to check the process of elimination; we build asylums for the imbecile, the maimed, and the sick; we institute poor-laws; and our medical men exert their utmost skill to save the life of every one to the last moment. There is reason to believe that vaccination has preserved thousands, who from a weak constitution would formerly have succumbed to small-pox. Thus the weak members of civilized societies propagate their kind. No one who has attended to the breeding of domestic animals will doubt that this must be highly injurious to the race of man. It is surprising how soon a want of care, or care wrongly directed, leads to the degeneration of a domestic race; but excepting in the case of man himself, hardly any one is ignorant as to allow his worst animal to breed.[35]

We can separate any moral criticism of Darwin from a criticism of natural selection or how it functions in Neo-Darwinian theories. There is a broader point to appreciate that transcends a strict Darwinian philosophy: if morality does involve objective norms of fittingness, then it appears that one needs to go beyond evolutionary biology to ground or find a place for those norms. Darwin quite explicitly acknowledged the contingent nature of evolution. Consider Darwin's famous bee thought experiment:

32. Charles Darwin, *The Descent of Man* (New York: Crowell, 1874), 27.
33. Ibid. 6.
34. Ibid. 148.
35. Ibid. 138–9.

If, for instance, to take an extreme case, men were reared under precisely the same conditions as hive-bees, there can hardly be a doubt that our unmarried females would, like the worker-bees, think it is a sacred duty to kill their brothers, and mothers would strive to kill their fertile daughters; and no one would think of interfering. Nevertheless, the bee, or any other social animal would gain in our supposed case, as it appears to me, some feeling of right and wrong, or a conscience. For each individual would have an inward sense of possessing certain stronger or more endearing instincts...an inward monitor would tell the animal that it would be better to (follow) one impulse rather than the other...the one would have right and the other wrong.[36]

If we believe that our sense of right and wrong are completely accounted for by natural selection, the deeply disturbing conclusions cited by Elijah Millgram give us reason to be cautious about relying on survivability or natural tendencies as a foundation for ethics. Millgram cites: "that some human females are fine-tuned by natural selection to murder their infants in a suitable range of circumstances...that human males are fine-tuned to rape women in a suitable range of circumstances...that humans value occupying dominant positions in hierarchies to a degree not compatible with justice of any kind."[37]

In looking at some of the naturalist's explanation of how we fit in the natural order, it is important not to neglect that it is *in* our experience that we seek explanations. It is this need to find a fitting explanation that leads both the naturalist and the theist (and presumably anyone who is curious), to acknowledge the longing we feel for reason and at-one-ment. Recognizing the allure of a non-anthropomorphic understanding of the universe, which does entail the aesthetic judgment of scale, we can agree that we are not the center of the universe. Yet, it is our predicament that as Thomas Nagel says:

Without God, it is unclear what we should aspire to harmony with. But still, the aspiration can remain, to live not merely the life of the creature one is, but in some sense to participate through it in the life of the universe as a whole...Having, amazingly, burst into existence, one is a representative of existence itself—of the whole of it—not just because one is part of it but because it is present to one's consciousness. In each of us, the universe has come to consciousness, and therefore our existence is not merely our own.[38]

36. Charles Darwin, *The Descent of Man* (New York: American Home Library Company, 1902), 137–8.
37. E. Millgram, "Life and action," *Analysis* 69, no. 3 (2009): 557–64.
38. Thomas Nagel, *Secular Philosophy and the Religious Temperament* (Oxford: Oxford University Press, 2010), 6.

The theistic Galapagos

I noted earlier that the use of the crane and the skyhook were images of origins, used to illustrate an explanation for how what exists exists. Nagel uses the term "harmony," another word for fittingness, to acknowledge our sense that we are not only part of something much larger than ourselves, but that we want to be an agent in that something larger, to be both accountable and counted.

It is fitting, I think, to ask what is the origin of our desire to feel at home in the world. A question about origins begins with the admission that a question of this kind begins with prior assumptions, which are by nature, metaphysical. If I say I have a strong intuition that if we know someone's or something's origin (the root of consciousness, the beginning of poetry, the historical Jesus), *we will know something important that bears on our understanding of these things,* I have at least one prior assumption. I am assuming that there is (revelatory, as in, revealing) meaning between what has crossed my path, both literally and in my mind, and from where or what this creature, this rock, this sea, this fear and this joy originates. Meaning here is not just an answer to cause and effect, the chicken or the egg. (To know the answer to that question might be called gaining information, an entirely different quest, important as it is. Information does not provide values; I have to place value on information.) Rather, it is a desire to see fittingness between something's origin and the value you place upon it. Perhaps origin will reveal the cause, the purpose or the proper magnitude of your attention. When you learn that the failure of a friend to keep an important promise originated in the midst of a personal crisis, and was not due to a lapse of care or unspoken anger, you have valuable knowledge in thinking through the meaning of the event.

Theism offers an understanding of the cosmos rooted in meaning. It provides a framework in which the desire for wholeness makes sense and is not a futile side effect of purposeless mechanisms. In a stark naturalist world, the quest for fitting habitation (in our subjective experience) would have to be some kind of misleading internal sparkplug that generates a longing for what you, in fact, can never have.'

For strict naturalists like Daniel Dennett and the Churchlands, our home is in the processes of the natural world and we are reducible to them. Problems of the existential kind, questions of consciousness don't really exist because those questions are themselves reducible to physics. Consciousness as we normally think of it, the way by which I have any experiences at all, is eliminated. Dennett and the Churchlands would have us eliminate the evident world of experience, and I would argue, there-by meaning, as I believe that experience *is* meaning, in all of its terrifying and consoling manifestations. Under ordinary but tragic circumstances we can readily identify with fitting responses. Think of someone you love who is dying. In the subsequent grief you feel the immeasurable weight of absence. Grief is felt as profoundly fitting in its density and weight.

This longing for fittingness between our experience and what we value is found in all forms of literature. Proust, who dwelled for hundreds of pages as a self consumed with longing and lost presences, still could not find fulfillment for his longing, illusory all:

> The bonds that unite another person to ourselves exist only in our mind.
>
> Memory as it grows fainter relaxes them, and nothwithstanding the illusion by which we fain be cheated and with which, out of friendship, politeness, deference, duty, we cheat other people, we exist alone.[39]

The longing found in the nostalgia that awakened Proust, could only result in absurdity in the relationship between human life and non-human life in the picture held up by the existentialist Albert Camus. Here is where Camus finds the absurd:

> At this point of his effort man stands face to face with the irrational. He feels within him his longing for happiness and for reason. The absurd is born of this confrontation between human need and the unreasonable silence of the world. This must not be forgotten. This must be clung to because the whole consequence of life can depend on it. The irrational, the human nostalgia, and the absurd that is born of their encounter—these are the three characters in the drama that must necessarily end with all the logic of which an existence is capable.[40]

Camus' picture has logic, hopeless as it is. He is convinced that outside of a reason, an answer to why what we desire and what we confront, our situation of longing (for justice, fulfillment and at-one-ment) is absurd. In this picture, what is reasonable to want, what reason seeks, is mocked by a universe with no reasons.

---

39. Marcel Proust, *The Sweet Cheat Gone* in *Remembrance of Things Past* Vol. 6, trans. C. K. Scott Moncrieff and Terrence Kilmartin (New York: Random House, 1981), chap. 1.
40. Camus, *The Myth of Sisyphus*, 21.

Habitat for humanity

We have long been, I believe that we still are, guests of creation. We owe it to our host the courtesy of questioning.[41]

So ends George Steiner's book *Grammars of Creation*, appearing at the close of a lengthy and elegant series of questions interrogating the layers of accrued meaning in the word "creation" in philosophy, science, religion, and art. Creation is a dawning, an origin, and the ultimate origination. In the West we have traditionally understood creation to be the act of bringing into being that which was not, or might never have been. To create in this sense, is to originate.

If we align ourselves with the naturalist account of origins, we have seen that the cost is to see the meaning and nature of our being as originating in that which has no consciousness, purpose or intrinsic meaning. In the the-istic worldview, it is in the provisions of origins that we can ground good-ness and meaning, and perhaps even come to terms with the conflicting set of experiences that Camus articulated: on the one hand we have a sense that the world is not the way it should be (events occur that ought not to occur) but this seems to hint at some way they could be reconciled. Can there be reconciliation between what we desire in happiness, justice and reason, and making sense of "what am I doing here?"

"At home in the world" is a phrase that at once locates place and how one exists. "Home" here is being oneself, losing self-consciousness, being at one with, anticipating not dreading. "The world" is where I want my home to be. Steiner's assumption that we are but guests of creation is an image of transcendence in so many ways. Not only does he believe our guest status carries a moral duty to ask questions about why we are here or why we exist at all, our status as guests leaves us looking for a host. Science is an endeavor that is always going forward (as equally fascinated with origins as any other practice), "knowledge begetting knowledge." Art, philosophy and theology are not progressive in that sense. So this question about the origins of the desire to feel, or be, at home in the world is a perennial one:

The intuition—is it something deeper than even that?—the conjecture, so strangely resistant to falsification, that there is "other-ness" out of reach gives

---

41. Steiner, *Grammars of Creation*, 338.

to our elemental existence its pulse of unfulfilment [sic]. We are creatures of a great thirst. Bent on coming home to a place we have never known.[42]

Theism is the proposal that our home is in God,

Although my chapter is an essay in the aesthetics of naturalism versus theism, rather than an essay in analytical philosophy, I have argued that the Dennett-Dawkins images or metaphors of the crane and the skyhook are not viable. I have gone on to propose that theism offers a better account of values and our desire to be at home (or find fitting habitation) in the cosmos. Theism remains profoundly challenged by evil for it must affirm the gravity of evil as something abhorrent to God while affirming God's power as a creator and redeemer. In Anthony O'Hear's depiction of the Christian narrative of the incarnation, we may see a hint of how Jesus the man may suffer without knowing of a greater redeeming wholeness, and yet such a wholeness does exist. Suffering or evil is neither accommodated nor obscured, but there may be redemption in which those who suffer may be transformed. This, I take it, (and on this point I am in agreement with O'Hear) is the object of desire and faith, rather than decisive argument.

> It is as if there are two poles to God's creation, God and the absence of God and both are in their own ways divine, part of the necessary economy of divine creation. Here and now we on earth may be said to participate in the pole of absence, as God did (does) Himself in the incarnation and the Cross. On a logical level there is something paradoxical about this ultimate expression of God's kenosis—Christ on the Cross—in which the man Christ, the ultimate incarnation of God and His purpose, cannot be said to be consciously aware that He is God. Yet, at another level, He must know, dispositionally at least, for is it God who suffers, not a man who is not God. Paradoxes of this sort—if indeed it is a paradox—are not unknown to us. We all experience self-doubt at times we know—deep down—there is not real need for it. Negatively we understand the notion of self-deception perfectly well, while the phenomenon of the divided self is clinically recognized, even if it is hard to explicate philosophically. What the incarnation suggests is that in becoming man, God, in addition to all else, in the Agony in the Garden and in the desolation on the Cross takes on the burden of being a divided self.
>
> Existentially, religiously, though, God/Christ knowing and not knowing what and who he is as He suffers makes perfect sense, and can be seen as necessary, for it is in this final self-emptying that God gathers up creation and—in the mythological economy—accepts it and restores it to the Father.

---

42. Steiner, *Grammars of Creation*, 20.

The negative aspect of creation—which exists—is not railed at—but it is accepted as intrinsic to that very gift which creation is, as necessary to it.[43]

In the phrases "economy of divine creation" and "the mythological economy," I take "economy" to refer to some harmonious arrangement or scheme of interacting elements. Our desire to be at home in the world might find its fulfillment in a picture of a restored creation. Yet in creating two economies, a divine economy and a mythological economy, O'Hear gives us a way to imagine how our sense that things are not as they should be is what creates our deepest longings, the desires of our mind, and this is experience we might allow ourselves to trust.

Both theists and naturalists have a deep passion to be concerned for origins and perhaps, as major worldviews, both worldviews stem from a common intuition about the illuminating nature of origins.

The image of the Galapagos that Melville created is monochromatic and eccentric, but it expresses how we do not just inhabit places, but we internalize them according to a host of prior assumptions, needs, and a desire to make sense of how we fit into the natural world. Dawkins' fly-over the Galapagos draws on the language of enchantment and discovery, but he is interested in keeping the questions limited to the parameters of properly understood scientific investigation. This is appropriate in the laboratory, and has led to many, many goods, not the least, knowledge that substantially fills out our relationship to the natural world. Nagel leaves us with another challenge, and I think it is a challenge to inhabit the question that leads us into deeper mysteries, the mysteries that are persons and why we want to know what our nature is, and what is the meaning that existence, not just life, does not *have,* but *is.*

43. Anthony O'Hear, "Why, Creation and Theodicy."

Figure 11.2 Isla Genovesa Tourists. © Jonathan Wells 2011

Index